Aligning Religious Law and State Law

Leiden Studies in Islam and Society

VOLUME 18

The titles published in this series are listed at *brill.com/lsis*

Aligning Religious Law and State Law

Negotiating Legal Muslim Marriage in Pasuruan, East Java

By

Muhammad Latif Fauzi

BRILL

LEIDEN | BOSTON

Cover illustration: *Akad nikah* in the office, led by an informal *modin*.

The Library of Congress Cataloging-in-Publication Data is available online at https://catalog.loc.gov
LC record available at https://lccn.loc.gov/2023018201

Typeface for the Latin, Greek, and Cyrillic scripts: "Brill". See and download: brill.com/brill-typeface.

ISSN 2210-8920
ISBN 978-90-04-51610-6 (paperback)
ISBN 978-90-04-51611-3 (e-book)

This book is printed on acid-free paper and produced in a sustainable manner.

For Ivo, Neva, and Queena

Contents

PART 2
Legal Practice

Figures and Tables

Figures

Tables

Acknowledgements

The process of making this into a book has been challenging. This book is based upon my doctoral dissertation at Leiden University. Behind me, different layers of people have helped me in numerous ways. Let me simply describe what my promotors have done for me. Prof. Dr. Adriaan Bedner has given me intensive and passionate supervision and has contributed significantly to the finalisation of this book. Prof. Dr. Léon Buskens has provided me with theoretical frameworks on the scholarly discourse about Shariʿa, law and society.

Research of this book could not have been possible without the support of the 5000 Doktor Scholarship of the Ministry of Religious Affairs of the Republic of Indonesia. I would like to convey my sincere thanks to the Ministry that had provided me with generous funds and the kind assistance and relevant support for this academic journey. I would like to express my gratitude to the family law group discussion at Van Vollenhoven Institute. The conversations have enriched me with insightful ideas on questions and relevant issues of doing family law. The members of this group, Al Farabi, Dr. Annelien Bouland, Dr. Arfiansyah, Dr. Hoko Hori, Judith van Uden, Mies Grijns, Nada Heddane, and Dr. Nadia Sonneveld, have carefully read and given important remarks on my chapters.

I am indebted to Dr. Margreet van Till, the coordinator of exchange programmes in the faculty of Humanities, Leiden University, for her assistance. I am grateful to my colleagues at LIAS and KITLV, Dr. Ade Jaya Suryani, Adrian Perkasa, Aminudin Siregar, Dr. Grace Leksana, Dr. Nor Ismah, Dr. Taufiq Hanafi, Dr. Syahril Sidik, and Dr. Yanwar Pribadi for the friendship and mutual supports. I would also like to thank colleagues in Berlin: Dr. Syaifuddin Zuhri, Dr. Zacky Khairul Umam, Dr. Dyah Wirastri, Dr. Stijn van Huis and Dr. Dominik Müller for their invaluable inputs. I wish to thank scholars, namely Prof. Dr. Nico Kaptein, Dr. David Kloos, Dr. Ward Berenschot, Dr. Upik Djalins, and Prof. Dr. Henk Schulte Nordholt for their inputs during my presentation in KITLV. A number of colleagues in PCINU Belanda deserve my sincere gratitude for having provided emotional and communal support, mainly KH. Nur Hasyim Subadi, KH. Hambali Ma'sum, KH. Ahmad Naf'an Sulhan, KH. Budi Santoso, Dr. Fachrizal Afandi, Dr. Fahrizal Yusuf Affandi, Muhammad As'ad, Yus Boersma, Dr. Ibnu Fikri, M. Shohibuddin, Dr. Yance Arizona and Ahmad Afnan Anshori. I also wish to thank my friends in Al-Hikmah mosque in The Hague, namely H. Bahrul Munif and Nana Supriatna for their valuable support.

I would like to express my gratitude to professors and colleagues in UIN Raden Mas Said Surakarta from whom I have obtained moral support. My apologies if I may not be able to name all of you, but let me try to thank a few people personally. The rector, Prof. Dr. Mudofir, the ex-dean of Sharīʿa faculty, Dr. M. Usman, the current dean, Dr. Ismail Yahya, Dr. Lukman Fauroni, Dr. Zainul Abas, Dr. Fauzi Muharram, Sulhani Hermawan, Dr. Sidik and some others are influential in my intellectual development. I would also like to thank my colleagues in the postgraduate program at UIN Yogyakarta. In addition, I would like to thank Rosemary Robson for proofreading my manuscript.

In the field, I would like to convey my greatest gratitude to my acquaintances and friends in Pasuruan. Pak Rudy, Mas Subadar, and Mas Hamzah always welcomed me when I did fieldwork in the office of KUA. I wish to particularly thank Dewi and Khoirul for their help to interview people about their marriage experiences. I wish to acknowledge the help of people in Sumbersari, among others Nisa, Ahmad, Iin, Alfi, Saiful and Gus Ja'far, who provided me with a nice place to stay at his Pesantren Miftahul Falah. My key informants, namely Umi Hanik, Haji Misbahul, Haji Hamim, Gus Rokib, Kyai Ghofur, and Ustadz Syukron have been essential in supporting me with a wealth of information for my study. I am also grateful to some NGO activists and organisations in Bangil, namely Mas Faizin, Cak Lutfi, Mbak Arofah and Mas Sihab in STAPA Centre and Cak Ali Sadikin in OBH YRPP. They have made my fieldwork livelier.

Finally, on a personal note, I wish to thank all members of my family for their tremendous encouragement to finish my study. My most profound appreciation is devoted to my parents, H.M. Hasibun and Hj. Maisyaroh, my brother and sister, my parents-in-law, the late M. Nasiruddin and Sulastri. Finally, this book is dedicated to my greatest inspirations and love: my wife, Ivo Latifah and our beloved daughters, Neva and Queena, who have always been the sources of patience, joy and encouragement.

Some chapters of this book have been previously published elsewhere. An earlier version of Chapter 4 was published as 'Actors and Norms in an Islamic Marriage: A Study of Madura Community in Rural Eastern East Java,' *Journal of Indonesian Islam* 13 (2) (2019): 297–325. A slightly different version of Chapter 5 appeared as 'Registering Muslim Marriages: *Penghulu*, *Modin*, and the Struggles for Influence,' *al-Jamiʿah: Journal of Islamic Studies* 57 (2) (2019): 397–424.

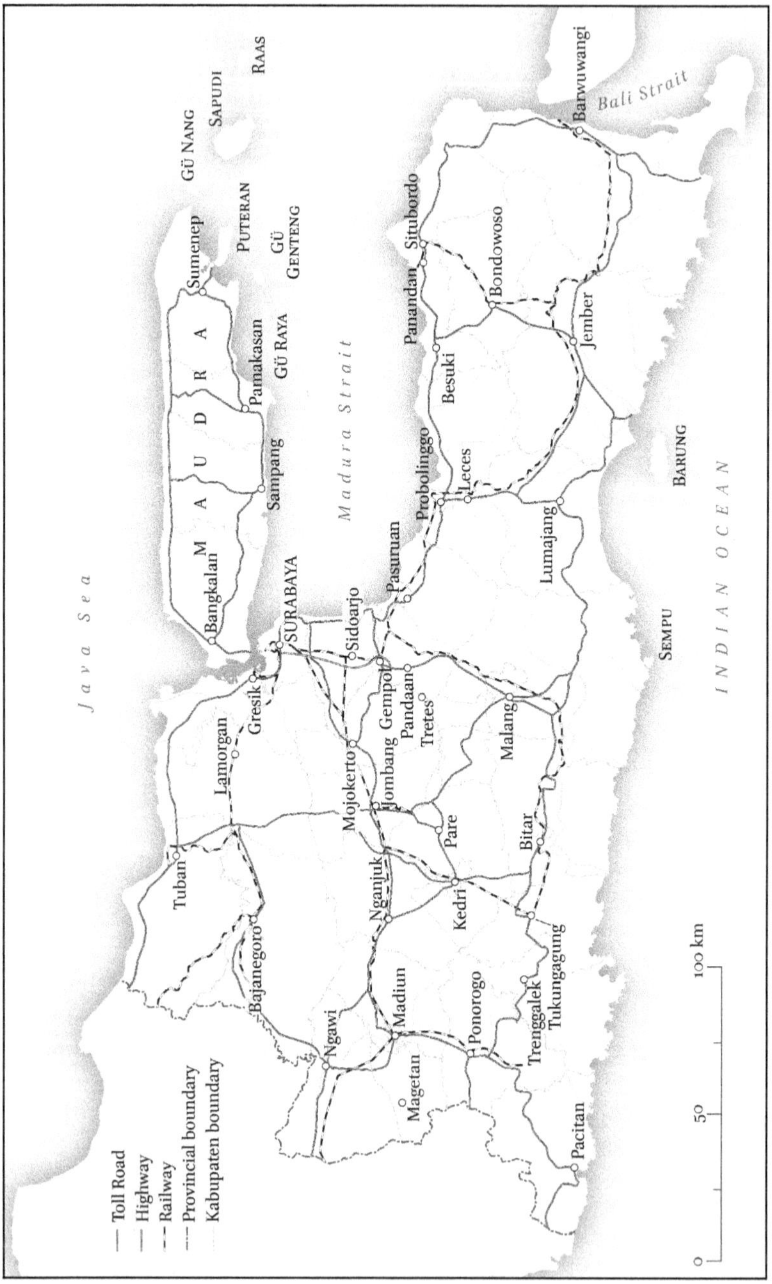

Map of East Java, modified from CartoGIS ANU

Abbreviations

BP4	Badan Penasihatan, Pembinaan dan Pelestarian Perkawinan, National Board for Counselling, Fostering and Perpetuation of Marriage
KMA	Keputusan Menteri Agama, the Decree of the Minister of Religious Affairs
KUA	Kantor Urusan Agama, the sub-district office of religious affairs that deals with marriage registration and other religious matters such as *ḥajj* and family life.
MASYUMI	Majelis Syuro Muslimin Indonesia, was a major Islamic political party in Indonesia during the Liberal Democracy Era in Indonesia (17 August 1950–5 July 1959) and was eradicated in 1960 by President Sukarno for supporting the PRRI rebellion
MUI	Majelis Ulama Indonesia/the Council of Indonesian Ulama, a semi-official council for Indonesian 'ulama' established in 1975
NU	Nahdlatul Ulama, the largest traditionalist Muslim organisation in Indonesia founded by Kyai Hasyim Asy'arie (d. 1947) in 1926
PETA	Pembela Tanah Air, Defenders of the Homeland, established in 1943 to assist the Japanese colonising Indonesia.
PMA	Peraturan Menteri Agama, the Regulation of the Minister of Religious Affairs
PNI	Partai Nasional Indonesia, the Indonesian National Party that had existed before Indonesia's independence
PKI	Partai Komunis Indonesia, the Communist Party of Indonesia, a communist party in Indonesia during the mid-20th century and was banned in 1965 by President Soeharto.
PPN	Petugas Pencatat Nikah, marriage registrars
PPPN	Pembantu Petugas Pencatat Nikah, the marriage registrar's assistants
RUU HMPA	Rancangan Undang-undang Hukum Materiil Pengadilan Agama Bidang Perkawinan, the Bill of Islamic Court's Material Law on Marriage

CHAPTER 1

Introduction

1 Unregistered Marriage and the Plurality of Legal Norms

In 2012, Fikri, the head of a district (*Bupati*) in West Java province, married a seventeen-year-old teenager, Oktora. It was an illegal polygynous marriage in the eyes of the state. Fikri did not have permission from the local Islamic court to take a second wife. The marriage lasted only four days and ended in a unilateral repudiation (*talak*).[1] In a live television interview, Fikri explained why he had divorced Oktora, Fikri believed Oktora was no longer a virgin when she married him. He drew an analogy between the bride and clothes. "It is like when you buy new clothes. If something is damaged, you can return it." Most people found his analogy irritating and distasteful. The marriage attracted extensive print and online media coverage, elicited a wave of public rumours and was the topic of legal debates. Following the public protests and a people's march, the local parliament set up a special committee (*panitia khusus*) to investigate Fikri's conduct. Most of the political factions in the parliament concluded that the *Bupati* was guilty of misconduct.[2] On account of his violation of the Marriage Law, the *Bupati* was considered to have broken his oath of office (*sumpah jabatan*). Later, the Indonesian Supreme Court endorsed the parliament's decision. Fikri finally stepped down.

Fikri deliberately avoided registering his marriage. This would suggest that he regarded the validity of marriage only from a restricted religious point of view. In his eyes, as most Indonesians say, marriage is more than a legal contract between two parties.[3] It is an important communal and spiritual affair. Fikri brushed aside the significance of legalising his marriage as the state law

---

1 Although his marriage lasted for a limited time, it was not a *mutʿah* marriage. *Mutʿah* is taken from an Arabic term, *mutʿa*, that literally means pleasure or enjoyment. A *mutʿah* marriage is a marriage where a man agrees to give a woman something for a specified period in return for her sexual favour. The institution of temporary marriage was prohibited by the second caliph, ʿUmar ibn Khaṭṭāb, who viewed it as fornication. This view is perceived to be fallacious by Shiʿi Muslims, who have continued to practice temporary marriage. Shahla Haeri, *Law of Desire: Temporary Marriage in Shiʿi Iran* (Syracuse, N.Y.: Syracuse University Press, 2014), 50.

2 Tempo.co, "Kasus Fany, Bupati Garut Terancam Kena Sanksi Golkar," *Tempo.Co*, last modified 2012, accessed March 15, 2016, https://nasional.tempo.co/read/445735/kasus-fany-bupati-garut-terancam-kena-sanksi-golkar/full&view=ok.

3 Ziba Mir-Hosseini, "Marriage," *Encyclopedia of Islam and the Muslim World* (New York: Macmillan, 2004), 430.

 | DOI:10.1163/9789004516113_002

required, because he was not able to present permission to perform a polygynous marriage granted by an Islamic court. His polygynous marriage did not qualify for registration under Indonesian law. Family law reform in the Muslim world has undergone significant change over the past century. It has become a source of contestation between conservative or traditionalist Islamic views and modernist egalitarian ones.[4] It has largely focused on restrictions on a husband's right to enter into a polygamous marriage, limiting a husband's right to unilaterally declare his wife divorced, raising the minimum age of marriage, and expanding a wife's ability to get a divorce at her initiative.

According to Welchman, Western scholarship perceives family law as the last stronghold of the Sharīʿa, arousing an image of the forces against different powers (secularist reform, European colonialism, and state authority).[5] The process of codification of laws and the reorganisation of judicial systems began in the Middle East in the end of the nineteenth century under the Ottomans and continued in the twentieth century under European colonial power and in the independent states that emerged afterwards.[6] The new political elite of independent states determined the supremacy of their own authority and their own legal systems. Meanwhile, other normative systems and the traditional elites were incorporated into the state's legal and political systems.[7] State interference with Sharīʿa became complicated.

Throughout the Muslim world, a myriad of local norms and local actors have influenced the implementation of Muslim marriage.[8] Compliance with local norms and the involvement of local actors in a marriage ceremony are essential elements in obtaining social acceptance of marriage. According to legal anthropologists, family relationships are more the domain of social norms than formal legal requirements.[9] In this regard, marriage remains an essential part of the social and moral fabric.[10] However, in the modern nation state, social accept-

4 Ann Black, Hossein Esmaeili, and Nadirsyah Hosen, *Modern Perspectives on Islamic Law* (Cheltenham: Edward Elgar Publishing, 2013), 108.

5 Lynn Welchman, *Women and Muslim Family Laws in Arab States: A Comparative Overview of Textual Development and Advocacy* (Amsterdam: Amsterdam University Press, 2007), 11.

6 Ibid.

7 Jan Michiel Otto, "Introduction: Investigating the Role of Sharia in National Law," in *Sharia Incorporated: A Comparative Overview of the Legal Systems of Twelve Muslim Countries in Past and Present*, ed. Jan Michiel Otto (Leiden: Leiden University Press, 2010), 27.

8 Dawoud Sudqi el-Alami, *The Marriage Contract in Islamic Law in the Shari'ah and Personal Status Laws of Egypt and Morocco* (London: Graham & Trotman, 1992).

9 Elizabeth S. Scott, "Social Norms and the Legal Regulation of Marriage," *Virginia Law Review* 86, no. 8 (2000): 1903.

10 Maria Platt, *Marriage, Gender and Islam in Indonesia: Women Negotiating Informal Marriage, Divorce and Desire* (Oxon and New York: Routledge, 2017).

ance is not sufficient. The nation state has claimed the right to uphold the legal validity of marriage by introducing the obligation to register marriages. One reason is that state law in many Muslim countries applies egalitarian gender norms. Furthermore, the state has the right to resort to legal enforcement of divorce when family relationships break down.

In Indonesia, the relationship between social acceptance and religious norms is indivisible. Social acceptance is unquestionably determined by the upholding of religious principles in the marriage ceremony. As noted, many people regard social acceptance as more important than state recognition, perhaps because the state applies restrictions to certain marriage practices, such as polygyny, yet religious norms do not. According to Nadia Sonneveld, from a social point of view, there is no obvious difference between a legal marriage and an illegal marriage, as long as it is socially acceptable.[11] Moreover, many Muslims regard traditional mechanisms as sufficient to deal with daily marital disputes. It is why the relationship between traditional mechanisms and state sovereignty in post-colonial Muslim societies has attracted the attention of legal anthropologists.[12]

On a practical level, three different legal bodies, namely Sharīʿa law, state law, and customary law, co-exist and interact in an Islamic triangle.[13] These legal bodies have different understandings of the religious, legal, and social validity of a marriage. In Indonesia, marriage without registration is popularly known as *nikah sirri*, a secret marriage. According to classical Muslim jurists, *nikāh al-sirr* is impermissible. It is a marriage contract concluded in the absence of male witnesses that includes neither publicity (*iʿlān*) nor a festive meal (*walīma*).[14]

11 Nadia Sonneveld, "Rethinking the Difference Between Formal and Informal Marriages in Egypt," in *Family Law in Islam: Divorce, Marriage and Women in the Muslim World*, ed. Maaike Voorhoeve (London: I.B. Tauris, 2012), 77–107.

12 A large number of scholarly works discuss the position of Sharīʿa in the different nation states, e.g., Clark B. Lombardi, *State Law as Islamic Law in Modern Egypt: The Incorporation of the Sharīʿa into Egyptian Constitutional Law* (Leiden: Brill, 2006); Morgan Clarke, *Islam and Law in Lebanon*: Sharīʿa *within and without the State* (Cambridge: Cambridge University Press, 2018); Jan Michiel Otto, ed., Sharīʿa *Incorporated: A Comparative Overview of the Legal Systems of Twelve Muslim Countries in Past and Present* (Leiden: Leiden University Press, 2010).

13 Léon Buskens, "An Islamic Triangle: Changing Relationships between Sharīʿa, State Law, and Local Customs," in *ISIM Newsletter*, vol. 5 (Leiden: Institute for the Study of Islam in the Modern World, 2000), 8.

14 According to classical Maliki scholars, marriage without two male witnesses is valid as long it is announced publicly (*iʿlān*). Khoiruddin Nasution, *Status Wanita Di Asia Tenggara: Studi Terhadap Perundang-Undangan Perkawinan Muslim Kontemporer Di Indonesia Dan Malaysia* (Leiden: Indonesian-Netherlands Cooperation in Islamic Studies (INIS), 2002), 139.

Diverging from this classical concept, *nikah sirri* in Indonesia refers to a religious marriage that is not registered.[15] Such a marriage is performed in the presence of local religious leaders (*kyais*) and witnesses in compliance with Islamic law but without the supervision of an official marriage registrar.[16] For many and perhaps most Muslims, the religious validity of a *nikah sirri* is more important than the validity of marriage authorised by the state.

The state requires the registration of every marriage. The Kompilasi Hukum Islam (Compilation of Islamic law, henceforth referred to as the Kompilasi), a significant reference work for judges in Islamic courts, states that registration is designed to protect the institution of marriage. The act of registration makes a marriage legally valid. If a marriage is legally valid, it must be religiously valid because, according to the Indonesian Marriage Law, a marriage cannot be registered unless it satisfies religious requirements. However, registration is not one of the legal conditions (*rukun*) of an Islamic marriage. Although an unregistered marriage has no 'legal effect,' it is not necessarily void. The legal obligation of registration established in Law 22/1946 on the Registration of Islamic Marriage, Divorce, and Reconciliation does not affect the lawfulness of an unregistered marriage as long as it was concluded according to the Islamic requirements.[17] Bowen refers to the complicated relationship between religious validity and state recognition as 'dual validity.'[18]

A marriage may also be validated by the social acceptance of persons living together in a form that is commonly recognised as a marriage. Mir-Hosseini calls this 'a socially valid marriage.'[19] In practice, social acceptance is often linked to religious validity. In Java, if a Muslim marriage is valid according to Islam, it is assured of social acceptance. Social acceptance is important to avoid social stigma. Thus, marriage acts as a social norm that regulates sexual relations. Grijns and Horii argue that if a teenager becomes pregnant, marriage is the only acceptable solution.[20] Hence marriage defines female sexuality. Parker

15 Eva F. Nisa, "The Bureaucratization of Muslim Marriage in Indonesia," *Journal of Law and Religion* 33: 2 (2018): 291–309.

16 Silvia Vignato, "'Men Come In, Men Go Out': Single Muslim Women in Malaysia and Aceh," *Social Identities* 18: 2 (2012): 239–257.

17 Stijn Cornelis van Huis, "Islamic Courts and Women's Divorce Rights in Indonesia: The Cases of Cianjur and Bulukumba" (PhD Dissertation. Leiden University, 2015), 95.

18 John R. Bowen, *Shari'a, State, and Social Norms in France and Indonesia* (ISIM Paper no. 3. Leiden: Institute for the Study of Islam in the Modern World, 2001), 10.

19 Ziba Mir-Hosseini, *Marriage on Trial: Islamic Family Law in Iran and Morocco* (London and New York: I.B. Tauris, 2000), 145.

20 Mies Grijns and Hoko Horii, "Child Marriage in a Village in West Java (Indonesia): Compromises between Legal Obligations and Religious Concerns," *Asian Journal of Law and Society* 5, no. 2 (2018): 7.

et al., for instance, describe the experience of being a *janda* (a widow or a divorcée) in Indonesia as a gendered experience. They argue that widows (*janda mati*) and divorcées (*janda cerai*) are denounced as immoral because they epitomise the opposite of an ideal marriage.[21] These studies suggest that marriage and divorce are a gendered phenomenon that has to do with sexual morality.

If we now return to Fikri, we understand that his unregistered marriage has to do with the perception of Sharīʿa and the state. The practice of unregistered marriage is not uncommon or exclusive to Indonesia. In many Muslim majority countries, the practice of unregistered marriage is common. Those performing an unregistered marriage regard registration as an invention of the modern state. Unregistered marriage demonstrates that there still is continuity in the tension between Sharīʿa law and state law. In Egypt, the tension between state law and religious law on marriage leads to the practice of *ʿurfī* (customary) marriage.[22] Similarly, in Morocco, non-registration leads to so-called *fātiḥa* marriages.[23] The participants in an unregistered marriage attach more importance to the Sharīʿa than to the state law. They value the validity of marriage exclusively from the perspective of Sharīʿa, i.e., marriage renders sexual relations between a man and a woman licit.[24] According to Hallaq, Muslims perceive marriage as the key to maintaining social harmony and the cornerstone of the entire Islamic order.[25] Abaza, Mir-Hosseini, and Hallaq emphasised that Sharīʿa is a social matter because it relates to how people perceive it.

Indonesia, which is blessed with a myriad of local cultures, provides a preexisting foundation on which Islamic law can be understood, practised, and taken as a point of orientation by Muslims in multiple ways. It means that Muslim society in Indonesia is crisscrossed by competing norms, social orders, and claims about how people should live in an appropriately Islamic way and

---

21 Lyn Parker, Irma Riyani, and Brooke Nolan, "The Stigmatisation of Widows and Divorcees (Janda) in Indonesia, and the Possibilities for Agency," *Indonesia and the Malay World* 44, no. 128 (2016): 27–46.

22 Mona Abaza, "Perceptions of *ʿUrfi* Marriage in the Egyptian Press," *ISIM Newsletter* 7 (2001): 20–21.

23 An unregistered marriage is referred to as *fātiḥa* because the couples are solemnized by recitation of the *fātiḥa*, the first *surah* of the Qur'an. See Mir-Hosseini, *Marriage on Trial: Islamic Family Law in Iran and Morocco*, 32. Underage marriage is often not registered, see Paul Scott Prettitore, "Family Law Reform, Gender Equality, and Underage Marriage: A View from Morocco and Jordan," *Review of Faith and International Affairs* 13, no. 3 (2015): 39.

24 Ziba Mir-Hosseini, "Nikah," *Encyclopedia of Islam and the Muslim World* (New York: Macmillan, 2004), 510.

25 Wael B. Hallaq, *Sharīʿa: Theory, Practice, Transformations* (Cambridge: Cambridge University Press, 2009), 271.

about what they should become.[26] Bowen sheds new light on the fact that Muslims are challenged by competing legal systems in which negotiation is an irrevocable instrument.[27] From his view, negotiation is the key concept. People have to cope with the pressure caused by the significant growth in the demand for the greater participation of women in education and skilled employment[28] to redefine the rights and duties of women and men and promote women's equality. This new understanding has challenged the perceived knowledge of Islamic law and traditional scriptural interpretations.

Based on this background, this book addresses these questions: *How does the Indonesian state regulate Muslim marriage? How do people practise and negotiate the state regulations on Muslim marriage? How do local officials deal with their practices? What role do informal intermediaries play in this process, in Pasuruan, East Java particularly?* The book first elucidates how the Indonesian state governs Muslim marriages. Since the early days of independence, the Indonesian government has included marriage, divorce, and reconciliation among Muslims in its steady march towards greater bureaucratisation. However, as bureaucratisation develops over time, this study investigates what legal reforms the state has set in motion, how local officials interpret and implement the state law, and how religious leaders respond to these legal reforms. It also addresses how the practices adopted by Muslims reveal their responses, how state officials deal with their practices, and in what ways intermediaries play a role in this process. This book addresses marriage practices in a Muslim community in Pasuruan to understand the implementation of marriage registration in a local setting.

By looking at local practices in Pasuruan, this book offers a critical perspective on the relationship between locally based legal norms and the modern legal norms promoted by the state. The title of this book, *Aligning Religious Law and State Law*, represents the complicated situation in Pasuruan in which Muslims face religious, legal, and traditional norms on marriage with overlapping applicability. Although Muslims undoubtedly adhere to religious law, they

---

26 Franz Von Benda-Beckmann, *Property in Social Continuity: Continuity and Change in the Maintenance of Property Relationships through Time in Minangkabau, West Sumatra* (The Hague: Martinus Nijhoff, 1979); Franz Von Benda-Beckmann and Keebet Von Benda-Beckmann, "Islamic Law in a Plural Context: The Struggle over Inheritance Law in Colonial West Sumatra," *Journal of the Economic and Social History of the Orient* 55, no. 4/5 (2012): 771–793.

27 John R. Bowen, *Islam, Law, and Equality in Indonesia: An Anthropology of Public Reasoning* (Cambridge: Cambridge University Press, 2003).

28 Linda Rae Bennett, *Women, Islam and Modernity: Single Women, Sexuality and Reproductive Health in Contemporary Indonesia* (London and New York: RoutledgeCurzon, 2005).

do not necessarily oppose state law because state law is generally not contradictory to the principles of Sharīʿa. However, when it comes to the obligation of legal marriage through registration, for instance, they may have an inconsistent attitude. In some cases, mainly where documents required for marriage registration are hard to produce, they will consider marriage registration not obligatory, arguing that religious norms provide no specific regulation on registration. On the contrary, when they need a marriage certificate, they will find ways to acquire it. Simply, they negotiate state law to achieve a local conception of an ideal form of religious and legal marriage.

The state has pursued many ways to deal with Muslim marriage in its attempts to realise a modern interpretation of *maṣlaḥa* (common good). However, they maintain their interpretation of the articulation of *maṣlaḥa* in marriage. Their understanding results from religious texts or other cultural norms and emerges from a lived engagement with a multitude of ideas, expectations, and local norms. In this framework, this book employs 'everyday practice,' an important analytical category, in its attempt to take "a more nuanced look at Muslims' religious lives"[29] without incurring any unnecessary dichotomies. Employing this approach, I examine people's involvement in and experiences of marriage legality and subject these to interpretations.

This study suggests that the relationship between the state actor and religious leaders is not a matter of competition but a mutual adjustment. In other words, there is no clear-cut competition between them. There is, of course, a particular segment of religious leaders who oppose the state law, mainly those who reject the foundation of the nation state, but the majority accept both the state and the state law. Two conditions explain why the former have chosen to resist. The first occurs when they think the state law goes against fundamental tenets laid down in Sharīʿa or when the state law introduces something explicitly impermissible according to Sharīʿa, such as allowing same-sex marriage or totally prohibiting polygyny. However, this would seem to be nearly impossible in Indonesia because, to a large extent, the legal reforms have carefully considered what is permissible and impermissible according to Sharīʿa.

In most cases, and this is the second form of resistance when the state law is too rigid to deal with practices which are socially acceptable, religious law offers a way out. People assume that religious law offers a version of *maṣlaḥa* and has the virtue of flexibility, especially in tackling problems of sexual mor-

29 Samuli Schielke and Liza Debevec, "Introduction," in *Ordinary Lives and Grand Schemes: An Anthropology of Everyday Religion*, ed. Samuli Schielke and Liza Debevec (New York and Oxford: Berghahn Books, 2012), 4.

ality such as *zinā* and teenage pregnancy. In this case, marriage is the only acceptable solution. Because people perceive marriage as a religious ceremony, religious law is required.

Another point that this study suggests is that the state's attempt to reform both Muslim marriage law and its marriage bureaucracy has preserved the informality of legal implementation. This informality is important as it offers a capacity to reconcile people's personal interests in religious and state law. It opens a door for the roles played by informal actors in helping ordinary people and negotiating their desire to observe their religion with all propriety and to seek state recognition. On the central state level, this informality is frowned upon as it makes inroads into the government's policy of establishing clean governance.

2 Muslim Marriage: Sharīʿa Law, State Law, and Bureaucratisation

For the majority of Muslims, marriage is "more than a mere contract."[30] It exceeds a private contract between two individuals. It also serves as an important familial, communal, and even spiritual event. The appropriate legal confirmation of marriage requires more than just compliance with the state's procedural forms of registration. It requires a religious ceremony held before a qualified official who solemnises the union and before a community that witnesses the new couple commencing a new chapter in their lives together.[31] Because these communal and religious dimensions of marriage are more important to many people than the formally conferred civil status, the relationship between the state procedures and the religious law is an unresolved topic of debate. This persisting tension means that the relationship between the two is a recurring theme in the study of Islamic law and society.[32] The relationship between them is key to understanding the varied dimensions of Muslim practice in Indonesia. It is therefore important to understand the position of Sharīʿa, *fiqh* (Islamic legal opinions), and the state law in Indonesian life.

---

30 Joel A. Nichols, "Religion, Family Law, and Competing Norms," in *Negotiating State and Non-State Law: The Challenge of Global and Local Legal Pluralism*, ed. Michael A. Helfand (Cambridge: Cambridge University Press, 2015), 198.

31 Ibid.

32 Baudouin Dupret, "Legal Pluralism, Plurality of Laws, and Legal Practices: Theories, Critiques, and Praxiological Re-Specification," *European Journal of Legal Studies* 1, no. 1 (2007): 1–26; Arskal Salim, *Contemporary Islamic Law in Indonesia: Shariʿah and Legal Pluralism* (Edinburgh: Edinburgh University Press, 2015).

Sharīʿa, *fiqh*, and state law interrelate with each other at specific points. God has set down Sharīʿa to be obeyed by Muslims.[33] Literally, Sharīʿa means 'way,' 'path,' or 'the road to a watering place.'[34] It is, therefore, defined as God's law, setting out the way of life a Muslim should follow. However, many Muslim scholars choose to emphasise the legal side of Sharīʿa.[35] Although Sharīʿa can be said to contain law, it embraces elements and aspects that are not, strictly speaking, law.[36] In *Marriage on Trial*, Mir-Hosseini describes Sharīʿa as forming "the basis of family law, though reformed, codified and applied by a modern legal apparatus."[37] Furthermore, she argues that as divine law, Sharīʿa has constituted the backbone of Muslim society.[38] The next concept is *fiqh*. While Sharīʿa comes from God through the verses of the Qur'an, *fiqh* (which means understanding) is the interpretations made by human beings of those Qur'anic legal verses which have imprecise, multiple meanings. *Fiqh* includes opinions of 'ulama' who, by their religious piety and learning, have become competent to interpret the scriptural sources and derive laws.[39] *Fiqh* is relative and subjective and varies according to the reasoning of different individuals. Differing opinions among jurists are inescapable.

The final factor is state Islamic law. Summing this up in relatively simple terms, it is a codification of Sharīʿa or *fiqh* and is limited to a particular aspect of them. Of course, this position assumes the crucial role of the state in the legislation. Lombardi remarks that, under certain conditions, a government could legitimately impose its preferred understanding of God's law and hence could force its citizens to observe the government's interpretation in preference to their own interpretations.[40] However, it is impossible to ignore that there is still room for a Muslim to choose potential rules of behaviour rooted in an understanding of God's law. Arabi came up with the idea of positivisation, that is, the process of the integration of Sharīʿa into the modern state political struc-

33 Qur'an 45:18.

34 Joseph Schacht, "Shariʿa," in *First Encyclopedia of Islam*, ed. M.Th. Houstma et al. (Leiden: Brill, 1987), 320–324.

35 Arskal Salim, *Challenging the Secular State: The Islamization of Law in Modern Indonesia* (Honolulu: University of Hawai'i Press, 2008), 11.

36 Bernard G. Weiss, *The Search for God's Law: Islamic Jurisprudence in the Writing of Saif Al-Dīn Al-Āmidī* (Salt Lake and Herndon: University of Utah Press and International Institute of Islamic Thought, 2010), 1.

37 Mir-Hosseini, *Marriage on Trial: Islamic Family Law in Iran and Morocco*, 8.

38 Ibid., 4.

39 Frank E. Vogel, *Islamic Law and Legal System Studies of Saudi Arabia* (Leiden/Boston: Brill, 2000), 7.

40 Lombardi, *State Law as Islamic Law in Modern Egypt: The Incorporation of the Sharīʿa into Egyptian Constitutional Law*, 19.

ture, which is allowed from a religious perspective as long as not it does not lead to the abandoning of the ethical and religious spirit of Islam.[41] The state may impose its interpretation provided it does not command Muslim citizens to disobey God and provided the object of the law is to advance the welfare of citizens.[42]

2.1 *Sharīʿa Law*

According to Hallaq, the introduction of the nation state and how it should deal with Sharīʿa has been the most ubiquitous problem in the legal history of the modern Muslim world.[43] For centuries, Sharīʿa, an intricate notion that comprises God's commands,[44] has reigned supremacy in Muslim societies.[45] Nevertheless, a considerable debate has arisen over how Sharīʿa law, as prescribed in the classical treatises, should respond to the changing social life and adjust its management of social order. Different legal interpretations in Sharīʿa make it difficult to present a unified language of law and produce more decisive rules devised to create legal certainty. The local political powers have had the right to make and apply rules and regulations in an indirect initiative to provide 'uniformity of the law' among different legal schools.[46] This legal-cum-political right of the ruler, popularly known as *siyāsa sharʿiyya*, has grown into an important instrument by which such a leader can advance their judicial authority. In practice, *siyāsa sharʿiyya* granted the ruler the authority to legislate as a complement to Sharīʿa law when the religious texts offered no opinion about a specific matter. Similarly, new rules could be created as long as

---

41 Oussama Arabi, *Studies in Modern Islamic Law and Jurisprudence* (The Hague: Kluwer Law International, 2001), 194.

42 Lombardi, *State Law as Islamic Law in Modern Egypt: The Incorporation of the Sharīʿa into Egyptian Constitutional Law*, 19.

43 Hallaq, *Sharīʿa: Theory, Practice, Transformations*, 359.

44 Rudolph Peters, "From Jurists' Law to Statute Law or What Happens When the Shariʿa Is Codified," *Mediterranean Politics* 7, no. 3 (2002): 82–95; Aharon Layish, "The Transformation of the Sharīʿa from Jurists' Law to Statutory Law in the Contemporary Muslim World," *Die Welt des Islams* 44, no. 1 (2004): 85–113; Salim, *Challenging the Secular State: The Islamization of Law in Modern Indonesia*, 13–14.

45 Early in the ninth century, Sharīʿa was the greatest subject of Islamic scholarship. Renowned as *fiqh* (literally *al-fahm* or understanding). It represents the intellectual efforts of Muslim jurists to understand the legal substance written in the holy texts. This intellectual enterprise, comprising a set of norms, commentaries and stipulations and laid down in the works of classical-medieval Muslim jurists, eventually developed into an established system of Islamic legal scholarship. Hallaq, *Sharīʿa: Theory, Practice, Transformations*

46 Layish, "The Transformation of the Sharīʿa from Jurists' Law to Statutory Law in the Contemporary Muslim World," 87–88.

considered necessary for the attainment of the common good.[47] This judicial authority also required the incorporation of religious piety and knowledge of Sharīʿa.

As a consequence, the formation of state Islamic law has involved power relations and encompassed the multifaceted social, political, and legal narratives in society over the last two centuries.[48] Scholars have argued that the dominant influence of European modernity in shaping Islamic legal institutions has meant a struggle in power relations. The state power could replace religious authorities in the administration of private affairs. Hallaq argues that because the state has played a decisive role in controlling the direction of Sharīʿa, it has diminished the institutional independence of religious scholars to formulate a legitimate interpretation of Sharīʿa.[49] In other words, Sharīʿa has moved towards its demise in the light of the shifts in the conception of legal authority introduced by the modern nation state. Nevertheless, many authors have shown that the codification of Islamic law still allows different legal opinions within Islam to struggle to find a true articulation of Sharīʿa.

The modern legal approach, characterised by a tendency towards a hierarchical, administrative understanding of the law, has influenced the legal conceptions in Sharīʿa.[50] The moral values and legal elements enshrined in religious law have become a more restrictive administrative state code. Furthermore, the fact that the idea of legal reform derives from the rise of Western scholarship in Islamic law has had the consequence of a misunderstanding of how Islamic normativity ought to function in the legal reform process.[51] The state power and religious authorities have worked together to select wide-ranging jurists' laws. At least two consequences have become apparent, even though the legislation has been no more than codifying preferred *fiqh* doctrines. First, religious scholars have experienced a struggle to reach an authoritative legal interpretation within their own circle. Second, despite the involvement of traditional Islamic jurists in preparing the contents, there have been persistent challenges to the state's authority to legalise religious law. The legitimacy of

47 Vogel, *Islamic Law and Legal System Studies of Saudi Arabia*, 173–174.

48 Iza R. Hussin, *The Politics of Islamic Law: Local Elites, Colonial Authority, and the Making of the Muslim State* (Chicago and London: The University of Chicago Press, 2016), 7.

49 Wael B. Hallaq, "Can the Shariʿa Be Restored?," in *Islamic Law and the Challenges of Modernity*, ed. Yvonne Y. Haddad and Barbara F. Stowasser (Walnut Creek: Altamira Press, 2004), 21–53.

50 Mohammad Fadel, "State and Sharia," in *The Ashgate Research Companion to Islamic Law*, ed. Rudolph Peters and Peri Bearman (Surrey, England: Ashgate, 2014), 94.

51 Léon Buskens, "Sharia and the Colonial State," in *The Ashgate Research Companion to Islamic Law*, ed. Rudolph Peters and Peri Bearman (Surrey, England: Ashgate, 2014), 212.

legislated Islamic law has emerged as a question because the ultimate decision about the content of the codification has lain in the hands of the state's political power.

In scholarly terms, the institutionalisation of Sharīʿa which has taken place in Muslim majority states, including Indonesia, has been a political and practical encounter.[52] This situation is not exclusive to Indonesia. Buskens has noted that the making of Moroccan family law has involved public and political debates.[53] In relation to this, Hallaq argues that the transformation of Sharīʿa into codified Islamic law results in what he termed 'great synthesis.'[54] This expression means that Islamic law has incorporated two aspects: traditionalism, that is, the ideas and norms indicated in the sacred texts, the Quran and prophetic traditions, and rationalism in the forms of scholarly consensus and analogical reasoning. A negative side to this legal-political process is that it has diminished the open scholarly discourse of Sharīʿa[55] with respect to the pre-existing different *fiqh* schools.

The legal reform of Islamic personal status (*aḥwāl shakhṣiyya*) in Indonesia has been far-reaching,[56] although it has involved the contestation of divergent religious and non-religious outlooks. Various scholars have contributed to our insights into particular contexts of this contestation. Jan Michiel Otto has argued that, despite the use of Sharīʿa as the basis of the Indonesian marriage law, some provisions have encroached upon the patriarchal norms of classical doctrine.[57] Cammack has remarked that the codifying of the Islamic

---

52 Léon Buskens, "Recent Debates on Family Law Reform in Morocco: Islamic Law as Politics in an Emerging Public Sphere," *Islamic Law and Society* 10, no. 1 (2003): 71; Léon Buskens and Baudouin Dupret, "The Invention of Islamic Law: A History of Western Studies of Islamic Normativity and Their Spread in the Orient," in *After Orientalism: Critical Perspectives on Western Agency and Eastern Re-Appropriations*, ed. Jean-Claude Vatin and François Pouillion (Leiden: Brill, 2014), 47.

53 Buskens, "Recent Debates on Family Law Reform in Morocco: Islamic Law as Politics in an Emerging Public Sphere," 123.

54 Wael B. Hallaq, *The Origins and Evolution of Islamic Law* (Cambridge: Cambridge University Press, 2005), 122.

55 Léon Buskens, "A Medieval Islamic Law? Some Thoughts on the Periodization of the History of Islamic Law," in *O Ye Gentlemen: Arabic Studies on Science and Literary Culture. In Honour of Remke Kruk*, ed. A. Vrolijk and J.P. Hogendijk (Leiden: Brill, 2007), 472.

56 Bowen, *Islam, Law, and Equality in Indonesia: An Anthropology of Public Reasoning*; Euis Nurlaelawati, *Modernization, Tradition and Identity: The Kompilasi Hukum Islam and Legal Practice in the Indonesian Religious Courts* (Amsterdam: Amsterdam University Press, 2010); Mark Cammack, "The Indonesian Islamic Judiciary," in *Islamic Law in Contemporary Indonesia: Ideas and Institutions*, ed. R. Michael Feener and Mark Cammack (Cambridge (Mass): Harvard University Press, 2007), 146–169.

57 Jan Michiel Otto, "Sharia and National Law in Indonesia," in *Sharia Incorporated: A Com-*

court law has created unstable accommodation between the modernists and the traditionalists in Islam and has changed the government's attitude towards Islam.[58] Furthermore, Hefner has also remarked that Sharīʿa has been an arena of contestation in Indonesian society. These remarks suggest that Sharīʿa is not a singular interpretation but includes understandings derived from complicated factors, including conservative religious orthodoxy and *maqāṣid* (higher aims)-based approaches to Sharīʿa.[59]

2.2 *State Law*

In the early years after independence, the Indonesian state devoted most of its attention to the administration of civil matters. Hence, it was in this period that marital relations came under the control of the state, and this shift has led to political and religious debates over the last four decades.[60] A key turning point has been the enactment of the Marriage Law in 1974.[61] This Law made family relations subject to the state by requiring civil registration, although religious doctrines still influenced the substantive rules of the Law.

The contest between religious law and state law on marriage has resulted in a number of compromises. They include the legal obligation of marriage registration, the regulation of the minimum ages of marriage, polygyny, and the judiciary's role in family law matters. The Law conceptualises marriage at the crossroads between religious precepts and state administration.[62] The Law

---

parative Overview of the Legal Systems of Twelve Muslim Countries in Past and Present, ed. Jan Michiel Otto (Leiden: Leiden University Press, 2010), 433–490.

58 Mark Cammack, "Indonesia's 1989 Religious Judicature Act: Islamization of Indonesia or Indonesianization of Islam?," *Indonesia* 63, no. April (1997): 143–168.

59 Robert W. Hefner, "Sharia Law and Muslim Ethical Imaginaries in Modern Indonesia," in *Sharia Dynamics: Islamic Law and Sociopolitical Processes*, ed. Timothy P. Daniels (Cham: Springer International Publishing, 2017), 91–115.

60 Mark Cammack, Lawrence A. Young, and Tim B. Heaton, "Legislating Social Change in an Islamic Society: Indonesia's Marriage Law," *The American Journal of Comparative Law* 44, no. 1 (1996): 45–74; Mark Cammack, Helen Donovan, and Tim B. Heaton, "Islamic Divorce Law and Practice in Indonesia," in *Islamic Law in Contemporary Indonesia: Ideas and Institutions*, ed. R. Michael Feener and Mark Cammack (Cambridge, MA: Harvard University Press, 2007), 99–127.

61 Kate O'Shaughnessy, *Gender, State and Social Power in Contemporary Indonesia: Divorce and Marriage Law* (London and New York: Routledge, 2009); Nancy J. Smith-Hefner, "The New Muslim Romance: Changing Patterns of Courtship and Marriage Among Educated Javanese Youth," *Journal of Southeast Asian Studies* 36, no. 3 (2005): 441–459.

62 Cammack, Young, and Heaton, "Legislating Social Change in an Islamic Society: Indonesia's Marriage Law"; June S. Katz and Ronald S. Katz, "Legislating Social Change in a Developing Country: The New Indonesian Marriage Law Revisited," *American Journal of Comparative Law* 26, no. 2 (1978): 309–320.

decrees that a marriage can be valid only once it has been performed in compliance with the principles of the religion of the bride and groom. Conformity with religious prescription is a must and unavoidable. However, in addition to religious compliance, a marriage must be authorised by the state through registration.[63] The contest between religion and the state in divorce is not as strong as that in marriage. Women in Indonesia often have no choice but to go to court to petition for divorce or request a divorce decree or certificate.[64] They have to depend on the state authority to declare their divorce status. As a consequence, those who wish to obtain a divorce extrajudicially also have to go to court if they want to get a formal divorce certificate.

Legal and human rights approaches are often brought into play to support the substance of marriage registration.[65] The problems caused by unregistered marriage, for instance, have been closely connected with violations of the rights of women and children born out of legal wedlock. This approach is in line with the general orientation of the legal reform after the 1998 political transition, albeit it has had a less revolutionary impact on Islamic family law, which has strengthened the continuing improvement of the position of women in the matrimonial sphere.[66] Nonetheless, public debates still revolve around the contest between religious validation and legal authorisation. This features very strongly in *fatwā* discourses.

Various issues and cases relating to family law have to do with how the legal norms imposed by the state are interpreted, practised, and negotiated by legal actors, be they judges, litigants, or lawyers. Facts emerging from court hearings, judges' decisions, and court reports have been the source of many heated debates in Indonesia. The problem revolves around how a judge of the Islamic court, bound by state laws, refers to a normative understanding of classical *fiqh* treatises or how he goes about adopting norms to introduce change into local practicalities.

---

63 Nani Soewondo, "The Indonesian Marriage Law and Its Implementing Regulation," *Archipel* 13 (1977): 283–294.

64 Euis Nurlaelawati, "Muslim Women in Indonesian Religious Courts: Reform, Strategies, and Pronouncement of Divorce," *Islamic Law & Society. 2013* 20, no. 3 (2013): 256.

65 Jayne Curnow, "Legal Support Structures and the Realisation of Muslim Women's Rights in Indonesia," *Asian Studies Review* 39, no. 2 (2015): 213–228; Ingrid Westendorp, "Personal Status Law and Women's Right to Equality in Law and in Practice: The Case of Land Rights of Balinese Hindu Women," *Journal of Human Rights Practice* 7, no. 3 (2015): 430–450.

66 Mark Cammack, Adriaan W. Bedner, and Stijn Cornelis van Huis, "Democracy, Human Rights, and Islamic Family Law in Post-Soeharto Indonesia," *New Middle Eastern Studies* 5 (2015): 1–32.

My study finds that, in terms of marital administration, the government has endeavoured to initiate legal changes through civil administration. Aware that any proposal for legal reform is always sure to spark controversy, the government has thought it best to begin to approach Muslim marriage within the framework of citizens' rights. Hence, the government deals with a marriage's legal status not directly but with the consequence of an altered legal status to the rights that a citizen can claim (Chapter 1). This shift has enabled the government to improve the efficacy of its marriage bureaucracy and encouraged people to depend more fully on its authority in seeking to arrange their marital affairs. Nevertheless, this effort has not entirely changed people's behaviour in particular societal contexts (Chapter 5).

Alongside the role of the civil administration in this direction, Islamic courts have also remained a significant factor in helping women obtain their rights. Studies done by John Bowen,[67] Stijn van Huis,[68] and Euis Nurlaelawati[69] have indicated the important role Islamic courts played in protecting women's rights. Bowen notes, "… but judges on Islamic and civil courts alike have tried to balance claims made in the name of Islam against those made in the name of *adat* …"[70] Studying legal cases in the Isak community in Aceh, Bowen concludes that judges in both public and Islamic courts have translated cultural ideas of fairness and agreement, namely social consensus, into their justification of gender equality.[71]

Furthermore, focusing on the functioning of Islamic courts in West Java and South Sulawesi, Stijn van Huis has argued that Islamic courts demonstrate the same tendency towards granting a divorce on the concept of a 'no-fault divorce,' in which the judges adopt a lenient approach towards divorce. This change means that women now have an equal position in divorce proceedings irrespective of their social standing. More importantly, Islamic courts now have enough room to create legal changes through reinterpretations of Islamic concepts in judicial processes.[72] Nevertheless, this positive development does not

67 Bowen, *Islam, Law, and Equality in Indonesia: An Anthropology of Public Reasoning*, 6.

68 van Huis, "Islamic Courts and Women's Divorce Rights in Indonesia: The Cases of Cianjur and Bulukumba."

69 Nurlaelawati, "Muslim Women in Indonesian Religious Courts: Reform, Strategies, and Pronouncement of Divorce"; Nurlaelawati, *Modernization, Tradition and Identity: The Kompilasi Hukum Islam and Legal Practice in the Indonesian Religious Courts*.

70 Bowen, *Islam, Law, and Equality in Indonesia: An Anthropology of Public Reasoning*, 6.

71 John R. Bowen, "Fairness and Law in an Indonesian Court," in *Islamic Law in Contemporary Indonesia: Ideas and Institutions*, ed. R. Michael Feener and Mark E. Cammack (Cambridge, MA: Harvard University Press, 2007), 170–192.

72 van Huis, "Islamic Courts and Women's Divorce Rights in Indonesia: The Cases of Cianjur and Bulukumba," 263.

necessarily determine the future of legal reform. Any legal reforms still need to maintain certain normative boundaries in the judicial tradition of Islamic courts if they are to be accepted. Nurlaelawati, who studied the use of the Kompilasi by judges in Islamic courts, found that the judges are often inclined to go along with the interests of those seeking justice in the courts, and their attitude means that transgressions against the rules interpreted by the State are unavoidable.[73]

The key role played by Islamic courts is evident in other Muslim countries too. In the context of 'progressive' Tunisian family law, Maaike Voorhoeve has argued that the implementation of state-promoted family law has a wide diversity where judicial discretion is significant on different levels of the state.[74] In the Egyptian context, Lindbekk has suggested that judicial practice in divorce shows a move towards an increased standardisation in the implementation of family law because of a closer unity between state law and religious morality, which is advantageous to women's interests. The critical finding of these studies is the increasing roles played by state agencies in protecting women's legal status and rights. My study also confirms these findings when it examines the quest for the state recognition of unregistered marriages (Chapter 6).

By contrast, O'Shaughnessy, who studied divorce cases in Indonesia from 1974 to 2005 based on court reports and printed sources, arrived at very different conclusions. She argues that the Marriage Law was designed to discourage divorces by making the terms for acceptance in courts and their administration more complicated. O'Shaughnessy has concluded that women's divorces during and post-Soeharto era could be construed as a threat to the state power's ideology of marriage and family. She said, "divorce was publicly and legally constructed as a menace to local and national stability."[75] I agree with Bowen's, Van Huis's, and Nurlaelawati's arguments on the roles of Islamic courts in protecting women's rights. By contrast, I find O'Shaughnessy's conclusion a bit unnecessary. My findings suggest that judicial divorce is not a danger to social stability. Instead, by seeking judicial divorces, women can define their legal status and claim citizens' rights and obtain proper access to state services.

---

73 Nurlaelawati, *Modernization, Tradition and Identity: The Kompilasi Hukum Islam and Legal Practice in the Indonesian Religious Courts*, 224.

74 Maaike Voorhoeve, "Judicial Discretion in Tunisian Personal Status Law," in *Family Law in Islam: Divorce, Marriage and Women in the Muslim World*, ed. Maaike Voorhoeve (London: I.B. Tauris, 2012), 199–229.

75 O'Shaughnessy, *Gender, State and Social Power in Contemporary Indonesia: Divorce and Marriage Law*, 199.

Researchers have also paid attention to the extent to which a Muslim marriage is linked to people's orientations on the understanding of what constitutes a good marriage, especially on the micro-Muslim community level. In social practice, religious laws have been prioritised, while local cultures (*adat*) are often entangled with Islamic tenets.[76] Many studies on child marriage,[77] marriage and religion,[78] marriage among educated urban Muslim teenagers,[79] and informal marriage and gender[80] have proposed the centrality of religious law. Summing up their study of child marriage, Grijns and Horii conclude that religious interpretations made by conservative Muslim groups in their efforts to deal with adolescent sexuality sustain the continuing practice of child marriage. In line with this argument, Nisa emphasises that religious piety and religious homogamy are important factors shaping marriage in certain Muslim communities. Bianca Smith, who studied divorce among women who live in *pesantren*, remarks that these women possess religious capital to avoid the state law on marriage.[81] In this *pesantren*, these women petitioned divorce informally and remarried in an Islamic manner, outside the formal procedure.

Moreover, Platt has explored why the Marriage Law as a project of modernity has failed to impact the Indonesian island of Lombok. The variety of women's experiences she has come across indicates the centrality of community-based law in shaping the marital trajectories for women.[82] Her finding on the centrality of community-based law is very relevant to my study. In terms of the everyday practice of marriage in the community I am studying, I found a sim-

76 Harry J. Benda, "The Structure of Southeast Asian History: Some Preliminary Observations," *Journal of Southeast Asian History* 3, no. 1 (1962): 120; M.B. Hooker, *Islamic Law in Southeast Asia* (Singapore: Oxford University Press, 1984), 8–15; Kristine Kalanges, *Religious Liberty in Western and Islamic Law: Toward a World Legal Tradition* (Oxford: Oxford University Press, 2012), 4.

77 Grijns and Horii, "Child Marriage in a Village in West Java (Indonesia): Compromises between Legal Obligations and Religious Concerns."

78 Eva F. Nisa, "Marriage and Divorce for the Sake of Religion: The Marital Life of Cadari in Indonesia," *Asian Journal of Social Science* 39, no. 6 (2011): 797–820; Myengkyo Seo, "Falling in Love and Changing Gods: Inter-Religious Marriage and Religious Conversion in Java, Indonesia," *Indonesia and the Malay World* 41, no. 119 (2013): 76–96.

79 Smith-Hefner, "The New Muslim Romance: Changing Patterns of Courtship and Marriage Among Educated Javanese Youth."

80 Platt, *Marriage, Gender and Islam in Indonesia: Women Negotiating Informal Marriage, Divorce and Desire*.

81 Bianca J. Smith, "Sexual Desire, Piety, and Law in a Javanese Pesantren: Interpreting Varieties of Secret Divorce and Polygamy," *Anthropological Forum* 24, no. 3 (2014): 37–41.

82 Platt, *Marriage, Gender and Islam in Indonesia: Women Negotiating Informal Marriage, Divorce and Desire*, 148.

ilar tendency to accord religious norms and the fundamental roles played by informal actors, namely *kyais* and *pengarep* (Chapter 4).

2.3 *Bureaucratisation*

Indonesia is a secular democratic country that has a Muslim-majority population. Although it is not an Islamic state, the centrality of Muslims in sociopolitical life is undoubtedly visible. Muslim groups have regularly pushed for a greater political and legal role for Islam.[83] Indonesian independence did not result in any important change in the status of Islamic rules as state law in Indonesia. However, as Cammack argues, "Muslims successfully resisted subsequent legislative efforts to change the substance of Islamic marriage law."[84] The state finds it important to deal with Muslims' interests in its attempts to realise a modern interpretation of *maṣlaḥa* (common good). The state bureaucratisation of Muslim marriage is one of the various areas where the state intervenes in religious affairs.

We should look at the bureaucratisation of Muslim marriage by requiring its registration as one of the ways in which the state is implementing its ideas of legal validity. Women's groups have regarded the government's intervention in marriage through bureaucratisation as a significant move to emancipate family law.[85] Nisa has argued that the issue of legal marriage has consistently presented a substantial problem for the government,[86] and the frequency of unregistered marriage "has been the real test of the bureaucratisation of religion in Indonesia."[87] In its efforts to achieve a balance, the government's efforts to accommodate people's understandings of Islam have led it to occupy an ambiguous position on the issue of unregistered marriages.

Numerous scholars have delved into this issue. Dominik Muller has defined the bureaucratisation of religion (Islam) as the way "state actors have empowered state-funded 'administrative' bodies in diverse ways to guide and influence Islamic discourses and regulate matters of religion and morality in

---

83 Simon Butt, "Islam, the State and the Constitutional Court in Indonesia," *Pacific Rim Law & Policy Journal* 19, no. 2 (2010): 279.

84 Mark Cammack, "Islamic Law in Indonesia's New Order," *International and Comparative Law Quarterly* 38, no. 1 (1989): 56.

85 June S. Katz and Ronald S. Katz, "The New Indonesian Marriage Law: A Mirror of Indonesia's Political, Cultural, and Legal Systems," *American Journal of Comparative Law* 23, no. 4 (1975): 653–681; Siti Musdah Mulia and Mark Cammack, "Toward a Just Marriage Law: Empowering Indonesian Women through a Counter Legal Draft to the Indonesian Compilation of Islamic Law," in *Islamic Law in Contemporary Indonesia: Ideas and Institutions* (Cambridge, MA: Harvard University Press, 2007), 129–145.

86 Nisa, "The Bureaucratization of Muslim Marriage in Indonesia," 309.

87 Ibid., 291.

the public sphere following their political interests."[88] Researching religious education in Egypt, anthropologist Gregory Starrett argues that the state objectifies religion and functionalises religion when it imposes bureaucratic categories. This functionalisation refers to "processes of translation in which intellectual objects from one discourse come to serve the strategic or utilitarian ends of another discourse."[89] Of course, this leads to the question of what purposes and whose interests the bureaucratisation of Islam serves.[90] For their part, Sezgin and Künkler argue that governments are interested in managing religion for socio-economic and social-engineering purposes.[91] These ideas about the bureaucratisation of Islam help understand the political dimension of actors involved in marriage registration, whom I present in Chapter 5.

In the end, the bureaucratisation of Muslim marriage is invariably concerned with how the state interacts with 'ulama' in a given setting. We know from Stijn van Huis's study that, in mid-nineteenth-century West Java, a relationship between the colonial state, the indigenous *priyayi* (social elites), and the landowning class of *kyai*s (traditional religious leaders) came to an end when the colonial government tried to increase its control of the autonomous *kyai*s. It inevitably led to a tense relationship between the *kyai*s on the one hand and the colonial government and the *priyayi* on the other.[92] Despite their predicament, the *kyai*s managed to maintain their position, lived in rural areas, and enjoyed their status as the social elite. They commenced a social process of making a distinct community and producing a particular type of Islamic understanding. After Indonesia declared its Independence, the Ministry of Religious Affairs tried to incorporate *kyai*s into its ranks. Still, it did not significantly change their autonomous behaviour in their dealings with everyday religious matters since many of them still viewed the state institutions as competition to their religious authority.

Examining this relationship has led Nurlaelawati to a different conclusion, namely that *penghulu*s, state-promoted Islamic leaders who have jurisdiction

88 Dominik M. Müller, *The Bureaucratization of Islam and Its Socio-Legal Dimensions in Southeast Asia: Conceptual Contours of a Research Project* (Halle, 2017), 2.

89 Gregory Starrett, *Putting Islam to Work: Education, Politics, and Religious Transformation in Egypt* (Berkeley: University of California Press, 1998), 9.

90 Mirjam Künkler, "The Bureaucratization of Religion in Southeast Asia: Expanding or Restricting Religious Freedom?," *Journal of Law and Religion* 33, no. 2 (2018): 193.

91 Yüksel Sezgin and Mirjam Künkler, "Regulation of Religion and the Religious: The Politics of Judicialization and Bureaucratization in India and Indonesia," *Comparative Studies in Society and History* 56, no. 2 (2014): 472.

92 Read chapter 5 of van Huis, "Islamic Courts and Women's Divorce Rights in Indonesia: The Cases of Cianjur and Bulukumba."

over marital affairs, and the KUA (Kantor Urusan Agama, Office of Religious Affairs), an office on a sub-district level that deals with Muslim marriage registration, have been an agency which intermediates the relationship between 'ulama' and the Islamic courts. She argues that the KUA officials consider themselves the guardians of Sharī'a rather than state officials. The KUA's views on marital problems are rooted in local society.[93] However, my study seems to confirm Van Huis's remarks. Rather than taking sides with the *kyai*s, *penghulu*s stand on the side of the state. They do not act as the bridge between 'ulama' and the Islamic court. On the other hand, some *kyai*s still preserve their own perception of religion and challenge the state law when it has interfered too much in people's religious lives (Chapter 4).

In this study, my goal is to understand how the state agencies interpret and implement the state laws on marriage. Therefore, I look at the role played by *penghulu*s and the whole everyday bureaucracy of the KUA. Besides my interest in the state *penghulu*s, I also analysed the position of *modin*s, village religious officials dealing with Muslim marriage informally, who, in my opinion, act as the fundamental informal actors. I use street-level bureaucrats to represent both *penghulu*s and *modin*s. They are frontline officials who interact directly with Muslim citizens and function as an essential link between the government and the people.[94]

*Modin*s are responsible for intermediating people with both state law and religious law. In other words, *modin*s assist in adjusting people's religious orientation towards the state law. In terms of marriage administration, *modin*s, appointed by the village head, worked as PPPN (*Pembantu Petugas Pencatat Nikah*, the marriage registrar's assistant). Their main task was to assist the work of PPN (*Petugas Pencatat Nikah*, the marriage registrar), that is the head of the KUA. In the last few years, the central government has discharged their position as the marriage registrar's assistant (Chapter 2). However, the loss of their legal status as the marriage registrar's assistant has not affected their socially acknowledged roles in the marriage ceremony (Chapter 5).

Furthermore, I also look at the judicial practices in the local Islamic court and examine how judges deal with socially disruptive problems like *isbat nikah* (retrospective authentication of marriage) for unregistered or informal marriages. *Isbat nikah* is a judicial procedure introduced by the Kompilasi which allows people to legalise their unregistered marriages retroactively. Upon the approval of *isbat nikah*, unregistered marriages turn into legal marriages.

93 Nurlaelawati, *Modernization, Tradition and Identity: The Kompilasi Hukum Islam and Legal Practice in the Indonesian Religious Courts*, 189.

94 Michael Lipsky, *Street-Level Bureaucracy: Dilemmas of the Individual in Public Services* (New York: Russell Sage Foundation, 2010), 3.

What follows is a visualisation of the relationship between legal norms and agencies in a Muslim marriage at different levels of society:

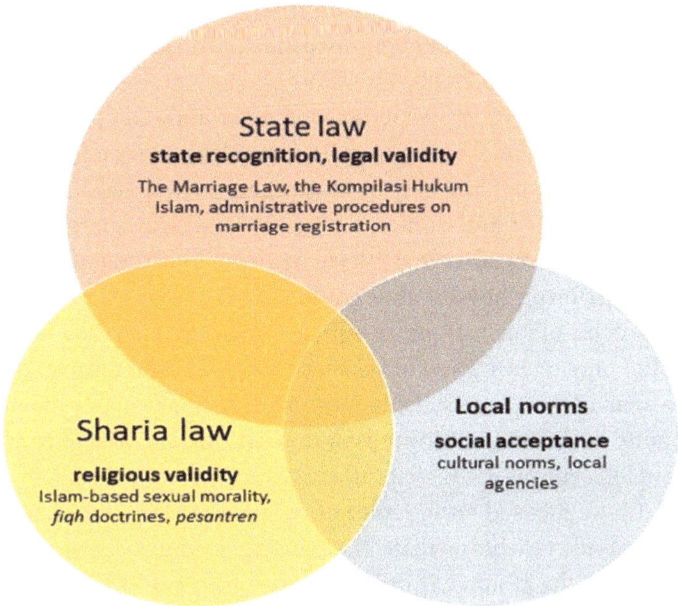

FIGURE 1 Relationship between legal norms and agencies in Muslim marriage in Indonesia

3 Focus and Setting

This book deals first and foremost with the bureaucratisation of Muslim marriage and its practical dimensions. Before launching into it, it is essential to explain how I have approached Islamic law on marriage. This book regards Islamic law on marriage as a system of norms constructed and transformed over time by the activities of individuals and larger social processes. This approach follows Dupret's assertion that Islamic law is found not only in the diverse legacy of Sharīʿa and *fiqh* treatises but also in what people, mainly Muslims, think about Islamic law. The task of researchers, in his view, is not to claim whether or not people's conception and practices comply with the pristine religious teachings but to describe in what ways they conceptualise Islamic law.[95]

95 Baudouin Dupret, "What Is Islamic Law? A Praxiological Answer and an Egyptian Case Study," *Theory, Culture & Society* 24, no. 2 (2007): 79–100.

Besides focusing on the debate on legal reform, this book investigates the practices and the negotiations which are an integral part of Muslim marriage. As already stated earlier in this Introduction, the second question can be developed into: how do local people on the northern coast of rural eastern Java practise and negotiate state regulations on Muslim marriage in their everyday lives? Here, I use 'everyday' to emphasise what Schielke and Debevec have called the openness of practices and experiences[96] to attain a better understanding of the daily practice of Sharīʿa. The term 'everyday' guides our attention towards the ways in which Muslims produce their own modernity[97] in everyday life.[98] Applying this framework, the practice of Muslim marriage is placed at the intersection of social, cultural, legal, and economic practices.[99]

First of all, the discussion on 'how the state governs' centres on more detailed enquiries into the process of law-making, the implementation of laws on marriage, and charts the bureaucratisation of marriage. Secondly, the term 'practise' refers to how marriage is perceived and performed in the everyday life of a Muslim community in Pasuruan. It tries to capture the role and influence of Sharīʿa and those of local norms in the shaping of marriage practice. To achieve this research goal, I have focused on the roles of religious leaders (*kyais*) and *pengarep* (voluntary brokers who mediate the communication between the families of the bride and the groom). Thirdly, the term 'negotiate' refers to the interaction between the state and society within the parameters of the state norms. This book investigates the legitimacy of the *penghulu*s, the position of *modin*s and how local people deal with them. 'Negotiate' also refers to the ways in which villagers seek the legalisation of their unregistered marriages, either in the KUA or in the Islamic court.

This book is also conceptually indebted to Bowen's idea of public reasoning. This theoretical concept provides the basis for an inclusive public dialogue in pluralistic societies,[100] in the sense that it attempts to discover a sphere of overlapping discourses and shared ideals on marriage, both vertically upwards from

96 Samuli Schielke and Liza Debevec (eds), *Ordinary lives and grand schemes: an anthropology of everyday religion* (New York and Oxford: Berghahn Books, 2012).

97 Modernity is understood as an age that began with the emergence and expansion of capitalism, industrialisation, scientific rationalism, nationalism and state claims to military power and the surveillance of citizens. Anthony Giddens, *The Consequences of Modernity* (Chicester: Polity Press, 1991).

98 Armando Salvatore and Dale F. Eickelman, "Muslim Publics," in *Public Islam and the Common Good*, ed. Armando Salvatore and Dale F. Eickelman (Leiden: Brill, 2004), 3–27.

99 Benjamin Soares and Filippo Osella, "Islam, Politics, Anthropology," in *Islam, Politics, Anthropology*, ed. Benjamin Soares and Filippo Osella (London: Royal Anthropological Institute, 2010), 1–22.

100 Bowen, *Islam, Law, and Equality in Indonesia: An Anthropology of Public Reasoning*.

the village level to the national scene and horizontally across between different normative systems. This idea leads me to ask a more theoretical question: *What can we learn from the practices and the negotiations in such a given society?* By posing this question, I expect to relate the issue of Muslim marriage to a broader debate about Sharīʿa and the nation state and the bureaucratisation of marriage.

At this point, I need to clarify the important distinction between 'Islam' and 'Muslim' as I have used these terms in this book. In Indonesia, Islam is expressed in different forms. Diverse kinds of Islam are (re)produced in society, and there is no single 'essentialist' Islam based on religious texts and Islamic history.[101] That is why I prefer the term 'Muslim marriage' instead of 'Islamic marriage.' The community I have studied practises a variant of Islam, which is close to so-called traditionalist Islam. It is an Islam that encourages the observance of one of the four schools in Sunni Islamic jurisprudence and at the same time gives great respect to religious leaders (*kyai*s) and the traditional Islamic schools (*pesantren*) they run as centres of learning. However, in the social realm, their religious activities are quite accommodating towards local traditions. Secondly, the word 'Muslim' is to emphasise the diversity in the practices of marriage. This is because, according to Benjamin Soares, by focusing on local culture, Islam as an object of study seems to become a plural phenomenon.[102]

I opted for Pasuruan as the setting of my research. Pasuruan is a regency in East Java province whose majority of inhabitants live in Muslim communities. They generally show a strong orientation towards practicing so-called traditional Islam,[103] especially that associated with Nahdlatul Ulama (NU), an Islamic organisation established in Surabaya in 1926 that promotes a motto 'preserving good old (Islamic) traditions and observing new better traditions.' This religious orientation is shaped by the fact that many Pasuruan residents' roots lie in the island of Madura, where the NU is also very influential.[104] However, my research focuses on Sumbersari (a fictitious name), a sub-district in Pasuruan. The majority of the people who live here are pious believers (*santri*). Culturally this community has developed into what is popularly known as a *pendhalungan* (mixed) society. The people speak Madurese and Javanese or

---

101 Michael Gilsenan, *Recognizing Islam: Religion and Society in the Modern Middle East* (London: I.B. Tauris, 1982).

102 Benjamin F. Soares, "Notes on the Anthropological Study of Islam and Muslim Societies in Africa," *Culture and Religion* 1, no. 2 (2000): 277–285.

103 Zamakhsyari Dhofier, *The Pesantren Tradition: The Role of the Kyai in the Maintenance of Traditional Islam in Java* (Tempe: Arizona State University, 1999), xix.

104 Yanwar Pribadi, *Islam, State and Society in Indonesia: Local Politics in Madura* (London and New York: Routledge, 2018).

a mixture of these and Indonesian with a Madurese accent. Only the younger generation born in the 1980s and thereafter can speak Javanese.

One specific feature of this community is the importance of maintaining patron-client ties. The patron is a *kyai* and his clients are the people in general. *Kyai*s are traditional religious leaders who are paid the greatest respect by the community for their religious learnedness. Most of them lead *pesantren* (traditional Islamic schools). *Kyai*s are invested with religious authority and, referring to Geertz, also play the role of the cultural broker.[105] The existence of *kyai*s and *pesantren* has contributed to the continuation of adherence to traditional Islam, which is also supported by *madrasah diniyah*, an out-of-school institution teaching subjects related to Islam. Children attend this *madrasah* in the afternoon after they have finished formal school in the morning. In this *madrasah*, they learn the Quran and other Islamic subjects. In Pasuruan, the Regent has issued a decree which obliges children at primary and secondary schools, who do not board in *pesantren*, to attend this *madrasah*. A more detailed explanation of the research setting comes in Chapter 3.

4 Method

This book is an anthropological (or social-legal) study of the implementation of marriage law in a Muslim community. I did open, lived, and dialogical fieldwork to ensure the depth of people's personal experiences. This choice had to do with doing justice to the people with whom I have been working. To understand people's everyday practices, I lived in a village, interacted with local people, and participated in social activities. For data collection, this study employed some methods, ranging from participant observation, open interviews, and case studies. I also used life history to describe the informant's experiences in concluding marriages.

Recording and making notes are important in ethnographic work. However, in my fieldwork, the use of each has been entirely dependent upon the situation. I had to reconsider whether or not making recordings of interviews with my interlocutors could make them feel uncomfortable and interrogated. I also tried to avoid making notes in detail during the interview because it could hinder the interview process. In this situation, I jotted down some key ideas and worked up the notes afterwards. I conducted my fieldwork in separate periods, namely seven months in 2017 (January to July), four months in 2017 and 2018 (November to February), and two months in 2019 (January to February).

105 Clifford Geertz, "The Javanese Kijaji: The Changing Role of a Cultural Broker," *Comparative Studies in Society and History* 2, no. 2 (1960): 233.

I divided my interlocutors into three hierarchal groups. The first group was the village level, which included women (unmarried, married, widows and divorcées), children, parents, men, religious leaders (*kyai*s), village religious officials (*modin*s), village officials (*pamong desa*), heads of neighbourhoods, and marriage brokers (*pengarep*).

The second group was the sub-district level which includes the KUA, the state body whose function is to register and legalise Muslim marriage. I conducted interviews with *penghulu*s and the officials of the KUA of Sumbersari in Pasuruan district, collected data on marriage practices in 2015 and 2016 based on official records, made categorisations, highlighted cases remarkable in an administrative sense, and discovered their context. One central question addressed was the extent to which the KUA plays a role in interpreting and performing the state rules on marriage and negotiates with the variety of religious and cultural norms in society. To make a comparison with Sumbersari, I also studied other KUAs in different districts such as Jember, Surabaya, and Yogyakarta.

Researching a government institution like the KUA is not always easy. In my efforts, I contacted my senior, who acted as the manager of the KUA in the town of Pasuruan. He introduced me to his fellow coordinator in the Pasuruan regency. This contact gave me access to the local KUA in Sumbersari. I used informal interaction when dealing with the head of the KUA and his staff. Based on informal interaction, I obtained the information I needed. This fieldwork was quite effective because sometimes I was allowed to lodge in the KUA, enabling me to extend my interaction and have good talks with its officials. Doing fieldwork in the KUA also helped me to get to know *modin*s. I also attended several monthly religious gatherings (*pengajian*), which they held.

The third group was the district and the upper level, which included state institutions (the Central and District Department of Religious Affairs and the Office of Civil Registration), the judges (local Islamic court), and religious institutions. My questions deal with their decisions, *fatwās*, and guidance pertaining to a Muslim marriage.

Pasuruan regency was not new to me, but Sumbersari was. My fieldwork began through my acquaintance with a lady, Umi, a graduate of an Islamic university in Surabaya whose bachelor's thesis dealt with the incidence of *nikah sirri* in Sumbersari. With the assistance of Umi, I managed to interact with local people. This process became more manageable as numerous young women of Sumbersari were Umi's friends when they studied in *pesantren* years earlier. With their help, I conducted interviews with ordinary villagers about their experiences in marriage. I also contacted Ali Sadikin, an NGO activist who has focused on women's issues in the area. Ali Sadikin introduced me to a number of active women. From their information, I understood how social structure works in practice and to what extent personal agency contributes.

It is worth noting that I used different identities depending on what kind of institution I was addressing. When visiting *kyai*s or *pesantren*, I had to use a religious identity. My status as a member of the NU in the Netherlands gave me advantages. At least, I was not treated as a 'different' person because most of them are also members of the NU. When doing fieldwork in the Islamic court, I used a more formal approach, as was expected of me. My position as a lecturer in the Sharīʿa faculty of an Islamic university in Central Java was advantageous. In general, the relationship between Sharīʿa faculties and Islamic courts is close because it is the faculty that produces judges and clerks of the court.

In addition to the interviews, I also did participant observation in social activities prior to and during a marriage ceremony (*akad nikah*), either in the KUA office or at a location outside it. I focused on the registration process, the verification of documents (*rafak*), the actors involved, and the handling of the marriage contract (the position of *penghulu*s and *modin*s). I also attended court hearing at a local Islamic court.

5 Structure of the Book

This book begins with an introductory chapter that explains the background to this book and presents an overview of key concepts. Eight chapters of this book are divided into two parts. The first part is concerned with law and institutions. It investigates public debates about the norms expected in Islamic marriage on the national level and issues arising from the bureaucratic reform of the administration of Muslim marriage. The first part consists of two chapters: Chapter 3 and Chapter 3.

Chapter 2 centres on continuity and change in the shaping of legal norms on Muslim marriage. This chapter seeks to elucidate the current developments by which the state simultaneously deals with the issues of the legal validity of a marriage and the protection of citizens' rights. In the Indonesian context, the public discourse about *nikah sirri* (unregistered marriage) has epitomised the dichotomy between the religious and legal validity of an Islamic marriage. This chapter argues that the state-led modernisation of Islamic marriage in Indonesia has moved away from the legal norm about the dual validity of a marriage, religiously and legally, to a legal policy on legal identity and citizens' rights. The state has not necessarily made attempts at legal reform by modernising traditional *fiqh* norms on marriage by passing legislation. Instead, it has chosen to endorse its bureaucracy to encourage the possession of civil documents such as marriage or birth certificates that protect citizens' rights. In this process, the question of the legal validity of marriage becomes irrelevant. However, an unprecedented consequence of this development is a conflict between state legal norms.

Chapter 3 delves into the modernisation of the bureaucracy in charge of administering Muslim marriage. In this chapter, I look at the bureaucratic reform of Muslim marriage administration and how it affects everyday practice of administration in the KUA. It is worth noting that there have been a series of efforts made by the Ministry of Religious Affairs to reform the KUA to introduce more efficient management. To reinforce the religious nature of the KUA, the Ministry of Religious Affairs sanctions *penghulu*s the only official eligible head of the KUA. In the spirit of good governance, the government has eradicated the informal administration fee and standardised the disparities in administration fees. Marriage registration has been integrated into the civil administration system.

The second part, consisting of four chapters, focuses more on legal practice. It addresses the functioning of the state law and the state institution and how local society deals with them. On a practical level, it elucidates the ways the state agency interprets and implements the relevant legal norms in its everyday bureaucracy and tries to understand how it deals with people's orientations towards Islamic marriage. In this part, I seek to present plentiful pictures of the people's individual orientations towards marriage and examine the state and non-state authorities' roles in dealing with marriage practice.

Chapter 4 offers an introduction that can assist in understanding the socio-economic history, the religious and cultural life and the development of Islam in Pasuruan. It first sets the scene by delineating the historical development of Pasuruan, including the history of Madurese migration and the historical development of Islam. Secondly, it addresses current cultural, religious, and political life. The last section centres on specific elements of the community in which I did my fieldwork.

Chapter 5 is concerned with the interaction between legal and social norms affecting marriage and how the actors negotiate marriage in a patrimonial social setting. In this chapter, I elucidate the roles played by religious leaders and social actors such as *pengarep*. This chapter suggests that marriage remains a religious concern, a sacred ceremony that sets a higher value on the involvement of religious authorities than those of the state. This chapter has discovered an internal heterogeneity in the relationship between the agency of the actors involved, cultural norms, and the social structure in selecting whom to marry.

Chapter 6 analyses the interaction between the state and society in marriage registration. It deals with the position of the KUA and the roles of street-level bureaucrats: *penghulus* and *modins* in marriage registration. In this chapter, I argue that the KUA, as the state agency in charge of Muslim marriage registration, needs to maintain its image as a body capable of supporting the proper balance between marriage, religious tradition, and modern administration. In the meantime, the state has terminated the role of *modins* as informal intermediaries on the grounds of public service and good governance. The bureaucratic reform had led to a dilemma as people have had to try to negotiate it to fit their own interests.

Chapter 7 deals with unregistered marriage and the search for state recognition. This chapter focuses on cases of participants in unregistered marriages who have sought state recognition by registering their marriage at the KUA or obtaining an authentication (*isbat nikah*) from an Islamic court. These cases have enabled me to think critically about the relationship between civil documents, state recognition, and citizens' rights from the perspective not only of the people but also of the other side: the state apparatus and the judges. Because some of the cases involve problems arising from a lack of documents, they suggest another aspect to take a look at administrative transgressions and judicial discretion. This chapter argues that people are not concerned about the legality of marriage. They request legalisation to define the legal status of their marital relationship because there is a need for them to do so. They are concerned with the benefits which accrue from the possession of civil documents.

This book ends with a concluding chapter (Chapter 8) in which I summarize and discuss my research finding. By looking at the implementation of legal norms on marriage, the functioning of marriage bureaucracy, and the people's attitudes towards state recognition of marriage in the local setting, this book suggests that Indonesia is experiencing a continuing process of the penetration of state law into society. The government has used a citizens' rights approach to control marriage practice. This citizens' rights approach helps guide people towards compliance with the state legal framework. Furthermore, the central state is also endeavouring to remove all forms of informality from the procedures involved. Nevertheless, it seems it is an uphill battle to reduce informal intervention. Moreover, in terms of the legalisation of unregistered marriages, we have witnessed the decision by judges of Islamic courts and *penghulus* at the KUA to adopt a lenient approach towards the rules governing marriage. In some instances, *penghulus* turn a blind eye to the rules while the judges are ready to exercise judicial discretion to grant state recognition to a marriage.

PART 1

Law and Institution

CHAPTER 2

Regulating Muslim Marriage: A Shift to Citizens' Rights-Based Approach

1 Introduction

Since the establishment of the KUA, the legal and religious validity of Muslim marriages and the relationship between them have been subject to debate in Indonesia. This chapter addresses a variety of questions concerning actors, discourse, and process. They are the following: *Who has been involved in the debates? What language has been used? How does the state deal with the different interpretations produced by Muslim leaders?* In essence, these questions reproduce the insistence common among Muslims in Indonesia that the state's codification of Islamic marriage law should still include a religious component. This is an important requirement for the majority of Muslims for whom the Sharīʿa is the frame of reference they believe should be their guide to morality and human relations. Their concern is not unfounded since the legal transformation from uncodified Sharīʿa law to the codified form of Islamic law has unquestionably expunged religious norms.[1] The elephant in the room is that Muslim majority countries cannot escape the need to systematise uncodified Sharīʿa into Islamic state law to deal with the various problems thrown up by modern development.

An important part of this chapter looks at the continuity and change in the formulation of legal norms on Muslim marriage in Indonesia, particularly since the fall of Soeharto in 1998. Its principal focus is the roles of the state and Islamic authorities in their struggle to define what makes an appropriate Islamic marriage in Indonesia on both national and sub-national levels. In this chapter, I wish to analyse laws, political processes, local regulations, and religious opinions.

I emphasise that the articulations of Sharīʿa laws on marriage and their embodiment in a legal code continue to feature in negotiations between the state and religious authorities about different legal norms. Although this is a persistent problem in numerous Muslim majority countries, the Indonesian experience offers some interesting, unique features. While the process of legal

1 Peters, "From Jurists' Law to Statute Law or What Happens When the Sharīʿa Is Codified," 90.

 | DOI:10.1163/9789004516113_003

reform has involved the secularisation of religion in state law, the post-New Order era has witnessed the increasing application of religion-inspired ideas in national and sub-national laws. Unquestionably, the government has faced a steep learning curve in its pursuit of legal reform through legislation because of the resistance from certain Islamic authorities. In this predicament, in line with the outgrowth of the human rights movement and bureaucratic reform, the judiciary and government bureaucracy have been important agents in facilitating reform without causing a confrontation with religious norms.

This chapter includes the following sections. Section 2 sketches how the Indonesian state deals with Muslim marriage and examines the notion of legal marriage according to state law. Section 3 focuses on the post-New Order development. In this section, I problematise the use of Islam as identity politics and how this fact has influenced legal reform on matrimonial matters on national and sub-national levels. Section 4 deals with the contestation of *maṣlaḥa* in legal discourses in the form of *fatwās* on marriage registration produced by Islamic organisations in Indonesia. Section 5 analyses the reforms introduced by the executive power in response to insistence on the protection of citizens' rights.

2 Legal Marriage: Dilemmas and Compromises

In the nineteenth century, along with the establishment of nation states and the implementation of European legal frameworks, the political rulers of numerous Muslim countries intervened in the application of Sharīʿa.[2] This intervention resulted in the incorporation of Sharīʿa norms, predominantly those relevant to personal status, into a legal framework.[3] Certain Muslim groups supported the formation of Islamic family law.[4] The majority of Muslims regard the reform of Islamic family law as a means of preserving Sharīʿa law.[5] In practice, legal reform generated problems because *fiqh* has never been a law code ratified by legislative authority. To achieve legal uniformity, governments in many Muslim countries must transform Sharīʿa from scattered, locally administered

2 Hallaq, *Sharīʿa: Theory, Practice, Transformations*, 2.

3 Hussin, *The Politics of Islamic Law: Local Elites, Colonial Authority, and the Making of the Muslim State.*

4 Paolo Sartori and Ido Shahar, "Legal Pluralism in Muslim-Majority Colonies: Mapping the Terrain," *Journal of the Economic and Social History of the Orient* 55, no. 4/5 (2012): 637–663.

5 Mir-Hosseini, *Marriage on Trial: Islamic Family Law in Iran and Morocco*, 12; Welchman, *Women and Muslim Family Laws in Arab States: A Comparative Overview of Textual Development and Advocacy.*

laws into state-centred Islamic legal codes. Codification has transformed what Muslims regard as divine norms into positive law.[6]

The Dutch colonial administration enforced legal systems on different segments of society.[7] Muslims were subject exclusively to Islamic family law, except for cases concerning maintenance (*nafkah*) and the division of property upon divorce and inheritance. Europeans and Christians were governed by Dutch law, while *adat* (customary) law was for natives. The legal classification of non-natives and non-Europeans was unclear.[8] *Adat* courts and Islamic courts remained under colonial control, although they enjoyed judicial autonomy.

Muslims in Indonesia have to negotiate Sharīʿa with the pre-existing practices, customs[9] and local rulers. The present Indonesian *taklik talak* (conditional divorce) formula,[10] signed by a husband at the time of marriage and enclosed on the last page of a marriage certificate, is one outcome of the long historical development of Islamic law, in progress since the end of the sixteenth century.[11] In the pre-colonial period, under the Islamic kingdom of Mataram in seventeenth-century Java, this legal procedure was found in a slightly different context. The earliest form of this conditional divorce agreement was called *janji dalem* or *janjining ratu* (the royal promise).[12] The word '*dalem*' represented the relationship between the ruler and the groom. The *penghulu*s read out the promise and asked whether or not the groom acquiesced in those mentioned above. The groom only needed to answer 'yes' or 'no' and only rarely did the groom refuse.[13]

---

6 Buskens and Dupret, "The Invention of Islamic Law: A History of Western Studies of Islamic Normativity and Their Spread in the Orient," 36.

7 Daniel S. Lev, "Colonial Law and the Genesis of the Indonesian State," *Indonesia* 40, no. 2 (1985): 61.

8 Ibid., 62.

9 C.A.O. van Nieuwenhuijze, "The Legacy of Islam in Indonesia," *The Muslim World* 59, no. 3–4 (1969): 210–219.

10 Scholars argued *taklik talak* was inspired by the sixteenth-century Shāfiʿī book, *Taḥrīr*, by Zakariyyā al-Ansārī (d. 926/1520) and subsequently elaborated by the Egyptian scholar al-Sharqāwī (1737–1812) in his book *Ḥāshiya al-sharqāwī*. See Azyumardi Azra, "The Indonesian Marriage Law of 1974: An Institutionalization of the Shariʿa for Social Changes," in *Shariʿa and Politics in Modern Indonesia*, ed. Arskal Salim and Azyumardi Azra (Singapore: Institute for Southeast Asian Studies, 2003), 76–95.

11 Cammack, Donovan, and Heaton, "Islamic Divorce Law and Practice in Indonesia."

12 Hisako Nakamura, *Conditional Divorce in Java* (Harvard: Islamic Legal Studies Program Harvard Law School, 2006).

13 Different regional versions of *janji dalem* can be found in A.H. van Ophuijsen, *De Huwelijksordonnantie En Hare Uitvoering* (Leiden: Firma P.W.M. Trap, 1907).

Sharīʿa pronouncements relating to marriage and divorce were the domain of *penghulus*. On the highest level (*kabupaten*) was *penghulu ageng* (the great *penghulus*), who also presided over judicial sessions in the *surambi* (forecourt) of the mosque. On the sub-district level (*kecamatan*), *naib* (deputy) performed this religious function. On the lowest level, *modins* (village religious officials) performed a religious function. The substantive laws applied in court were based upon several Shāfiʿī *fiqh* books. The *penghulus* exemplify the close relationship between Islam and Javanese custom.[14] Given the long-established political and religious power of *penghulus*, in 1835, the colonial administration formally recognised the *penghulus*' jurisdiction in family law.[15] Later, in the 1880s, the *penghulus* were absorbed into the Dutch colonial administration.[16]

The principle of 'to each his own law'[17] was in practice during the colonial era. Muslims were subject exclusively to Islamic family law, with the exception of law cases concerning maintenance (*nafkah*) and the division of property upon divorce and inheritance. Europeans were governed by Dutch law, while *adat* law was for those considered natives. The natives were fragmented into various groups with various requirements. Christians requested assimilation into Dutch law, the local aristocracies and elites claimed a privileged procedure, and the legal classification of non-natives and non-Europeans was indistinct.[18] The *adat* and Islamic judicial systems remained under the control of the colonial regulation, although they enjoyed judicial autonomy.

In the late colonial period at the end of the nineteenth century, the demands for the institutionalisation of Islam increased. The first ordinance on the obligation of marriage registration came into force in 1896 in the form of *Staatsblad* (Law) 1895/198. This ordinance stipulated a general marriage registration procedure and emphasised that only registrars appointed by the Dutch had the authority to register marriages, divorces, and marriage reconciliations. The

---

14 R. Abdoelkadir Widjojoatmojo, "Islam in the Netherlands East-Indies," *The Far Eastern Quarterly* 2, no. 1 (1942): 48–57.

15 van Huis, "Islamic Courts and Women's Divorce Rights in Indonesia: The Cases of Cianjur and Bulukumba," 34.

16 In the colonial era, *penghulus* faced three pressures: (1) the religious obligation to ensure the proper application of the Sharīʿa; (2) their status as agents of the colonial government; and (3) their status as social leaders who uphold moral standards. In the early twentieth century, Muslim organizations regarded *penghulus* as colonial-sponsored civil servants with inadequate knowledge of Islam. Muhamad Hisyam, *Caught between Three Fires: The Javanese Pangulu under the Dutch Colonial Administration, 1882–1942* (Jakarta: INIS, 2001).

17 Lev, "Colonial Law and the Genesis of the Indonesian State," 61.

18 Ibid., 62.

registrars collected an administrative fee from their clients.[19] The second ordinance, *Staatsblad* 1929/348, appointed marriage registrars to reinforce marriage registration as a legal obligation for Muslims in Java and Madura. Finally, in 1937, the colonial state established the *Penghulu* Court, which exercised jurisdiction over marital disputes, but not inheritance and endowment disputes. In practice, these laws were ineffective.

The Ministry of Religious Affairs was established in 1946.[20] Non-Muslim nationalists opposed the establishment of this ministry. According to Lev, "the very existence of a Ministry of Religious Affairs seemed to justify and lend permanence to a state that was patently not Islamic in form and substance."[21] Although the Ministry of Religious Affairs was intended to be a body that would meet the interests of all religious communities, it was largely staffed by Muslims.[22] It offered employment opportunities to members of Muslim organisations, the majority of whom came from devout and non-privileged organisations.[23] In practice, the Ministry of Religious Affairs plays a role in mediating the gap between national law and Islamic law.[24] Moreover, despite its attachment to Islamic tradition and affiliation with the Shāfiʿī *madhhab*, the Ministry of Religious Affairs has initiated small reforms acceptable to the majority of Muslim organisations.[25] For example, the government prioritised the administration of Muslim private affairs, especially in Java and Madura, and placed it under the administrative jurisdiction of the Ministry of Religious Affairs. The government applied a legal sanction to people who perform a marriage ceremony without a state official in attendance.[26]

Law 22/1946 on the Registration of Islamic Marriage, Divorce, and Reconciliation was enacted as the first government regulation after Indonesian Independence. The Law applied only to Muslims in Java and Madura, but was later supplemented by Law 32/1954, which extended the jurisdiction to all Muslims

---

19 Stijn Cornelis van Huis and Theresia Dyah Wirastri, "Muslim Marriage Registration in Indonesia: Revised Marriage Registration Laws Cannot Overcome Compliance Flaws," *Australian Journal of Asian Law* 13, no. 1 (2012): 7.

20 Deliar Noer, *Administrasi Islam Di Indonesia* (Jakarta: Rajawali, 1983).

21 Daniel S. Lev, *Islamic Courts in Indonesia: A Study in the Political Bases of Legal Institutions* (Berkeley: University of California Press, 1972), 47.

22 Nieuwenhuijze, "The Legacy of Islam in Indonesia," 212.

23 Cammack, Bedner, and van Huis, "Democracy, Human Rights, and Islamic Family Law in Post-Soeharto Indonesia," 5.

24 Otto, "Sharia and National Law in Indonesia," 444.

25 Lev, *Islamic Courts in Indonesia: A Study in the Political Bases of Legal Institutions*, 50–53.

26 See article 3 of Law 22/1946 on the registration of Muslim marriage, divorce and reconciliation.

in Indonesia. The Law was an important step for the Ministry of Religious Affairs to take, as it unified the registration of Muslim marriage and divorce. The Ministry of Religious Affairs sought to assure Muslim marriages' legal certainty and stability by requiring official registration.[27]

Since 1946, the KUA has had the task to handle marriage registration. District administrations (*regentschappen*) were no longer responsible for appointing registrars and managing administration fees.[28] During the 1950s, the government attempted to reform substantive marriage law. In the 1960s, responding to pressures from Indonesian female activists, the courts strengthened the position of women in the family. In 1968, the Supreme Court handed down a judgment that gave Indonesians the right to divorce on the grounds of irreconcilable differences.

In the early years following Independence, the new state maintained the plurality of legal orders for almost three decades. The winds of change began to blow when the debate about the unification of substantive marriage laws escalated under the New Order. Debates over marriage laws continued to rage in the early years of the New Order[29] administration. One group demanded one law for all religious groups, while its opponents insisted on different laws consistent with the requirements of the different religious groups. Religious political parties endorsed different laws.[30] Convincing all the groups to agree on one law to all groups seemed an impossible task. Consequently, despite numerous proposals for marriage law reform, none reached the statutory law up to 1973.[31]

It was only under the Soeharto government that it was possible to introduce a bill before the House of Representatives on 31 July 1973. Among the issues that the government sought to control through unified legislation on marriage was population growth.[32] Cammack argued that the draft of the marriage law gave the Islamic courts an advantage: these courts would exercise firm con-

27 Nurlaelawati, *Modernization, Tradition and Identity: The Kompilasi Hukum Islam and Legal Practice in the Indonesian Religious Courts*, 51.

28 van Huis and Wirastri, "Muslim Marriage Registration in Indonesia: Revised Marriage Registration Laws Cannot Overcome Compliance Flaws," 9.

29 The term New Order was coined by the second Indonesian President Soeharto to characterize his regime from 1966 to 1998.

30 Soewondo, "The Indonesian Marriage Law and Its Implementing Regulation."

31 Katz and Katz, "The New Indonesian Marriage Law: A Mirror of Indonesia's Political, Cultural, and Legal Systems."

32 Adriaan W. Bedner and Stijn Cornelis van Huis, "Plurality of Marriage Law and Marriage Registration for Muslims in Indonesia: A Plea for Pragmatism," *Utrecht Law Review* 6, no. 2 (2010): 178.

trol over the administration of marriage and divorce; and it included provisions regulating substantive areas not previously stipulated as being under the jurisdiction of Islamic courts, e.g., marital property, spousal support, and child custody.[33]

It is not clear who drafted the bill before the President endorsed it.[34] Although President Soeharto certainly did instruct the Ministry of Justice to draft the bill on the basis of the state philosophy known as *Pancasila*,[35] the Ministry of Religion was excluded from participation in preparing the draft bill.[36] Furthermore, Muslim leaders felt that they had been side lined from the process. This is possibly why some of the articles proposed in the Bill were rejected by Muslim groups as contravening Islamic doctrines. Islamic political parties and younger Muslims[37] criticised the government and made it clear that it would have to make some delicate compromises. The new Marriage Law introduced essential changes that promoted political stability and initiated social reform in Indonesia.[38]

The Law was passed in 1974 and came into force a year later. By accommodating the ideas of reformist Muslims, the new Marriage Law strengthened state authority to regulate and control family affairs. In brief, the state staked its claim to place its officials in a vital position as guardians of socio-religious change at the expense of non-state agencies.[39] In addition, the state addressed substantive issues relating to marriage in the language of state law,[40] avoiding questions about plural legal norms, religious affiliations, and local ethnic attachments.[41] The Law covers a wide range of matters arising from the dissolution of marriage. One important step is the abolition of the husband's right to unilateral repudiation (*talak*) and the provision that divorce must be subject to

33 Cammack, "Islamic Law in Indonesia's New Order," 58.

34 Katz and Katz, "The New Indonesian Marriage Law: A Mirror of Indonesia's Political, Cultural, and Legal Systems," 660.

35 O'Shaughnessy, *Gender, State and Social Power in Contemporary Indonesia: Divorce and Marriage Law*, 30.

36 Katz and Katz, "The New Indonesian Marriage Law: A Mirror of Indonesia's Political, Cultural, and Legal Systems," 659.

37 Soewondo, "The Indonesian Marriage Law and Its Implementing Regulation," 285.

38 Katz and Katz, "Legislating Social Change in a Developing Country: The New Indonesian Marriage Law Revisited."

39 Katz and Katz, "The New Indonesian Marriage Law: A Mirror of Indonesia's Political, Cultural, and Legal Systems"; Ratno Lukito, "Sacred and Secular Laws: A Study of Conflict and Resolution in Indonesia" (PhD Dissertation. McGill University, 2006), 244–245.

40 M.B. Hooker, "State and Syarîah in Indonesia, 1945–1995," in *Indonesia: Law and Society*, ed. Timothy Lindsey (Sydney: Federation Press, 1999), 97–110.

41 Cammack, "Islamic Law in Indonesia's New Order," 61.

court review. The Law grants both husband and wife an equal right to petition for a divorce. Despite these changes, most Muslims were satisfied that the Law accommodated Islamic teachings.

The state marriage legislation led to a dramatic shift in perceptions and patterns of marriage.[42] The Marriage Law defines a marriage contract as a religious marriage, not a civil marriage. Article 2 stipulates that marriage is not valid unless it is performed in a religious ceremony. Conformity with religious prescriptions is, therefore, unavoidable. However, in addition to religious solemnisation, marriage also must be authorised by the state through registration. Registration is not one of the legal conditions of marriage. Non-compliance with state regulations renders a marriage null and void, both civilly and officially. Consequently, a husband and a wife may not apply for or be issued a marriage certificate. However, failure to register a marriage does not affect its validity in religious terms. In other words, the Marriage Law conceptualises marriage as a combination of religious precepts and state administration.[43]

Politically, this Law influenced the subsequent direction of the relationship between Islam and the state. Earlier attempts to impose a secular, unified marriage law enforced in a general court failed. Therefore, instead of curtailing Islamic law and courts, the government decided to support Muslims in their desire to manage their own family affairs.[44] Beginning in the mid-1980s, however, there was a radical shift in the New Order government policy towards Islam on several issues.[45] This changing attitude crystallised in the enactment of Law 7/1989 on Religious (Islamic) courts, which now serves as the legal basis for the independence of Islamic courts.[46] The Law places Islamic courts on the same footing as other courts. Legal practitioners believe that the Law improves the application of Islamic law.

With the support of the central government, Muslim elites submitted several new proposals for legal reform. The Ministry of Religious Affairs applied for the

42 O'Shaughnessy, *Gender, State and Social Power in Contemporary Indonesia: Divorce and Marriage Law*; Smith-Hefner, "The New Muslim Romance: Changing Patterns of Courtship and Marriage Among Educated Javanese Youth."

43 Mark Cammack, Lawrence A. Young, and Tim B. Heaton, "Legislating Social Change in an Islamic Society: Indonesia's Marriage Law," *The American Journal of Comparative Law* 44: 1 (1996): 45–74; Katz and Katz, "Legislating Social Change in a Developing Country."

44 Mark Cammack, "Islam, Nationalism and the State in Suharto's Indonesia," *Wisconsin International Law Journal* 17 (1999): 27–63.

45 R. William Liddle, "The Islamic Turn in Indonesia: A Political Explanation," *Journal of Asian Studies* 55, no. 3 (1996): 613–634.

46 Nurlaelawati, *Modernization, Tradition and Identity: The Kompilasi Hukum Islam and Legal Practice in the Indonesian Religious Courts*, 57.

drafting of a family law code that regulates Islamic courts. This idea was first voiced in 1985 by Bustanul Arifin, chairman of the Special Chamber of Islamic Law of the Supreme Court. With the approval of Muslim judges and Islamic court officials, the government agreed to compile the Kompilasi.[47] President Soeharto approved the proposal in 1991.[48] The Kompilasi charges all relevant state institutions to refer to it to resolve marital disputes, covering marriage, inheritance, and endowments laws.

The promulgation of the Kompilasi was the outcome of extensive conversations and negotiations between representatives of Islam and the state. The New Order government reasoned that taking an accommodating approach to marriage reform would reduce resistance from Islamic circles in the future.[49] Soeharto's personal desire to secure the political support of Muslim circles was one of the most important arguments.[50] From a political point of view, the Kompilasi is a product of the political intervention of the state in Islamic jurisprudence in Indonesia.[51] The authorisation of the Kompilasi means that the state has demonstrated its cordial relationship with Islam and its support of the process of Islamisation in the political domain.

Some provisions of the Kompilasi sustain the legal norms of the Marriage Law, but others introduce a new legal norm. Several provisions refer to *adat*. Of particular interest is the heir's right to inherit a grandparent's property if the heir's parents predecease their parents. The Kompilasi also stipulates that both a husband and a wife have rights to marital property when their marriage ends, in the form of joint property (*harta bersama, gono gini*). Despite such nods to state and *adat* law, the Kompilasi defines marriage in accordance with classical *fiqh* doctrine, that is, as a solemn agreement (*mīthāq ghalīẓ*) that serves

---

47 Abdurrahman, *Kompilasi Hukum Islam Di Indonesia* (Jakarta: Akademika Pressindo, 1992); Cik Hasan Bisri, ed., *Kompilasi Hukum Islam Dan Peradilan Agama Dalam Sistem Hukum Nasional* (Jakarta: Logos, 1999).

48 There are two main steps in the formation of the Kompilasi: collecting relevant data and legal drafting. The team divided research activities into several stages: studying thirty-eight *fiqh* texts of different *madhhabs*, predominantly the Shāfiʿī school, and the *fatwās* of Islamic organizations in Indonesia. With the assistance of a number of scholars from the State Institutes of Islamic Studies (IAIN, Institut Agama Islam Negeri), the team interviewed hundreds of *ulama* from ten areas in which an Appeals Court had been established. The team compared Islamic family laws in force in Indonesia with those in other Muslim countries.

49 Bedner and van Huis, "Plurality of Marriage Law and Marriage Registration for Muslims in Indonesia: A Plea for Pragmatism," 180.

50 Nurlaelawati, *Modernization, Tradition and Identity: The Kompilasi Hukum Islam and Legal Practice in the Indonesian Religious Courts*, 91.

51 Ibid., 89.

as a manifestation of obedience to God's commands and thereby qualifies as an act of worship (see article 2).

The Kompilasi refers to and reinforces article 2 of the Marriage Law, which states that a marriage must be registered to safeguard social and legal order. This means that the absence of marriage registration does not affect its religious validity. The Kompilasi acknowledges an unregistered marriage (*nikah sirri*) and provides a legal procedure called *isbat nikah*, i.e., filing a request to an Islamic court to legalise an unregistered marriage retrospectively. This *isbat nikah* procedure is a state compromise on *nikah sirri*. *Isbat nikah* enables the couples in a *nikah sirri* to claim legal identity documents that facilitate their access to state programs and formal education.[52]

In 2009, there were more than 13,000 *isbat nikah* requests to Islamic courts.[53] In 2012, this number rose to 31,927. My data from a regional Islamic court in East Java show that the number of *isbat nikah* cases is low (0–6 cases per year). In some villages in Pasuruan regency, approximately 20 percent of husbands and wives do not have a marriage certificate. Towards the end 2016, the Female Civil Servants' Association of Pasuruan arranged an *isbat nikah massal* (mass marriage authentication) programme in partnership with the sub-district Muslim marriage registration offices and *modins*. Public participation in the program was significant. The Bangil Islamic court legalised approximately 100 unregistered marriages. Similar programs have been implemented in other areas, including the capital city, Jakarta.[54]

3 Sharīʿa-Based Regulations and the Steep Stairway to Legislation

The political reform in Indonesia in 1998 has led to an increasing challenge to the state from conservative Islamic groups. Despite the agreed principle of the state based on the rule-of-law (*negara hukum*),[55] the question of whether Indonesia is secular or religious recurs at regular intervals. In the present cli-

52 Bedner and van Huis, "Plurality of Marriage Law and Marriage Registration for Muslims in Indonesia: A Plea for Pragmatism."

53 Cate Sumner and Tim Lindsey, *Courting Reform: Indonesia's Islamic Courts and Justice for the Poor* (New South Wales: Lowy Institute for International Policy, 2010).

54 "557 Pasangan Sudah Mendaftar Di Acara Nikah Massal Dan Isbat Nikah Di Malam Tahun Baru," *Tribunnews*, accessed March 4, 2019, http://www.tribunnews.com/metropolitan/2018/12/31/557-pasangan-sudah-mendaftar-di-acara-nikah-massal-dan-isbat-nikah-di-malam-tahun-baru.

55 Daniel S. Lev, "Judicial Authority and the Struggle for an Indonesian Rechtsstaat," *Law & Society Review* 13, no. 1 (1978): 43–44.

mate, Islam has increasingly become the most important frame of reference for many Muslims in Indonesia[56] and has become a source of identity politics. The rise of 'new Islamic populism'[57] has influenced the relationship between state sovereignty and Islam. This shift has been strengthened by the idea of a global and transnational *umma* (Islamic community), which has dramatically changed local understandings of what it means to be a true Muslim.[58] In this section, I discuss how the rise of Islam as a collective identity, after the fall of Soeharto, has influenced the regulations on marriage on both national and district levels.

Within the new framework of democratisation and regional autonomy, the emphasis on Islamic identity has become apparent in the introduction of Islam-based regulations at the district level. The existence of local regulations, which purportedly encourage the growth of a better Islamic society, impose additional conditions on those who wish to enter into a marriage. Since 2001, regencies like Solok, Payakumbuh (West Sumatra), Bulukumba (South Sulawesi), Kota Banjarmasin (South Kalimantan), have issued a local regulation on the obligation to read the Qur'an. The long and short of this requirement is that brides and grooms must be able to read the Qur'an. In Bulukumba, for instance, the proposal to adopt this regulation was voiced by a religious leader who was the incumbent head of the Ministry of Religious Affairs' District Office.[59] The ability to read the Qur'an as a new condition for the conclusion of an official marriage is indeed a new interpretation of certain aspects of Sharīʿa. These regional regulations demonstrate the complexity of social and political domains.[60] According to Buehler, the implementation of Sharīʿa-based regulations is a by-product of a simmering conflict over control of economic resources between state and local elites.[61] Alimi argues that the use of Sharīʿa

56 Noorhaidi Hasan, "The Making of Public Islam: Piety, Agency, and Commodification on the Landscape of the Indonesian Public Sphere," *Contemporary Islam* 3, no. 3 (2009): 229–250.

57 Vedi R. Hadiz, "A New Islamic Populism and the Contradictions of Development," *Journal of Contemporary Asia* 44, no. 1 (2013): 125–143.

58 Delmus Puneri Salim, *The Transnational and the Local in the Politics of Islam: The Case of West Sumatra, Indonesia* (Cham: Springer International Publishing, 2015).

59 Elsam, *Monitoring Perda Syariat Islam Di Bulukumba: Perda Nomor 06 Tahun 2003 Tentang Pandai Baca Tulis Al-Qur'an Bagi Siswa Dan Calon Pengantin* (Jakarta, 2008).

60 Michael Buehler, "The Rise of Sharīʿa by-Laws in Indonesian Districts: An Indication for Changing Patterns of Power Accumulation and Political Corruption," *South East Asia Research* 16, no. 2 (2008): 255–285.

61 Michael Buehler, "Elite Competition and Changing State–Society Relations: Shariʿa Policymaking in Indonesia," in *Beyond Oligarchy: Wealth, Power, and Contemporary Indonesian Politics*, ed. Michele Ford and Thomas B. Pepinsky (Ithaca, New York: Cornell Southeast Asia Program Publications, 2014), 174.

in South Sulawesi has to do with Muslims' perception of Sharīʿa as the performance of everyday rituals. According to him, Sharīʿa discourse of the elites tends to be intellectual, yet Sharīʿa of the ordinary Muslims tends to be theatrical and discursive.[62]

Be that as it may, the post-New Order legal reform has fuelled debates and conversations between Muslim groups. A legal draft called the Counter Legal Draft Kompilasi Hukum Islam (CLD KHI), proposed by a working group of young Muslims in 2004, signalled a progressive shift. The draft proposal was intended to complement the government's efforts to raise the status of Kompilasi to that of a law. The draft was controversial, drawing harsh reactions from conservative Muslim groups, mainly because it treats Islamic marriage as a civil contract, not a religious agreement.[63] Subsequently, the CLD KHI drafters proposed that marriage registration should be compulsory, and its omission would abolish the validity of a marriage.[64] Their conversations suggest that contestation of religious authority is continuing.

In the post-Soeharto era, a number of new regional laws were enacted that support religious-based ideas but have not been recognised in national law. When conservative Muslim groups emerged as the public face of Islam, these regional laws were interpreted as a threat to attempts to reform family law. The government attempted to introduce legal reforms in 2010. However, several major obstacles stood in the way of the government's effort to introduce financial penalties for permissible actions under Sharīʿa law. The general public rejected the draft law.

In 2010, the government proposed the Bill on the Material Law on Marriage in Islamic Courts (Rancangan Undang-undang Hukum Materiil Pengadilan Agama Bidang Perkawinan, RUU HMPA). This law, to be applied exclusively in Islamic courts, would replace the two-decades-old Kompilasi. Generally speaking, for the most part, the RUU HMPA sustains norms already stipulated in the Kompilasi, but puts forward new rulings (articles 143–153) pertaining to unregistered marriage, temporary marriage, polygyny, and out-of-court divorce. The law identifies illegal marriage practices as either violation (*pelanggaran*) or crime (*kejahatan*). The former is sanctioned by a fine or imprisonment, while the latter carries a lengthy prison term.

---

62 Moh Yasir Alimi, "Rethinking Anthropology of Shariʿa: Contestation over the Meanings and Uses of Shariʿa in South Sulawesi, Indonesia," *Contemporary Islam*, no. 2 (2018): 123–151.

63 Muhammad Latif Fauzi, "Islamic Law in Indonesia: Recent Debates on Islamic Family Law in the Reformasi Era (1998–2007)" (Leiden University, 2008).

64 R. Michael Feener, *Muslim Legal Thought in Modern Indonesia* (Cambridge: Cambridge University Press, 2007).

More details of the two categories are found in the following table:

TABLE 1 Categories of violations and crimes in the RUU HMPA

Violations	Crimes
A marriage not concluded in the presence of a marriage registrar (article 143)	Entering into a temporary marriage (*mut'ah*) (article 144)
A marriage to a second, third, or fourth wife without the official permission of an (Islamic) court (article 145)	Conducting an extramarital relationship with an unmarried woman that has led to a pregnancy and refusal to marry her (article 147)
A husband's unilateral repudiation out of court (article 146)	Performing a marriage and acting as an official marriage registrar and/or magistrate guardian without due authorisation (article 149)
A marriage registrar who infringes on his obligations (article 148)	Acting intentionally as a marriage guardian, even though not legally entitled to do so (article 150)

Some opponents argued that criminalisation was 'uncreative efforts' (*langkah malas*) of the legal drafters. It repeats the content of previous marriage laws. The 1946 Marriage Law introduced financial penalties for women who enter into an illegal marriage and imprisonment for religious leaders who marry them off illegally. Government Regulation 9/1975 stipulates that failure to register a marriage is punishable by a fine of Rp7,500. Law 23/2006 on Civil Administration introduced a civil penalty, a maximum of Rp 1,000,000, for anyone who fails to report their marriage within sixty days of its conclusion. However, no strict implementation of the Civil Administration Law has ever been attempted.[65]

In the post-Soeharto era, a number of new regional laws were enacted that support religious-based ideas but have not been recognised in national law.

65 van Huis and Wirastri, "Muslim Marriage Registration in Indonesia: Revised Marriage Registration Laws Cannot Overcome Compliance Flaws."

When conservative Muslim groups emerged as the public face of Islam, these regional laws were interpreted as a threat to attempts to reform family law. The government attempted to introduce legal reforms in 2010. However, several major obstacles stood in the way of the government's effort to introduce financial penalties for permissible actions under Sharīʿa law. The public rejected the draft law.

The only successful legal reform was in 2019 through the enactment of Law 16/2019. The law amended article 7 of the 1974 Marriage Law on the marriageable age, 16 for brides and 19 for grooms. The law makes 19 a marriageable age for both brides and grooms. Furthermore, the law makes it possible for parents who wish to deviate from this legal norm by filing a request for marriage dispensation to Islamic courts. They have to convince the judges and present an 'urgent reason' (*alasan sangat mendesak*) and 'adequate evidence' (*bukti-bukti pendukung yang cukup*). However, this reform seems unsuccessful to change people's behavior in marriage. Islamic courts receive a larger number of requests for marriage dispensation than before Law 16/2019 was enacted.

4 Contesting *Maṣlaḥa*

The reform of Islamic family law has always been an arena in which ʿulamaʾ seek to intervene through their *fatwās* (legal opinions). They have applied *ijtihād* (the process of making a legal decision by independent interpretation of Islam legal sources) to ensure that their involvement was, and remains, visible in formulating the material legitimacy and maintaining the religious legitimacy of a legal code. Although there is a growing tendency to promote the notion of *maṣlaḥa*,[66] the result of *ijtihād* is not always supportive of, indeed can even be in opposition to, the state way of thinking. By exerting their influence on Islamic legal matters, Muslim groups articulate their position on the relationship between Islam and state authority.

In this section, I investigate three *fatwās* on marriage registration. These *fatwās* were issued by major Islamic organisations in Indonesia, namely the Majelis Ulama Indonesia (MUI, the Indonesian Ulama Council), the Muhammadiyah, and the Nahdlatul Ulama. I selected these organisations considering their methods of legal reasoning and the special body of *iftāʾ* (*fatwā* giving): the

66 Felicitas Opwis, "Maṣlaḥa in Contemporary Islamic Legal Theory," *Islamic Law and Society* 12, no. 2 (2005): 182–223; Hefner, "Sharia Law and Muslim Ethical Imaginaries in Modern Indonesia."

Komisi Fatwa of the MUI, *Majelis Tarjih* of Muhammadiyah, and *Bahtsul Masail* of the Nahdlatul Ulama.

4.1 *The* MUI *Fatwā*

The government established the MUI in 1975 as a common platform that would unite different Islamic organisations, Muslim leaders and scholars. The MUI seeks to accommodate the interests of the political regime and Muslim communities.[67] Its *fatwā*s are intended to make religion close with the state. The MUI discussed unregistered marriage in the *Ijtima' Ulama* (Ulama Assembly) held in the Pesantren of Gontor, East Java, in May 2006. Two years later, the MUI issued *Fatwa* 10/2008, including its legal opinion on unregistered marriage. The MUI was careful in selecting terms to designate unregistered marriages to avoid ambiguities.

Although the term *nikah sirri* is widespread among Muslims in Indonesia, the *fatwā* introduces the concept of *nikah di bawah tangan* (unofficial marriage). The MUI argues that, in everyday practice, *nikah sirri* refers to a marriage that has deliberately been concluded in secret, without two witnesses (*shāhidayn*). This kind of marriage, according to the MUI, is invalid (*tidak sah*). The *fatwā* states that the majority of Sunni schools are in agreement that the presence of witnesses is a requirement for the validity of a marriage. Only the Mālikī school holds that publication (*iʿlān*) is sufficient, as a substitute for two witnesses.

Although the *fatwā* confirms the legal norm stipulated in state law, it also embraces 'dual validity.' It states that an unofficial marriage is (religiously) valid (*sah*), in regard to its compliance with the conditions (*syarat*, *rukun*) of Islam, but falls into the category of *haram* (unlawful) if it causes harm (*mudharat*). The *fatwā* defines harm as it applies to the husband's obligation to fulfil the rights of wives and children. The MUI did not openly declare unofficial marriages either harmful or immoral. Discussing the status of *haram*, Ma'ruf Amin, General Chairman of the MUI at the time, indicated that if a husband neglects his responsibilities, he will be regarded only as sinful. In its legal reasoning, the *fatwā* adopts the method of *sadd al-dharīʿa* (blocking the means to evil). It concludes that marriage registration is strongly recommended so as to protect Muslims from harm. The *fatwā* also refers to a statement by a nineteenth-century Javanese religious scholar, Muḥammad ibn ʿUmar al-Nawāwī: "an obligation (*wujūb*) must be considered to be absolutely compuls-

67 Syafiq Hasyim, "Majelis Ulama Indonesia and Pluralism in Indonesia," *Philosophy & Social Criticism* 41, no. 4–5 (2015): 487–495.

ory (*ta'akkada wujūbuh*); recommended activities (*mustaḥabb*) must be considered to be compulsory; and permissible activities (*jā'iz*) must be considered to be recommended, so long as it involves *maṣlaḥa*." According to the MUI *fatwā*, marriage registration is covered by the first category, which is obligatory.

4.2 *The* Majelis Tarjih Fatwā

The second *fatwā* was issued by the *Majelis Tarjih* of the Muhammadiyah, a modernist movement that, under the banner of reform (*tajdīd*) and purification, approaches the basic sources of Islam by means of independent rational investigation. In addition to the principle of the return to the Qur'an and Sunnah of the Prophet advocated by the Egyptian scholar Muhammad 'Abduh, Muhammadiyah encourages the use of reason. In the context of Sharīʿa law, this orientation is epitomised by *tarjīḥ*, an examination of several Muslim jurists' differing opinions to determine which is most consistent with the original Sharīʿa source.[68]

In 2007 the *Majelis Tarjih* of the Muhammadiyah issued a *fatwā* on *nikah sirri* that reinforced the state's legal norm on official marriage. Interestingly, this *fatwā* does not contain a clear-cut statement on the legal status of *nikah sirri*. Instead, it states that the function of marriage registration is to eliminate nonfulfilment of the required conditions in a marriage contract and to avoid forgery of the bride's identity and documents. Marriage registration is declared compulsory, by analogy (*qiyās*) to the obligation of debt registration (*mudāyana*). A marriage contract occupies a more important position than other contracts. The *fatwās* of the MUI and Muhammadiyah are both excellent examples of the use of the *maṣlaḥa* to address modern developments.

4.3 *The* Bahtsul Masail Fatwā

The Nahdlatul Ulama is an Islamic organisation that promotes a traditionalist view of Islam. Traditional religious leaders (*kyai*s) are vested with the authority to undertake legal reasoning. Its adherence to classical traditions is evident in its references to the four Sunni schools of law, most notably the Shāfiʿī. The Nahdlatul Ulama's *Bahtsul Masail* upholds the text-based reference (*madzhab qauli*) to 'books of high repute' (*kutub muʿtabara*) and attaches (*ilḥāq*) legal problems to cases in the books (precedents). It adds precedents set by pious ancestors (*madzhab manhaji*).[69]

---

68 Syamsul Anwar, "*Fatwā*, Purification and Dynamization: A Study of Tarjīh in Muhammadiyah," *Islamic Law and Society* 12, no. 1 (2005): 27–44.

69 Ahmad Zahro, *Tradisi Intelektual NU: Lajnah Bahtsul Masa'il, 1926–1999* (Yogyakarta: LKiS, 2004).

In the mid of 2010, following the introduction of the Bill on Islamic marriage, the Pesantren Deliberation Forum in Java and Madura (*Forum Musyawarah Pondok Pesantren se Jawa dan Madura*) held a *Bahtsul Masail* meeting in Pesantren Lirboyo, East Java. *Nikah sirri* and unofficial polygyny were the subjects of heated debates. The question raised in the forum was: "Is it justifiable to consider these practices as crimes?" This forum produced a *fatwā* on unregistered marriage.

The *fatwā* cites the opinion of the Syrian scholar, Wahbah al-Zuḥailī (1931–2015), recorded in his seminal work, *al-Fiqh al-islāmī wa adillatuh*. Under the heading "requests for the judge's permission (*idhn al-qāḍī*)," al-Zuḥailī remarks that polygyny is based on the permission of judges. The judge must determine whether or not a man who wishes to enter into a polygynous marriage has fulfilled the legal requirements, namely justice between wives and the ability to provide equal maintenance. Obtaining the permission of judges is a necessary step because, as al-Zuḥailī argues, people are likely to make improper concessions (*rukhṣa*).[70] In a word, al-Zuḥailī urges that the judge's permission is unavoidable.

The *fatwā* does not emphasise al-Zuḥailī's core point, i.e., the judge's permission. Instead, it seems more concerned with the judge's supervision of a personal relationship. Al-Zuḥailī notes:

> The control of the judge over personal status is useless. The judge might not be aware of the real reason why people do certain things in their marital life. Knowledge of the facts is supposed to expose the secrets of marital life, influence people's personal freedom, and control the will of a human being. Marriage is purely a personal matter, agreed upon by the man and the guardian of the woman. No one can change his intention and stand in the way of his values. The secrets of a household are known only to the couple.

The *fatwā* treats personal affairs as something that should be respected by judges. In the context of the criminal provisions in the Bill, the *fatwā* imposes a legal sanction on people who do not register their marriage. Here, the *fatwā* interprets *maṣlaḥa* in terms of the privacy of a husband and a wife. The *Bahtsul Masail* concludes that legal sanctions imposed on persons who conclude a *nikah sirri* or unofficial polygyny violate Sharīʿa.

70 Wahbah Az-Zuḥailī, *Al-Fiqh al-islāmī wa adillatuh*, vol. 7 (Beirut: Dār al-fikr, 1985), 172.

5 A New Direction: Citizens' Rights-Based Approach

From a religious perspective, unregistered marriage is a controversial topic. The government has attempted some ways to address this issue, one of which is through the enactment of Law 23/2006 on Civil Registration. The Law imposes legal sanctions on persons who do not report their marriage to the authorised institution. However, the problem does not lie in the absence of a legal norm but rather in its implementation.[71] Moreover, controversies over what makes a proper marriage have not been resolved. The government continues to depend on civil administration and court decisions.[72] The regulation over Muslim marriage has shifted from contention over what is an appropriate norm to be applied to Muslims to a legal policy on citizens' rights to legal identity.

Judges have played an important role in the state's attempts to protect children's rights. In the current legal framework, retrospective marriage legalisation through *isbat nikah* regulated by the Kompilasi has proved inadequate to accommodate the needs of a child born out of legal wedlock. This issue arose in 1993 when former *dangdut* (a genre of Indonesian folk music) singer, Aisyah Mochtar, claimed to have been married in a traditional Islamic ceremony to the Secretary of State, Moerdiono. Because of the 'informal' nature of the marriage, she could not validate the marriage and legitimise the son born of that marriage, Muhammad Iqbal Ramadhan. When Aisyah Mochtar submitted a request for legalisation of the marriage to an Islamic court, she was unable to provide valid proof of the marriage contract. Moerdiono never recognised the son, did not provide maintenance and divorced her informally. In 2010, she filed a request to the Constitutional Court for judicial review of the constitutionality of the Marriage Law stipulations, article 2 point 2 and article 43 point 1, which state that a child born out of wedlock has a legal relationship only with the mother.

The Constitutional Court amended article 43 (1) of the Marriage Law on the legal status of a child born out of wedlock. The article formerly stated, "a child born out of legal wedlock has a legal relationship with its mother and the mother's family only."[73] The judges held that this provision, based on the principle of equality before the law, contravenes the Constitution and that the

71 van Huis and Wirastri, "Muslim Marriage Registration in Indonesia: Revised Marriage Registration Laws Cannot Overcome Compliance Flaws," 15.

72 Bedner and van Huis, "Plurality of Marriage Law and Marriage Registration for Muslims in Indonesia: A Plea for Pragmatism," 182.

73 Simon Butt, *The Constitutional Court and Democracy in Indonesia* (Leiden/Boston: Brill Nijhoff, 2015), 125.

article curtails children's right to life, as guaranteed by the Constitution (article 28B point 2). The court stated that paternal recognition must be accorded to children born out of legal wedlock, provided it can be proven that they are related by blood to the father.[74] The decision provoked criticism. Islamic groups argued that the legalisation of children born out of wedlock can be interpreted as allowing extramarital sex. Taking a different tack, some feminist groups criticised the decision on the ground that it does not differentiate children conceived as a result of rape.[75] This Constitutional Court decision offers promise in terms of the legal status of children born out of wedlock, although it is not easy to implement. This case also reveals that the Constitutional Court is engaged in providing interpretations of Islamic law.

In 2005, civil society organisations came up with an idea to improve the protection of human rights. Their concern centred on civil registration. In conjunction with government agencies, they set up a common platform called Konsorsium Catatan Sipil (the Consortium for Civil Registration). Their goal was to help the government provide a national legal framework to reinforce the right to a legal identity. To this end, they prepared a Civil Registration Bill and presented the draft to the Ministry of Home Affairs. The bill was passed in 2006. This Law invests the Ministry of Home Affairs to coordinate inter-agencies in civil administration. However, from the government's point of view, legal identity is primarily an administrative affair.

A child's right to state recognition has become a central issue in Indonesian public debates. On the basis of the 2011 report of the Bureau of Statistics, the Ministry of Women's Empowerment and Child Protection claimed that the state does not formally recognise approximately 40 percent of Indonesian children. Since 2012, the acceleration of the possession of birth certificates has become a common agenda point in the government's program. Joko Widodo, the Indonesian president, included this issue in his *Nawa Cita* (nine visions), which states that the number of children under the age of eighteen years who possess birth certificates should increase from 78 percent in 2016 to 90 percent in 2020. In 2015, eight related Ministries were involved in compiling a Memorandum of Understanding (*Nota Kesepahaman*), designed to frame a policy to accelerate the government's efforts to protect a child's right to a legal identity. The Ministry of Home Affairs, the body responsible for issuing birth certificates

---

74 Tutik Hamidah, "The Rights of Children Born out of Wedlock: Views of Muslim Women's Organizations on Constitutional Court Judgement 46/2010," in *Women and Property Rights in Indonesian Islamic Legal Contexts*, ed. John Bowen and Arskal Salim (Leiden: Brill, 2018), 47–68.

75 The Jakarta Post, "Paternity Ruling to Apply in Rape Cases," April 7, 2012.

through the Office of Population and Civil Registration (*Kantor Catatan Sipil*), coordinates this partnership. The Commission on Indonesian Child Protection became actively involved in campaigning to repeal laws that delay the issuance of birth certificates for children. It criticised the law that requires people to register a child, arguing that the registration of a birth is a right and that the state must register births.[76]

In response to its campaign, the Ministry of Home Affairs issued Regulation 9/2016, which serves as a legal basis for the district-level office of the civil administration to enforce the program to accelerate the issuance of birth certificates. Article 4 of the Regulation states that "if the parents/guardian/rapporteur fail to procure a declaration of birth from a doctor/midwife, they can submit a letter of absolute responsibility (*Surat Pernyataan Tanggungjawab Mutlak*, SPTJM)." There are two kinds of these letters: for the child's birth data (*data kelahiran*) and for married couples (*pasangan suami isteri*). The first type of letter makes it possible for parents to obtain their child's birth certificate. The biological father declares that the child was born to a mother, his wife, and mentions the midwife's name. The regulation offers an alternative to parents who do not have a marriage certificate but wish to include their names on the birth certificate. The second type of letter declares that a husband and a wife have been united in marriage, approved by the bride's guardian and two male witnesses. This letter can serve as a substitute for a marriage certificate. Parents can claim the legal status of their marriage. These letters of absolute responsibility conflict with the legal norms of marriage registration and undermine the Islamic court's jurisdiction over marriage legalisation. This letter can be used to recognise a polygynous marriage, which represents a fundamental challenge to the court's authority.

Following this Ministry of Home Affairs' regulation on SPTJM, a number of local governments issued similar regulations. For instance, the mayor of Depok in West Java issued Regulation 25/2016 to safeguard the implementation of this MoHA policy. However, as I observed in practice, some East Javanese regencies do not implement this policy. Officials who reject it argue that they consider a marriage certificate issued by the KUA or civil registration office the most legitimate form of proof of the legal status of the offspring's parents. They even require the parents to include a marriage certificate when the latter want to update their family card (*kartu keluarga*). If they fail to present the marriage

76 KPAI, "Akta Kelahiran Adalah Hak Setiap Anak Indonesia, Batalkan UU Yang Persulit Pembuatan Akta Kelahiran!," accessed March 4, 2019, http://www.kpai.go.id/tinjauan/akta-kelahiran-adalah-hak-setiap-anak-indonesia-batalkan-uu-yang-persulit-pembuatan-akta-kelahiran.

SURAT PERNYATAAN TANGGUNG JAWAB MUTLAK (SPTJM) KEBENARAN SEBAGAI PASANGAN SUAMI ISTERI

Saya yang bertandatangan dibawah ini :

Nama	: ....
NIK	: ....
Tempat / Tanggal Lahir	: ....
Pekerjaan	: ....
Alamat	: ....

menyatakan bahwa :

Nama	: ....
NIK	: ....
Tempat / Tanggal Lahir	: ....
Pekerjaan	: ....
Alamat	: ....

adalah **suami / isteri** *) dari :

Nama	: ....
NIK	: ....
Tempat / Tanggal Lahir	: ....
Pekerjaan	: ....
Alamat	: ....

sebagaimana tercantum dalam Kartu Keluarga (KK) Nomor :..

Demikian surat pernyataan ini saya buat dengan sebenar-benarnya dan apabila dikemudian hari ternyata pernyataan saya ini tidak benar, maka saya bersedia diproses secara hokum sesuai dengan peraturan perundang-undangan dan dokumen yang diterbitkan akibat dari pernyataan ini menjadi tidak sah.

Surabaya, ...

Saksi I, Saya yang menyatakan ,

(..) ....

NIK ....

Saksi II,

(..)

NIK ....

Keterangan :

Lampiran ini digunakan dalam hal perkawinan tidak dapat dibuktikan dengan akta perkawinan atau akta nikah

*) coret yang tidak perlu.

FIGURE 2 SPTJM *Suami Isteri* (SPTJM of husbands and wives)
DUKCAPIL.JAKARTA.GO.ID

certificate, the legal status of the husband and wife is changed to 'unmarried' (*belum kawin*). Whereas the wife is first on the list, designated as the head of household, the husband is listed on the bottom row, identified as 'the other' (*lainnya*). In one interview, a KUA official said that the regulation on SPTJM infringes on the function of Muslim marriage registration, which falls under the authority of the KUA. Although children have a constitutional right, the government should not issue regulations that challenge the authority of the KUA to register a Muslim marriage.[77]

6 Conclusion

For the majority of Muslims, marriage is one of the most important aspects of their personal life because, without it, family is not possible. Muslim communities require that any modern reshaping of Islamic marriage should preserve its religious character as prescribed by Sharīʿa law. However, the Sharīʿa is not easy to define. The transformation of Sharīʿa substantive law into state law has created an arena that has scholarly, political, and practical dimensions. The struggles over state codification of Islamic law have been disrupted by the necessity for negotiations between the state and religious authorities. In the Indonesian context, these negotiations involve the issue of what makes a Muslim marriage valid.

In the colonial era, the Dutch administration required Muslims to register their marriages under the supervision of an official marriage registrar. The Dutch colonial policy was oriented towards producing new Islamic leaders who could be incorporated into its colonial administration. The Dutch policy was maintained by the post-colonial Indonesian government. The new Indonesian state established the Ministry of Religious Affairs and then issued a Law that regulated Muslim marriage and divorce. In 1946, Muslim marital matters came under the aegis of the Ministry of Religious Affairs. In 1974, the state unified the substantive legal rules pertaining to marriage to address the problem of the plurality of legal norms, religious affiliations, and local ethnic attachments.

The state adopted the principle of 'dual validity' to accommodate the demands of Muslim organisations. The Marriage Law defines a marriage contract as a religious ceremony but adds the legal obligation of registration. Furthermore, the Kompilasi corpus, which codified Muslim family law, not only endorsed the 'dual validity' principle as defined in the Marriage Law but also

---

77 Interview with Pak Zaki, an official at the KUA Sumbersari, Pasuruan, East Java.

introduced a new legal norm to deal with unregistered marriages. As one tactic in the battle to attain state recognition, Muslims may apply to an Islamic court for retroactive legalisation (*isbat nikah*).

Since 1998, religious based ideas have become increasingly prominent in Indonesia. Islam has been emerging as a collective identity while religious piety has been occupied by different political interests. As a consequence, since the 2000s, Sharīʿa-based regional regulations have emerged as the outcome of negotiations among political elites. These political elites champion Sharīʿa-based regulations as a viable means to form a better Muslim society. These regional regulations cover rules on public morality that challenge the regulations on Muslim marriage enshrined in the national law. A relevant example is a regional regulation on the ability to read the Qur'an as an obligatory condition before a marriage ceremony can be concluded.

Marriage registration remains an important issue. The Indonesian public perceives unregistered Muslim marriage (*nikah sirri* or *nikah di bawah tangan*) as an infringement of the rights of vulnerable women and children. In response, the government raised the status of the Kompilasi from a Presidential Instruction to a Law. It proposed a Bill on Islamic Marriage that included legal sanctions on certain infringements, for instance, people who do not register a marriage. The Bill has elicited harsh reactions and has been rejected by many conservatives. The future of the bill is uncertain.

By issuing *fatwā*s on legal reform, ʿulama' reclaim their religious authority. Their *fatwā*s reveal a new trend in Islamic law that takes *maṣlaḥa* as an important consideration in legal reasoning. By referring to *maṣlaḥa*, ʿulama' emphasise the important position of the state in administering marital relations. In the light of *maṣlaḥa*, marriage registration is a viable means to prevent social harm. Nevertheless, this *maṣlaḥa* orientation is challenged by a literal approach to classical Islamic texts. These two religious orientations are locked in a contest to shape the content of legal reform. Be that as it may, the different interpretations of the ʿulama' show that Sharīʿa is not a fixed body of legal rules.[78] This public debate has also produced "a degree of openness ... that appears to have transformed the country."[79] Unlike other *fatwā*-issuing bodies, the MUI, through its self-proclaimed identity as a civil society organisation, seeks to function as an 'official national *fatwā* body.'[80]

78 Hefner, "Sharia Law and Muslim Ethical Imaginaries in Modern Indonesia," 91.

79 Cammack, Bedner, and van Huis, "Democracy, Human Rights, and Islamic Family Law in Post-Soeharto Indonesia," 13.

80 Tim Lindsey, *Islam, Law and the State in Southeast Asia*, Vol. 1: In. (London: Tauris, 2012), 124.

The Indonesian government continues to improve the position of women in the matrimonial sphere and protect children's rights. Developments over the last decade suggest that the judiciary and the civil administration have made a meaningful contribution. The ruling on Muslim marriage has shifted from a legal norm on the validity of Muslim marriage to a state policy on the consequences of marriage registration for citizens' rights, primarily the rights of children to a legal identity. First, the judicial authority produces a legally binding interpretation of the legal status of a child based on the Constitution. This decision grants paternal recognition to children born out of wedlock. Second, because the legal status of children has become an important issue, a government body has issued a program to accelerate the acquisition of birth certificates. This policy appears to overlap with the existing rules on marriage registration because a marriage certificate is no longer important to prove the legal status of a marriage. Despite the conflict between the rules, in my opinion, this policy may be interpreted as a step forward in state formation.[81] It enables the state to expand its community service and protect individual rights and obligations based on national identity.

The next chapter deals with continuity and change in the laws and procedures governing marriage registration. It also analyses the bureaucratic reform of Muslim marriage. It investigates how the reform affects the implementation of marriage registration performed by the KUA on a sub-district level.

---

81 Michael G. Peletz, *Islamic Modern: Religious Courts and Cultural Politics in Malaysia* (Princeton: Princeton University Press, 2002).

CHAPTER 3

Reforming the Bureaucracy of Muslim Marriage

> *"Pemerintah berharap calon pengantin mendaftar sendiri, mengurus persyaratan dari desa langsung dibawa ke* KUA. *Tapi masyarakat belum siap. Secara tradisi mereka datang ke modin. Di sisi lain, petugas* KUA *juga minim turun ke desa untuk pemeriksaan status calon pengantin dan wali nikah. Situasi di masyarakat sangat rumit."*
>
> The government expects the couples to prepare the documents for marriage registration themselves and bring them from the village office to the KUA. However, people are not ready to do this yet. They go to *modins*, which is the tradition. Moreover, officials on the sub-district level seldom come into villages to examine the legal status of the couples and the marriage guardian. The social situation on the ground is extremely complicated.
>
> HAJI MUSTOFA, a *modin* in Sumbersari

1 Introduction

In the previous chapter, I explained that post-New Order Indonesia has been experiencing a rise in religious identity, which continues to contest the state's attempt to reform Muslim marriage through legislation. Nevertheless, at the same time, there is a tendency among ʿulamaʾ to speak of the concept of *maslaḥa*, which increasingly resembles the state's idea of public order. On the secular side of the coin, the non-religious state bureaucracy has emerged as an alternative force introducing reformatory ideas into strategic regulations. This bureaucratic reform has stimulated the government's public service institutions to strengthen citizens' rights.[1] Despite the conflicts arising from the state's insistence on legal norms for marriage registration and other problems such as

1 In 2010, the Indonesian government issued the main guideline for bureaucratic reform covering a period of 5 years. *Peraturan Presiden* (Presidential Regulation) 81/2010 On the Grand Design of Bureaucratic Reform of 2010–2015.

 | DOI:10.1163/9789004516113_004

the underperformance of bureaucrats,[2] this reform is an important step in the way the state is endeavouring to cope simultaneously with Islamic affairs and citizens' rights.

In this chapter, I try to get a grip on the practice of the state in which I look at the bureaucratic reforms in the administration of Muslim marriage and how these reforms affect the administration of marriage registration in society. To this end, the central question of this chapter is: In what ways does the reform improve the bureaucracy of Muslim marriage?

It is often said that the Ministry of Religious Affairs has to deal with more practical questions of religious identity or theological disputes about what 'proper' religion should be.[3] However, when it comes to Islamic marriage, religion has not been the overriding issue. The Ministry of Religious Affairs has been confronted with the problem of corruption. It has attempted to address this problem by instigating a series of reforms to reinforce its rational-legal authority[4] and legitimacy.[5] Although attempts at reform have so far been half-hearted, the state is under growing pressure to address the issue of citizens' rights. Political actors have agreed that Muslim marriage registration is an integral part of the civil registration system. Here we encounter the problem of falling between two stools. They define citizenship by expressing preferences in a way that modern, state-centric conceptions have strongly influenced.[6]

2 Nurdiana Gaus, Sultan Sultan, and Muhammad Basri, "State Bureaucracy in Indonesia and Its Reforms: An Overview," *International Journal of Public Administration* 40, no. 8 (2017): 658–669.

3 Sezgin and Künkler, "Regulation of Religion and the Religious: The Politics of Judicialization and Bureaucratization in India and Indonesia," 450.

4 Weber introduced this concept in response to the transition from medieval to modern societies and states in Europe. It refers to the authority which is legitimized by a rational-legal and interdependent division of labour, characterized by economic and occupational specialization and complex rational-legal systems, in which highly specialized bureaucracies are the norm. Weber called this rational justification of obedience to authority "domination by virtue of legality, by virtue of the belief in the validity of the legal statute and functional competence, based on rationally created rules." Max Weber, "Politics as a Vocation," in *From Max Weber: Essays in Sociology*, ed. Hans H. Gerth and C. Wright Mills (New York: Oxford University Press, 1946), 79.

5 Legitimacy is a central concept which defines how individuals accept power and conceive their obedience as a commitment. It is critical because it constitutes any normative claims made by a government. R. Stryber, "Legitimacy," *International Encyclopedia of the Social & Behavioral Sciences* (2001): 8700–8704.

6 Pamela J. Stumpo, "Challenging the Practice of the State, but Beholden to Its Image: Women's Activists, Academics, and the Public Take on Egypt's Citizenship Laws," in *The Everyday Life of the State: A State-in-Society Approach*, ed. Adam White (Seattle: University of Washington Press, 2013), 189.

According to Law 23/2006 on Civil Administration, marriage is a crucial life moment to which the legal obligation of registration is applied. A marriage certificate (*akta nikah* or *buku nikah*) issued by the KUA is deemed equivalent to a civil document (*dokumen kependudukan*). Embracing this modern approach, they have somewhat lost sight of the more traditional views on marriage which are still embedded in village life.

In this chapter, my purpose is to argue that the Ministry of Religious Affairs has endeavoured a series of reforms to redefine the position of the KUA, assuming it not just in its narrow sense as a religious bureaucracy but, more widely, as a public service institution. In this light, the KUA plays a role as a prominent government frontline public service agency helping the government protect the rights of citizens more effectively. However, in the eyes of its superior, the Ministry of Religious Affairs, religious issues to do with the marriage ceremony still take pride in place. The position of *penghulu*s lies at the core of the problem. It was when the head of the KUA did not necessarily have to be *penghulu*s, but now the Ministry of Religious Affairs has returned *penghulu*s to the core of the KUA bureaucracy to secure its religious credibility. This was the first reform.

Other changes have seen the elimination of informality and the concomitant charging of official fees for marriage registration. The state requires the KUA to be a centralised, powerful agency firmly in charge of marriage registration. It has attained its goal by diminishing the intermediary roles played by informal village religious leaders. However, in doing so, it has failed to appreciate the social importance of the latter. Lastly, the Ministry of Religious Affairs has struggled with the integration of civil administrative data into the marriage registration system. To sum it up in one sentence, the implementation of this series of reforms was more easily said than done.

This chapter starts with a historical sketch of the role of *penghulu*s and the position of the KUA since Indonesia declared its independence in 1945. Section 2 explores the historical path of the bureaucratisation of Muslim marriage in Indonesia. Section 3 focuses on the promotion of *penghulu*s as the key actors of the marriage bureaucracy. Section 4 deals with the core problems in the administration of Muslim marriage, i.e., corruption, informality, and the need for the reform. Section 5 examines Muslims' attitudes towards the reform. Section 6 addresses the complexities behind the introduction of an information system of marriage administration.

2 The Indonesian Muslim Marriage Bureaucracy

Scholars have argued that the emergence of a modern nation state has made religious affairs an integral part of state control. Deliar Noer's 1978 work emphasised that the position of Islam in Indonesia was not easy as it was subject to debate between secular and Islamic groups and competition in Muslim circles.[7] Gradually, the political process of administering Islam has proceeded to what is called state Islam,[8] a form of Islam endorsed by the state. Consequently, as they are embedded in religious affairs, the state actors have unavoidably reshaped marriage norms to tackle matters in the national interest, such as population control.[9] As Muller has remarked, this has been done by empowering "state-funded administrative bodies to guide and influence Islamic discourses in diverse ways."[10]

This section explores explicitly how the state deals with the administration of Muslim marriage. It examines the historical trajectory of the bureaucracy of Muslim marriage under the aegis of the Ministry of Religious Affairs. This bureaucracy is understudied, particularly when compared to topics related to marital dispute settlement by Islamic courts.[11] After the Indonesian state began to reform the Muslim husband's unilateral rights to divorce through the introduction of judicial divorce in 1974, the legal practices in Islamic courts have grown enormously in importance as a topic of debate. Matters have reached such a pitch that not just their practices but the very existence of Islamic courts have become the subject of political debate. Political pressure demanding the abolition of Islamic courts was nearly successful after Law 19/1948 on Judicial Power was enacted. Chapter 35 (2) of this Law decreed that the dispute between Muslims should be resolved under the jurisdiction of a general court.[12] The

---

7 Deliar Noer, *The Administration of Islam in Indonesia* (Ithaca, NY: Cornell Modern Indonesia Project, 1978).

8 Moch Nur Ichwan, "Official Reform of Islam: State Islam and the Ministry of Religious Affairs in Contemporary Indonesia, 1966–2004" (Tilburg University, 2006).

9 Maznah Mohamad, "Malaysian Sharia Reforms in Dlux: The Changeable National Character of Islamic Marriage," *International Journal of Law, Policy and the Family* 25, no. 1 (2011): 46–70; Nancy F. Cott, *Public Vows: A History of Marriage and the Nation* (Cambridge, MA: Harvard University Press, 2002).

10 Müller, *The Bureaucratization of Islam and Its Socio-Legal Dimensions in Southeast Asia: Conceptual Contours of a Research Project*, 2.

11 See, for instance, Nur Ahmad Fadhil Lubis, *Islamic Justice in Transition: A Socio-Legal Study of the Agama Court Judges in Indonesia* (Los Angeles: University of California, 1994).

12 Jaenal Aripin, *Jejak Langkah Peradilan Agama Di Indonesia* (Jakarta: Kharisma Putra Utama, 2013), 70.

imputation of this chapter was that Islamic courts had been integrated into the public courts. However, this Law never came into force.[13] It was superseded by the Emergency Law 1/1951 on the Jurisdiction and Procedures of the Civil Courts, which stipulated the continued existence of Islamic courts and the abolition of all indigenous *adat* courts.[14] Under these circumstances, the administration of Muslim marriage remained relatively free of political intervention.

The administration of Muslim marriage was set up simultaneously with the foundation of the Ministry of Religious Affairs by the Indonesian government on 3 January 1946, based on the Government Declaration (*Penetapan Pemerintah*) 1/S.D. 1946. The Ministry of Religious Affairs itself was, in fact, an extension of what had existed since the closing years of the nineteenth century in the Dutch East Indies, initially as the Office for Indigenous Affairs (*Kantoor voor Inlandsche Zaken*). This became the Bureau of Religious Affairs (*Kantoor voor Inlandsche en Arabische Zaken*) in early 1899.[15] In this period of administrative changes, the colonial administration reorganised the hierarchy of *penghulus*. These were government-sponsored officials charged with handling matters pertaining to Islamic affairs, including marriage and divorce, on district and sub-district levels.[16] *Penghulus* were answerable to *Bupati* (Regent). During the Japanese occupation from 1942 to 1945, this Office of Religious Affairs was renamed the *Shumubu* or *Kantor Oeroesan Agama*.[17] Prominent staff members of the former Dutch-established office continued to run its successor. Worried about the strength, or lack of it, of its control over religious leaders, the Japanese military administration decided to establish the *Shumuka* to expand the powers of the *Shumubu* in various regencies (*karesidenan*) in 1944.[18] The *Shumuka* was supposed to act as the coordinator of local 'ulama' but with the

13 According to Lev, Law 19/1948 Chapter 7 made no mention at all of a distinct jurisdiction for Islamic courts implying their demise. Lev, *Islamic Courts in Indonesia: A Study in the Political Bases of Legal Institutions*, 65.

14 Emergency Law 1/1951 on the Jurisdiction and Procedures of the Civil Courts. See also van Huis, "Islamic Courts and Women's Divorce Rights in Indonesia: The Cases of Cianjur and Bulukumba," 46.

15 Rini Rusyeni, "Fragmented Voices: The Personal Archives of the Advisors of Inlandsche Zaken, 1899–194" (Leiden University, 2017), 13.

16 Karel A. Steenbrink, *Beberapa Aspek Tentang Islam Di Indonesia Abad Ke-19* (Jakarta: Bulan Bintang, 1984). For further details about the *Kantoor voor Inlandsche Zaken*, read Husnul Aqib Suminto, *Politik Islam Pemerintah Hindia Belanda: Het Kantoor Voor Inlandsche Zaken* (Jakarta: LP3ES, 1985), 99–107.

17 Lev, *Islamic Courts in Indonesia: A Study in the Political Bases of Legal Institutions*, 44.

18 Ahmad Syafii Maarif, *Islam Dan Politik: Teori Belah Bambu, Masa Demokrasi Terpimpin, 1959–1965* (Jakarta: Gema Insani Press, 1996), 20.

obvious aim of exerting more control over them.[19] The *Shumubu* served as the foundation of the establishment of the Ministry of Religious Affairs in 1946.

Since 1946, the mission of the Ministry of Religious Affairs has been to be the most prominent agency responsible for the supervision of all matters related to marriage and reconciliation between Muslims.[20] The most apparent change which has taken place since the formation of the Ministry of Religious Affairs was the reorganisation of the existing judicial and executive institutions on both national and regional levels. On the basis of the Governmental Decree (*Penetapan Pemerintah*) 5/SD 25 March 1946, the Ministry of Religious Affairs took control of both lower Islamic courts and the Supreme Islamic Court (*Mahkamah Tinggi Islam*) from the Ministry of Justice. On the regional level of religious office, the name of the *Shumuka*, was changed to the Regional Religious Bureau (*Djawatan Agama Daerah*).[21] Ever since, *penghulus*, who had previously been subordinate to a *Bupati*, have fallen directly under the supervision of the Ministry of Religious Affairs.

The rules and regulations governing Muslim marriage were legally defined more clearly when the central government issued Law 22/1946 on the Registration of Islamic Marriage, Divorce and Reconciliation. The Law placed the practical implementation of Muslim marriage administration in the hands of the Marriage Registrar (*Pegawai Pentatat Nikah*). Article 1 (1) of the Law states: "A marriage which is concluded in accordance with the precepts of Islam, henceforth referred to as a marriage, is to be supervised by a marriage registrar who is appointed by the Minister of Religion or other designated officials."[22] On the practical level, this Law indirectly enjoined a division between *penghulu kabupaten* (regency *penghulu*) and *penghulu hakim* (judge or *qadi penghulu*). The role of the former was to act as the marriage registrar, while the latter was adjudicated on Muslim marital affairs in an Islamic court. A year or so later, this division was formally confirmed in the Decree of the Minister of Religion (*Keputusan Menteri Agama*, KMA) 6/1947 on 8 December 1947 pertaining to the division of tasks between the two institutions.[23]

In the late 1940s, the central government issued PP (*Peraturan Pemerintah*, Government Regulation) 33/1949 on the *susunan dan lapang pekerjaan* (the

19 Aiko Kurasawa, "Mobilization and Control: A Study of Social Change in Rural Java, 1942–1945" (Cornell University, 1988), 400–404.

20 Noer, *The Administration of Islam in Indonesia*, 18.

21 Mujiburrahman, *Feeling Threatened: Muslim-Christian Relations in Indonesia's New Order* (Amsterdam: Amsterdam University Press, 2006), 126.

22 Law 22/1946 on the Registration of Islamic Marriage, Divorce and Reconciliation.

23 Abdul Manan, *Pembaruan Hukum Islam Di Indonesia* (Depok: Kencana, 2017), 2–3.

structure and the tasks) of the Ministry of Religious Affairs. One of these was "to regulate, undertake and observe all aspects related to marriage registration, reconciliation and repudiation among Muslims." Practically, this function was overseen by the *jawatan nikah, talak, rujuk* (section on marriage, repudiation, and reconciliation).[24] An important aspect of this regulation was the designations of *kantor kenaiban kecamatan* (the office of the sub-district religious affairs) and *kantor kenaiban distrik* (the office of the district religious affairs). Both offices were supervised by the *kantor kepenghuluan kabupaten* (the office of the regency *penghulu*). The government officially restored the term *naib*,[25] as it had been applied in colonial times,[26] as the designation of the representative of the regency *penghulu* on a sub-district level.[27] In my view, this reorganisation can be seen as a government strategy to maintain its control over Muslim marriage without putting itself into too much trouble since people were already familiar with such institutions.

In 1947, the Muslim marriage bureaucracy also underwent a phase during which village-level informal religious officials were incorporated as official marriage functionaries. The government promoted the village-level religious officials, namely *kaum* (*modin, amil,* or *lebei*), to be PPPNTR (*Pembantu Pegawai Pencatat Nikah, Talak dan Rujuk* or Assistant of Marriage, Divorce and Reconciliation Registrars), to assist the marriage registrars on higher levels.[28] This process signified the bureaucratisation of traditional authorities. It transformed them into a modern organisational team whose main role was to bridge the relationship between the state and society.[29]

However, the office of *modins* was not solely the Ministry of Religious Affairs' affairs because it also fell under the aegis of the Ministry of Home Affairs. The reason was *modins* dealt with religious issues of village residents, which was assumed to make them part of the village administration. This village adminis-

---

24 This division was regulated by KMA 2 1185/KJ November 1946 and was then reaffirmed by PP 33/1949 on the structure and the task of the Ministry of Religious Affairs.

25 In the Sunni tradition of Islamic law, *naib* refers to the authorized representative of a *qadi* (judge) or local magistrate.

26 Lubis, *Islamic Justice in Transition: A Socio-Legal Study of the Agama Court Judges in Indonesia*, 85.

27 Clifford Geertz, *The Religion of Java* (Illinois: The Free Press, 1960), 202.

28 More details about their tasks and technicalities are regulated in the Instruction of the Minister of Religion 4/1947 regarding the obligations of a marriage registrar.

29 There is a variety of names given to this informal authority, such as *modin, kaum* (community leader) and *rois* (religious leader). Achmad Zainal Arifin, "Defending Traditions, Countering Intolerant Ideologies: Re-Energizing the Role of Modin in Modern Java," *Al-Jami'ah: Journal of Islamic Studies* 55, no. 2 (2017): 265–292; Pradjarta Dirdjosanjoto, *Memelihara Umat: Kiai Pesantren-Kiai Langgar Di Jawa* (Yogyakarta: LKiS, 1999), 195.

tration was, and is, under the control of the Ministry of Home Affairs. Therefore, according to *Maklumat Bersama* (the Shared Declaration) 3/1947 of the two Ministries, *modins* should be treated the same as a *pamong desa* (a village official). In the 1980s, especially following the issuance of Law 5/1975 on *Pemerintahan Desa* (Village Administration), the Soeharto regime incorporated *modins* into the village administration under the title *Kepala Urusan Kesejahteraan Rakyat* (*Kaur Kesra*, head of People's Welfare).[30] However, this did not apply to all of them.

In some villages in Pasuruan, there has been a division between *modin kawin* (marriage *modin*) and *modin kematian* (funeral *modin*). The village administration only incorporated *modin kematian* into its body, not *modin kawin* because the *Kantor Kementerian Agama Kabupaten* (the Ministry of Religious Affairs' District Office) already organised them. *Modins* were put in a problematic position with a foot in the camp of each of the two Ministries. Although they were entitled to identify themselves as PPPNTR, with the exception of those officially recognised as *pamong desa*, their legal status was never set out in black and white. Until recently (see Section 4 of this chapter), this ambivalent status is a cause of confusion.

The Ministry of Religious Affairs has passed down the official reform of Islam to lower-level agencies by exercising a strict mechanism of control to bring them into line with the policy of the central administration.[31] In the early 1950s, the designation of the KUA was the general designation of the Ministry of Religious Affairs branch office on a sub-district level whose primary task was to deal with the administration of Muslim marriage. In the subsequent transformation, this entailed *naib* who was responsible for *kantor kenaiban kecamatan*, being given equivalent status to the head of the KUA. The equivalence of *naib* with the head of the KUA can be seen in the elucidation to the Regulation of the Minister of Religion (PMA, *Peraturan Menteri Agama*) 1/1952 on *wali hakim* (magistrate-guardians). This regulation asserted that, because of his equivalent status to the head of the KUA, *naib* had the authority to act as magistrate-guardian if a biological guardian of a bride could not be present (*mafqūd*). Although the term *naib* is no longer currently in use, I have personally seen that local Muslims are still comfortable addressing the head of the KUA as *naib*.

The year 1955 signified a significant change in the bureaucracy of the Muslim marriage administration. The Regulation of the Minister of Religion 1/1955 on the obligations of marriage registrars restructured the organisation of the KUA.

30 Law 5/1975 on *Pemerintahan Desa* (village administration).
31 Sezgin and Künkler, "Regulation of Religion and the Religious: The Politics of Judicialization and Bureaucratization in India and Indonesia," 469.

It declared that marriage registration could only be done by *naib kepala* (head of *naib*), *naib* or *naib pengganti* (a substitute). In the same year, the Ministry of Religious Affairs also standardised the documents required to register a marriage, repudiation, and reconciliation. They included the marriage examination form (*daftar pemeriksaan nikah*), books for marriage registration, repudiation, and reconciliation (*buku pendaftaran nikah, talak, dan rujuk*) and a certificate of marriage, repudiation, and reconciliation (*surat nikah, talak dan rujuk*).[32]

Under its former jurisdiction, the KUA was vested with the authority to register divorce initiated by men (*talak*). A Muslim husband could divorce his wife simply by declaring a repudiation, which he was then required to register with the KUA.[33] Meanwhile when a wife demanded a divorce, but the husband could not or did not want to proclaim it, she had to petition for divorce, called *rapak*, in an Islamic court. In this regard, Hildred Geertz stated:[34]

"It is easy to get divorce in Java. Husband and wife usually notify the village religious official (the *modin*), who helps with weddings and divorces and conducts funerals. He then accompanies them to the sub-district religious official (the *naib* [the head of KUA]), who actually performs the marriages and divorces and keeps the records."

Nakamura has questioned the meaning of the phrase "performs the marriages and divorces and keeps the records." In her opinion, describing the role of the *naib* in officiating at marriages, divorces and keeping records is too narrow. As a religious official, the *naib* had a broader responsibility, guiding people to behave in accordance with Islamic law. When faced with instances of divorce, his first step was to advise the parties concerned and encourage them to reconsider the intention to dissolve their marriage. If the husband believed that divorce was the only way to improve the situation, he examined them both to see if the marriage dissolution could be legally approved according to Islamic law. After completing this examination, he recorded the divorce and issued a divorce decree.[35] Nakamura also noted that the KUA, the Islamic court, and BP4 were integral parts of the administration of Islamic law, even though they appeared to be mutually unrelated.[36]

---

32 PMA 15/1955 on Examples of Registration Forms for Marriage, Repudiation and Reconciliation of a Marriage.

33 Mark Cammack and R. Michael Feener, "The Islamic Legal System in Indonesia," *Pacific Rim Law & Policy Journal* 21, no. 1 (2012): 17.

34 Hildred Geertz, *The Javanese Family: A Study of Kinship and Socialization* (New York: The Free Press of Glencoe, 1961), 71.

35 Hisako Nakamura, *Divorce in Java: A Study of the Dissolution of Marriage among Javanese Muslims* (Yogyakarta: Gadjah Mada University Press, 1983), 107–108.

36 Ibid., 106.

The Marriage Law ushered in a significant change in the jurisdiction of the KUA. Since it has been in force, the KUA has no longer had to deal with a unilateral divorce pronounced by the husband. All divorces must be declared before an Islamic court. Consequently, the PPPNTR institution in the past has changed into the PPPN (*Pembantu Pegawai Pencatat Nikah* or the marriage registrar's assistant). Despite this fundamental change, the jurisdictions of the KUA and the Islamic court remain interrelated. The Islamic court delivers the divorce report to the KUA with which the parties' marriage was registered. The KUA then has to execute the court's decision of *isbat nikah* (retrospective marriage confirmation). Furthermore, the KUA also facilitates marital reconciliation (*rujūʿ*) between the husband and the wife during the prescribed waiting period (*ʿidda*) subsequent to the pronouncement of the divorce. The document of reconciliation is then presented to the Islamic court as legal proof of the annulment of their divorce.

3 The Re-centralisation of *Penghulu*

Since 1963, all matters related to Muslim marriage have been handled by the Directorate of *Urusan Agama Islam* (Islamic Affairs). As of 1967, this directorate came under the aegis of the Directorate General for *Bimbingan Masyarakat Islam* (Islamic Guidance). Other Muslim affairs such as Islamic education, Islamic courts and Islamic higher education were also run by the Directorate General.[37] This structure was reorganised again at the end of the 1970s. This reorganisation was deemed necessary because of the wide range of matters the Ministry of Religious Affairs had to cope with. The Directorate-General of Islam was split into two bodies to lighten the workload. The first, the Directorate-General for *Bimbingan Masyarakat Islam dan Urusan Haji* (the Guidance of the Islamic Community and Pilgrimage) deals with matters pertaining directly to religion, including marriage and pilgrimage. Meanwhile, Islamic education and Islamic courts were henceforth administered by the second body, called the Directorate-General for *Bimbingan Masyarakat Pembinaan Kelembagaan Agama Islam* (the Social Development/Advancement of Islamic Institutions).

For some decades, *Direktorat Urusan Agama Islam* (the Directorate of Islamic affairs) managed more than 5,600 KUA offices and more or less 8,000 *penghulus* throughout the nation. In 2010, the nomenclature of the body was changed

37 Regulated by KMA 56/1967 on the Structure, Tasks and Competences of the Department of Religion, dated 30 May 1967.

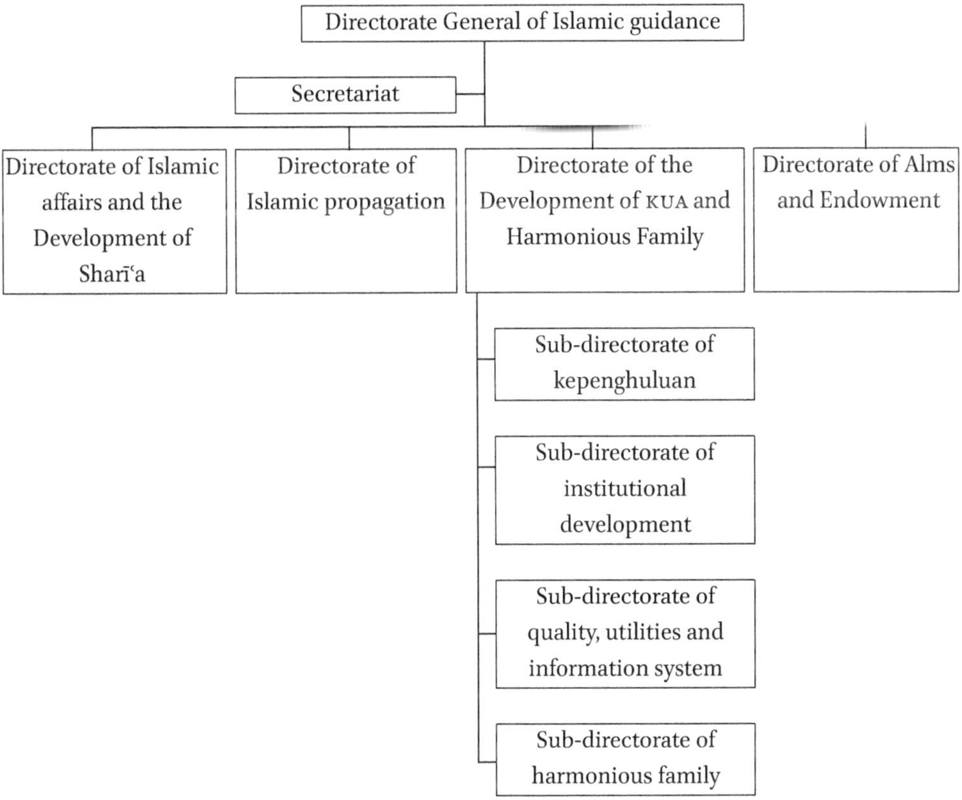

FIGURE 3 The structure of the bureaucracy of the KUA on the Ministry level according to the Regulation of the Minister of Religion 42/2016

to *Direktorat Urusan Agama Islam dan Pembinaan Syariah* (Directorate of Islamic affairs and the Advancement of *Sharīʿa*).[38] This change meant broadening the scope of the control of the directorate from focusing solely on marital affairs to covering mosque and *halal* matters. A decade later, another fundamental change occurred. The government decreed that a specialised body should undertake the organisation of marriage administration and familial affairs. The Ministry of Religious Affairs issued the Regulation of the Minister of Religion 42/2016 on Organisation and Operating Procedures of the Ministry of Religious Affairs, article 387, which affirmed the setting-up of a new directorate, namely *Bina Kantor Urusan Agama dan Keluarga Sakinah* (Office for

38 Kementerian Agama, *Profil Direktorat Urusan Agama Islam Dan Pembinaan Syariah* (Jakarta: Kementerian Agama RI, 2013).

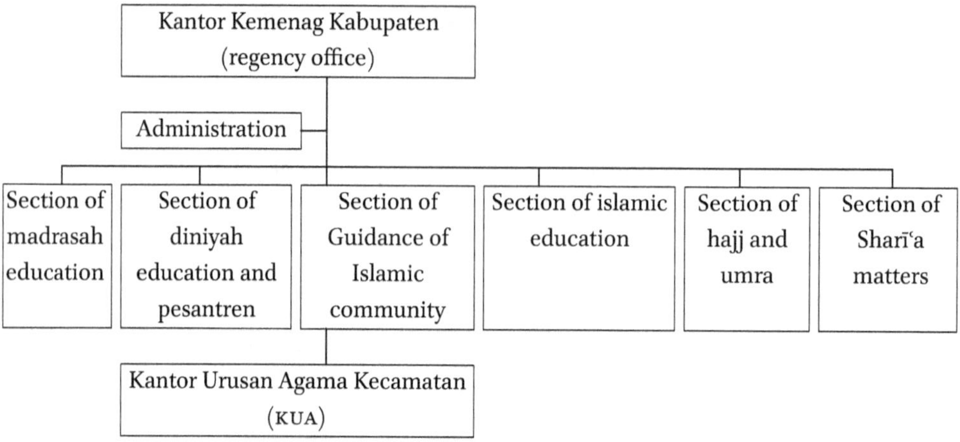

FIGURE 4 The structure of the regional and sub-district offices of religious affairs according to the Regulation of the Minister of Religion 42/2016

the Organisation of Religious Affairs and Harmonious Families/Family Cohesion).[39] With the passing of this regulation, the KUA was assured of its own specialised home on the national level.

In this structure, the KUA is under the control of *Kantor Kementerian Agama Kabupaten* (the Ministry of Religious Affairs' District Office). In the everyday running of the department, it is *kepala seksi* (the section head) of the *Bimbingan Masyarakat Islam* (Guidance of the Islamic Community), in *Kantor Kementerian Agama Kabupaten* who is responsible for overseeing the performance of the KUA offices.

Generally speaking, the KUA is responsible for handling Islam-related affairs in one sub-district. The registration and reconciliation of Muslim marriages lie at the very heart of its activities. Still, it also has other matters to deal with, such as the running of mosques, alms, property endowment and family harmony (*keluarga sakinah*). In its handling of marital affairs, the head of the KUA acts as a marriage registrar (*Pegawai Pencatat Nikah*, PPN). Article 2 of the Regulation of the Minister of Religion 11/2007 on marriage registration states that "the PPN is an official who verifies documents, supervises and registers marriage/reconciliation, administers husband-initiated divorce (*cerai talak*), wife-petitioned divorce (*cerai gugat*) and marriage counselling."

This regulation makes it quite clear that the KUA also undertakes marriage counselling and runs courses on preparation for marriage for brides and

39 PMA 42/2016 Organization and Operating Procedures of the Ministry of Religious Affairs.

grooms (*kursus calon pengantin*). In the past, counselling was the task of a body called *Badan Penasehat Perkawinan dan Penyelesaian Perceraian* (BP4, Board of Marriage Counselling and Divorce Settlement). The establishment of this advisory board was initiated locally in the course of the 1950s.[40] In 1962, it was unified nationally. In 1977, its name was changed to *Badan Penasihatan Perkawinan, Perselisihan dan Perceraian* (the Board of Marriage Counselling, Dispute Settlement and Divorce) based on the Decree of the Minister of Religion 30/1977 on Affirmation of the Acknowledgement of the Marriage Counselling, Dispute Settlement and Divorce. Since then, the board has been a semi-official body within the Ministry of Religious Affairs. Its principal mission is to lend assistance and solve marital disputes. Couples who wish to get a divorce are expected to attend the BP4 for counselling. Upon receiving confirmation of a break-down in marriage from the members of the board, declared in the form of *Naskah Penasihat* (Advisor's Note), the couples then go to the KUA to formalise their divorces.[41]

Since 1998, the Ministry of Religious Affairs was financially prevented from funding this board because of the shortfall in its budget. As a consequence, in 2009, following the 14th BP4 National Conference, BP4 was transformed into an independent organisation, whose staff members were high officials in the Ministry of Religious Affairs. Nevertheless, this board is still involved in Ministry programmes such as *kursus pra nikah* (pre-marital course).[42] In the wake of this change, the BP4 now focuses only on marriage counselling and is no longer involved in divorces. Therefore, the abbreviation BP4 now stands for *Badan Penasihatan, Pembinaan dan Pelestarian Perkawinan* (the Board for the Counselling, Fostering and Perpetuation of Marriage).[43]

Functions in the KUA are classified into three categories. They consist of the *kepala* (the head), functional officers (*pejabat fungsional*) who include marriage functionaries (*penghulus*) and the administrative staff. In the past, the KUA functionaries were simply categorised into the *kepala* and the *pelaksana* (officers). Under the 2001 Ministry of Religious Affairs Regulation, the head of the KUA is a structural position (*jabatan struktural*) that also serves as the PPN. In the past, any officials could be promoted to this position and they did

---

40 Lev, *Islamic Courts in Indonesia: A Study in the Political Bases of Legal Institutions*, 151.

41 Nurlaelawati, *Modernization, Tradition and Identity: The Kompilasi Hukum Islam and Legal Practice in the Indonesian Religious Courts*, 185.

42 In 2013, the Directorate-General on Islamic Guidance issued Regulation DJ. II/542 concerning the organisation of pre-marital courses which declares that BP4 is one of the organizers.

43 See the KMA 114/2009 on the officials of the Central BP4.

not have to be a *penghulu*.[44] *Penghulus* are trained, specialised marriage functionaries whose sole responsibility is to conduct a marriage ceremony. They do not have the authority to sign marriage certificates, although there has been a debate about it. The authority to sign marriage certificates is vested in the PPN. However, some argued that *penghulus* were allowed to authorise marriage certificates if the PPN delegated his mandate.

This dispute has now been resolved since the Ministry of Religious Affairs issued a new regulation on the reorganisation of the KUA in 2016.[45] The regulation stipulates that the head of the KUA is no longer a structural position (*jabatan struktural*) but is considered an additional task (*tugas tambahan*) that can be exercised exclusively by *penghulus*. In other words, it is now only *penghulus* who are eligible to act as head of the KUA. As a consequence, the head of the KUA who is not a *penghulu* has to meet certain standards attained by passing a set of competency training and tests to be a *penghulu*.[46] When they have passed the exams, they are awarded a certificate that declares their fitness to assume a functional position (*jabatan fungsional*) as *penghulus*.

This regulation has wrought some significant changes. Firstly, the regulation pragmatically endorses the uniformization of who should serve as the PPN. Secondly, even more importantly, it seems that the Ministry of Religious Affairs has demanded the reshaping of the position of *penghulus* placing him at the centre of the KUA so as to reclaim the KUA's specialisation in religious affairs. This development brings us back to the concept of *naib*. In the past, a *naib*, a religious person who acted as the representative of the regency *penghulus*, headed the *kantor kenaiban kecamatan*. Now it is the *penghulus* who are qualified in religious matters and are fully responsible for the KUA. Those heads of the KUA who are not *penghulus* are encouraged to take the certification examination to qualify as *penghulus*.

4 Corruption, Informality, and the Need for Reform

Over the last few years, the phrase *paradigma baru* (a new paradigm) has increasingly become the buzzword circulating among the functionaries of the KUA. The nub of this problem had to do with the complexities surrounding the

44 KMA 517/2001 on the reorganisation of the Sub-district KUA.

45 PMA 34/2016 on the organisation and the working procedures of the sub-district KUA.

46 See Peraturan Menteri Pendayagunaan Aparatur Negara (The Decree of the Minister for the Efficient Running of the Civil Service) PER/62 /M.PAN/6/2005 on the Functional Position of *Penghulu* and Their Credit Points.

informal administration fee, traditionally received by KUA marriage registrars, which was later defined by Anticorruption Law as an illegal charge (*pungutan liar*) or gratification. This illegal charge was the reason that the KUA found itself stereotyped as a corrupt institution.

In the colonial period, *penghulus* were confronted with financial predicaments. The 1882 Regulation concerning the Priest Councils in Java and Madura was issued for the very purpose of controlling the informal fees received by *penghulus* by stipulating that they be paid a salary. The fly in the ointment in the Regulation stipulated that only the chief *penghulu* would be salaried, while other *penghulus* were not. Unsurprisingly, the absence of a provision on their salaries meant that the regulation was ineffectual[47] and the *penghulus* remained dependent on *ongkos perkara* (legal fees). This income was administered as *kas masjid* (mosque fund).[48] In practice, the chief *penghulu* circulated a certain portion of *zakat* (alms fund) not only to religious officials and the people legally eligible to receive *zakat*, but also as a present to the Regent. Sometimes this generosity was extended distribution to European officials.[49]

The 1929 Marriage Ordinance, article 1 (5) laid down that *penghulus* could set discretionary fees of varying amounts based on the degree of solvency of the families concerned. Later, at the time of the introduction, the *penghulu-gerecht* (*penghulu* courts) replaced the *raad agama* (religious court) in 1931, and the colonial government tried to ensure that court officials were salaried. However, this intention was never implemented as the government budget was in a lamentable state as a consequence of the severe economic crisis in the 1930s.[50] Only from 1934 did *penghulus* begin to receive allowances, but not salaries.

In the mid-1950s, the problem had shifted from the provision of a salary for *penghulus* to the difference in the fee for a marriage ceremony in the office and a marriage conducted outside the office (*bedolan*). To officiate the latter, the *penghulus* had to attend a marriage ceremony held, for instance, at the bride's house. They charged extra for this, but no specific regulation could ensure a degree of uniformity in this matter. In Circular Letter (*Surat Edaran*) 2/B/1954

47 van Huis, "Islamic Courts and Women's Divorce Rights in Indonesia: The Cases of Cianjur and Bulukumba," 36; Lev, *Islamic Courts in Indonesia: A Study in the Political Bases of Legal Institutions*, 16.

48 Hisyam, *Caught between Three Fires: The Javanese Pangulu under the Dutch Colonial Administration, 1882–1942*, 62.

49 Ibid., 116.

50 Ibid., 163.

issued by the Jakarta Office of Religious Affairs in 1954,[51] *bedolan* featured as an important issue with regard to the legal status of the sum they received from the bride's families. Rather puzzlingly, the Circular seems to justify this extra charge. It emphasises that *penghulu*s in big cities were likely to receive a significant amount of money. In contrast, their counterparts in small towns and rural areas would enjoy smaller amounts of money.

Ever since, the *bedolan* fee has been subject to debate and conflicting legal norms. Each region has its approach to dealing with this matter. Numerous regencies introduced local regulations to legalise the practice of charging an additional fee in calculations of the *bedolan*. The Ministry of Religious Affairs turned a blind eye to this variation in the fee. The government regulation only mentions an administration fee of Rp. 30,000 is charged, irrespective of where a marriage ceremony was conducted.[52] For some decades, the additional fee has been the norm in society. Many people believe that the *penghulu*s deserve the fees due to their important role in a marriage ceremony.

For example, in Sidoarjo, East Java, in 2003 the *Bupati* issued a decree concerning the adjustment (*penyesuaian*) of the *bedolan* fee and the honorarium for the marriage registrar's assistant.[53] The letter referred to a higher regulation, namely the decision made by the Governor of East Java province which approved the *bedolan* fee and the honorarium for the marriage registrar's assistant.[54] The *Bupati*'s decree stipulated that the administration fee for marriage outside the office during working hours was Rp. 180,000, differing considerably from that in the government regulation. This *Bupati*'s regulation demonstrates that the administration fee for an Islamic marriage has become a concern not only to the *Kantor Kementerian Agama Kabupaten* but also to the local government. Moreover, the regulation orders the head of the *Kantor Kementerian Agama Kabupaten* to supervise the implementation of this regulation, even though his office falls under the control of the Ministry of Religious Affairs.

In response to the confusion caused by these different local regulations, the Ministry of Religious Affairs issued the Letter of Instruction 2/2004 on the improvements to the marriage service. The instruction emphasises the fixed

51 *Surat Edaran Jawaban Urusan Agama Jakarta* (Circular Letter from the Jakarta Office of Religious Affairs) 21/B/1954 on *bedolan*.

52 PP 51/2000 on the Non-tax Revenue of the Ministry of Religious Affairs.

53 *Keputusan Bupati Sidoarjo* (Decree of the Regent of Sidoarjo) 29/2003 on the Synchronization of the *Bedolan* Fee and the Honorarium of PPPN in Sidoarjo.

54 *Surat Gubemur Jawa Timur* (Letter of the Governor of East Java) 45113267/02112002 on Response to the Request for an Adjustment to the *Bedolan* Fee and the Honorarium of PPPN.

charge for a *bedolan* fee of Rp. 30,000 and strongly prohibited *penghulu*s from charging an administrative cost exceeding this; in a nutshell, advising them not to apply the local regulations.[55] Moreover, the central government also issued Regulation 47/2004 that replaced the previous Regulation 51/2000 but brought no changes in its wake. The Regulation still stipulated one tariff, Rp. 30,000, as the administration fee, irrespective of the variety of places in which a marriage ceremony (*akad nikah*) might be held. Heeding these regulations, the *Bupati* of Sidoarjo amended the 2003 local regulation in 2008.

Another variation on the *bedolan* fee was applied in the West Javanese regency of Subang. The Regent issued Regional Regulation 22/2006[56] whose purpose was to facilitate the carrying out of a marriage ceremony in society. It not only set the amount of *bedolan*, but specified the detailed allocation of the fee. It states that the *bedolan* fee, Rp. 250,000, including the official fee, Rp. 30,000. Nearly half of the fee was given to the KUA to cover its various requirements (*penghulu*, *modin*, marriage preparation course and other things), while around 34 percent of the fee was distributed to the *Kantor Kementerian Agama Kabupaten*. Interestingly, the local administration also enjoyed 10 percent of the fee. These regulations show that the *bedolan* has become a serious issue among *penghulu*s but, so far, there has been no specific regulation to amend the issue. Therefore, several regional governments have taken steps to deal with the matter in response to the conditions in their local areas.

Despite its awareness of the difficulties arising from the *bedolan* fee, the Ministry of Religious Affairs still acknowledges its existence, as shown by the Ministry of Religious Affairs' regulation 11/2007, which serves as the fundamental basis for the setting in training the procedures for marriage registration. Article 21 point (1) in this regulation asserts that a marriage ceremony should be held in the KUA office. Interestingly, point (2) stipulates that considering a request from the bride and with the marriage registrar's consent, a marriage can be held outside the KUA office. By this point, despite the absence of Religious Affairs' frontline national regulation and the abolition of local regulations on the *bedolan* fee, *penghulu* cannot reject any proposal for paying *bedolan* as it is allowed by the regulation. Accordingly, the statistics from the Directorate of Islamic Affairs of the Ministry of Religious Affairs indicate that the comparison between *nikah bedolan* and *nikah kantor* in the course of the first half of 2007

---

55 The Instruction of the Minister of Religious Affairs 2/2004 on the Improvement of Service in Sub-district KUA.

56 *Peraturan Daerah Kabupaten Subang* (Local Regulation Subang) 22/2006 on the *Bedolan* Fee.

was 981,536 (82%) for *nikah bedolan* and 221,367 (18%) for *nikah kantor*.[57] In Pasuruan, East Java, the marriage ceremony frequently happens at the bride's home, in which religious leaders lead the ceremony, while the KUA officials come to supervise and register it.

This issue came to a head when the police arrested a *penghulu*, Romli, in Kediri, East Java. He was prosecuted by the attorney of Kediri municipality for receiving *bedolan* fee and sentenced to one year's imprisonment and a fine of Rp. 50,000,000. It appeared that Romli had asked his financial administrator to record every single informal fee from the brides' families and this document was deemed to be admissible evidence that the attorney could submit to the court when bringing a charge of extortion against him. He was found guilty of charging a fee that differentiated between *nikah bedolan* and *nikah kantor*. The cost of the former was 225,000 and that of the latter 175,000. Romli received Rp. 50,000, regarded as the transfer cost, of each *bedolan* fee and Rp. 10,000 from every single marriage ceremony. Some portion of the fee was used to pay the salary of non-tenured administrators in the KUA and was also deposited with the marriage section at the *Kantor Kementerian Agama Kabupaten*. I happened to know that this regular deposit enabled the district office to pay allowances to the marriage registrar's assistant.

Romli was prosecuted under the Anticorruption Law of 2001. The informal fee was officially defined as unlawful gratification. Article 11 states that a state official is subject to a 5-year term of imprisonment or a fine ranging from 50 to 250 million rupiahs if he/she receives a gratification as a consequence of his/her position.[58] The judges decided that Romli was proved guilty. The decision agreed with the attorney's prosecution, sentencing Romli to one year's imprisonment and a fine of Rp. 50,000,000.

In mid-December 2017, I talked to Samsu Thohari, the head of a KUA in Surabaya who was the coordinator of the Forum of the Heads of the KUA of East Java. The forum was established after the Romli case had been filed with the court of Surabaya. Thohari argued that Romli was a good person that should not be prosecuted. Thohari and his colleagues perceived Romli's case as a kind of criminalisation of *penghulus* and condemned the Ministry of Religious Affairs for ignoring the situations on the ground with which *penghulus* were confronted.[59] They protested against the legal process by a mass strike rejecting the conclusion of a *bedolan* marriage involving *penghulus* throughout the province. In a

57 Departemen Agama RI, *Bimas Islam Dalam Angka 2007* (Jakarta: Direktorat Jenderal Bimbingan Masyarakat Islam, 2007), 24.

58 The decision of Surabaya General Court 04/Pid.Sus/2013/PN.Sby.

59 Interview with Samsu Thohari, 10 December, 2017.

FIGURE 5 *Penghulus*' strike demanding the release of Romli.
HTTPS://M.KBR.ID/MEDIA/?SIZE=810X450&FILENAME=/ARCHIVE/2013/12/16/PENGULUBESAR.JPG

pointed protest, they only solemnised marriages held in the office during working hours.

Thohari argued that Romli's gratification case should be understood in the framework of the central government's attempts to achieve good governance in the Ministry of Religious Affairs. In mid-2012, the Ministry of Religious Affairs was shaken by a corruption case arising from a project to print the Qur'an. In the same year, M. Yasin, the ex-deputy head of the Commission for the Eradication of Corruption (*Komisi Pemberantasan Korupsi*) was appointed Inspector-General of the Ministry of Religious Affairs. He later became an icon of the corruption eradication movement in all the working units under the Ministry of Religious Affairs. The KUA, as the Ministry of Religious Affairs' frontline public service institution, emerged as a major concern in the hoary practice of charging informal fees. In 2014, the Commission for the Eradication of Corruption designated the Ministry of Religious Affairs one of the 'red report' (*rapor merah*) Ministries on account of the lack of integrity of its functionaries.[60]

The imprisonment of Romli and the strike of his fellow *penghulus*, have become an important step on the road to eradicating corruption in marriage administration. An important figure in the Ministry of Religious Affairs dealing with *penghulus*, Anwar Saadi, told me that, through its failure to live up

60 https://tirto.id/biaya-nikah-dan-rapor-merah-kua-bGz3

to its responsibility, the government was ignoring the interests of *penghulus* and neglecting Muslim affairs in general.[61] Adding his weight to the discussion, Suryadharma Ali, the incumbent Minister, argued that people perceive the marriage ceremony to be a sacred event. They prefer to conduct it at home and it is common for people to give voluntary gifts to their *kyais* or *penghulus* for performing their religious roles in a marriage ceremony.

The first proposal the Ministry of Religious Affairs made was an additional budget to replace the informal fee received by *penghulus*. This proposal was not approved by the government. Instead, the government encouraged the Ministry of Religious Affairs to keep the people involved in the financial costs of marriage registration. From the outset, the government had been adamant that marriage registration can never be free of charge.[62] Under the supervision of the Coordinating Ministry for Human Development and Cultural Affairs, the government prepared a new regulation to accommodate its preference. According to Anwar Saadi, a high-rank official in the Ministry of Religious Affairs, the Ministry of Religious Affairs proposed some categories of administration fees. Firstly, those who want a marriage ceremony performed at the KUA office would have to pay Rp. 50,000. Secondly, those wishing to have an an-outside-office marriage ceremony have to pay Rp. 400,000. Thirdly, if the marriage ceremony was held on hired premises (*gedung*), the couple's family would have to pay even more. This initial proposal was rejected as too complicated and the proposal was simplified into two categories of fees. The first category remained the same, while the second and the third were fused into one with one charge, Rp. 600,000.[63]

The Commission for the Eradication of Corruption, the Parliament and the Ministry of Home Affairs then exerted pressure on the Ministry of Religious Affairs to change the first category by eliminating the fee. Their argument was premised on Law 23/2006 on Civil Administration. The Law stipulates that all Muslim citizens who conclude a marriage ceremony must report it to the subdistrict KUA within 60 days. According to the Law, a marriage ceremony constitutes one of the 'crucial life moments' (*peristiwa penting*) to which the legal obligation of registration is applied. Furthermore, article 79A of Law 24/2013, which is the revision of the previous Law 23/2006, states that "all matters as the consequence of the publication of civil documents (*dokumen kependudukan*) are free of charge". With regard to these provisions, a marriage certificate issued

61 Interview with Anwar Saadi, 13 December 2017.

62 http://www.tribunnews.com/nasional/2014/02/07/menkokesra-biaya-nikah-harus-tetap-ada

63 Interview with Anwar Saadi, 13 December 2017.

by the KUA is taken to be one of these civil documents (*dokumen kependudukan*) to which a citizen has an inalienable right. Muslim marriage registration is treated the same as civil registration applies to all citizens.

This has stirred up a considerable debate among KUA officials.[64] Most of them argue that a Muslim marriage certificate (*akte nikah*) is not the equivalent of a *dokumen kependudukan* because it requires a religious ceremony. The reason is twofold. Firstly, the official definition of *dokumen kependudukan* in Law 23/2006 refers specifically to documents of civil registration, which does not necessarily include marriage registration. Secondly, there is still a dichotomy between the registration of Muslim and non-Muslim marriages which has led to different procedures being applied. In contrast to the civil administration office, the KUA has the jurisdiction not solely to register a marriage ceremony but, more fundamentally, to ensure that it has complied with Islamic rules. Anwar Saadi confessed that the Ministry of Religious Affairs failed to negotiate the KUA officials' interests effectively in the meeting with different elements of the government.

To ensure the proper administering of civil administration and public service, the government issued regulation 48/2014 on the non-tax income of the Ministry of Religious Affairs which accommodates the last option. Article 6 states that every citizen who performs a marriage or brings about a reconciliation inside or outside the KUA office should not charge a registration fee. If a marriage ceremony is held outside the KUA office (*nikah bedolan*), the bride's family is obliged to pay an amount of Rp 600,000 as honorarium and transport costs.[65] The implementation of two types of fees is not without complexities. Some people in Pasuruan pragmatically strategise these fees to suit their interests.

They officially register a marriage ceremony as a *nikah kantor* to get a free charge, but in practice, they perform both *nikah bedolan* and *nikah kantor*. The *nikah bedolan* is first carried out without involving a *penghulu*. They generally see a marriage ceremony as a crucial stage that should be conducted under the guidance of a prominent religious leader, quite close to the issue of obtaining *barokah* (blessing). Hence, when organising a marriage ceremony, people ask a religious leader to lead the marriage ceremony. The *nikah kantor* is then carried out at the KUA office simply to get a marriage certificate. Sometimes, both cere-

64 This idea was, for instance, expressed by a *penghulu* in West Java, arguing that the management of administration fee should be decentralized because of the variety of conditions in each region; see http://kuagunungjati.blogspot.com/2015/06/analisa-biaya-nikah-berdimensi-ruang.html

65 See article 6 of Government Regulation 48/2014.

monies are performed on the same day. This practice has led to the practice of *akad nikah dua kali* (two times marriage ceremonies). I will delve more deeply into this issue in Chapter 5.

A few years before the arrest of Romli, the Ministry of Religious Affairs attempted to reduce the practice of informal fees, whose roots as the Ministry of Religious Affairs assumed had to do with the intermediary roles played by a marriage registrar's assistant.[66] As I explained earlier, a marriage registrar's assistant is a *modin* who has been authorised by the state to assist *penghulu*s in marriage affairs. The fly in the ointment is that, despite the official position of marriage registrar's assistants, they are not officially salaried. Although it was said that they receive allowances once every three months, when push came to shove, the local government allocated their allowances from the informal fees collected by the KUA.

In its attempt to get on top of the problem, the Ministry of Religious Affairs reformed the position of assistants of marriage registration. The Director General of Islamic Guidance initiated the reform in 2009.[67] It issued an instruction that orders the *Kantor Kementerian Agama Kabupaten* not to extend the contract of assistants of marriage registration or to make any new appointments unless they are needed. Rather than use an intermediary, the Ministry of Religious Affairs suggested people come directly to the KUA, with the marriage documents they have prepared themselves, without involving a *modin*. The subsequent policy statement issued in 2015[68] defined the boundaries of 'needed'. It only applies to remote areas. This policy was met with a wave of rejections in numerous areas. In Palembang, South Sumatra, for instance, the marriage registrar's assistant requested a hearing in the local parliament to secure their position.

Returning to the Romli case, the heart of the problem is that the role of a *penghulu* is critical in the administration of marriage. A *penghulu* is, referring to Lipsky, a frontline worker who interacts directly with citizens, a street-level bureaucrat.[69] Hence a *penghulu* is an essential link between the government and the people. In coping with everyday marriage administration, *penghulu*s are challenged by various traditions which are an inseparable part of any society. Quite often a *penghulu* receives a fee to which he is not entitled but which

66 As an effort, the Director General of Bimas Islam issued the Circular Letter DJ.II.I/3/HK.007/2757/2013 on the prohibition of collecting informal fees in marriage registration.

67 Instruction of the Director General of Bimas Islam DJ.II/113/2009 (10 February 2009) on the use of non-tax revenue funds and the reorganization of the PPPN.

68 Instruction of the Director General of Bimas Islam DJ. II/1/2015 on the promotion of PPPN.

69 Lipsky, *Street-Level Bureaucracy: Dilemmas of the Individual in Public Services*, 3.

seems legitimate given the extra work he has been required to do. We learn from Lipsky that as, a civil servant, a *penghulu* might have to work in situations that often require responses to the human dimensions of a situation.[70] If dedicated to his job, he might give his clients individualised and thorough attention. As the man-on-the-spot, he feels that he is best equipped to deal with local situations and when the central government attempts to change the *status quo*, he often tries to resist this intervention.

5 Muslims' Attitudes towards the Reform

In the context of Sumbersari in Pasuruan, East Java, where I did my fieldwork, the abolition of the position of marriage registrar's assistant did not affect whatsoever the practice of *modin*. Fighting to uphold their position, the *modin* have set up an association (*paguyuban*) called Samawa. Every month they meet at each other's houses. Sometime in January 2017, I attended one of their meetings. Although it was an informal gathering, it was spilling over with religious agenda. A recitation of *tahlil* (prayers to remember the dead) opened the meeting. Some issues came up in a discussion session afterwards.

Haji Hamim, the coordinator of this *paguyuban*, raised the issue of *wali* (guardianship). He argued that guardianship continued to cause problems because official documents cannot always be guaranteed to contain valid data about a citizen, especially in the matter of the biological relationship between a father and his daughter. Moreover, Haji Mustofa, a *modin* in Pasuruan, emphasised that it would be almost impossible for the government to monopolise the administration of marriage as long as the civil administration on the level of local society is not properly organised. Besides performing his religious duties, *modins* play an important role in verifying the biological relationship between the bride and the marriage guardian. In particular cases, as I discovered in my fieldwork, neither a birth certificate nor a family card can be taken as a proper guarantee of the actual relationship between biological parents and the child. In a nutshell, having to depend solely on a document that might happen to contain incorrect data opens plenty of room for conflict and requires extensive local knowledge.

For example, on one occasion, a bride registered a man, Pak Ahmad, as her marriage guardian. A neighbouring villager dropped a hint that the *modin* should double-check who could serve as the guardian in her marriage because

70 Ibid., 15.

Pak Ahmad was, in fact, not the biological father of the bride, even though on the family card Pak Ahmad is listed as her father. This raised the problem that, according to Islamic law, a stepfather is not legally entitled to act as a marriage guardian. The *modin* told Pak Ahmad that he could not take the role of guardian for his adopted child. Upset Pak Ahmad rejected the *modin*'s assertion as had always treated the bride as his daughter. The *modin* tried to convince Pak Ahmad of the conditions required for marriage according to Islamic law, but the latter refused to budge. The *modin* understood that he had to manage this matter carefully with a good deal of discretion, assuming that, if the biological father knew about the situation, he would confront Pak Ahmad.

In Sumbersari, rarely does a father give the bride in marriage himself. Most of the time, the father delegates his authority to a respected religious leader (*kyai*). The *modin* did not force Pak Ahmad to relinquish his wish but tactfully took Pak Ahmad to visit the *kyai* whom he preferred so that the former could delegate his rights (*tawkil wali*). Hence the matter seemed to have been resolved satisfactorily and a couple of days later, when the *modin* met the bride's biological father, again exercising his discretion, he invited him to visit the same *kyai* to do the same thing. The result was that, on the day of *akad nikah*, the *kyai* assumed the role of guardian and neither Pak Ahmad nor the biological father played any formal part.

This experience goes a long way to underline that Muslim marriage registration is much more than simply an administrative affair. It has wider dimensions, both religious and social. Because of these ramifications, a *modin*, the man-on-the-spot, remains a vital actor. The story I have just told shows very clearly that, in contrast to the limited capacity of the state, the *modin* played an important role in mediating the different interests in society. Firstly, he certainly assisted the *penghulu*s in the latter's main task, that is to ensure that a marriage ceremony was conducted under Islamic rules. Secondly, he was successful in preventing potential tension between Pak Ahmad and the father.

6 The Information System of Marriage Registration

Besides introducing this administration fee reform, the Ministry of Religious Affairs has also urged the KUA to improve its administrative system. In 2013, the Ministry of Religious Affairs introduced an information system for the Minister of Ministry marriage registration (*Sistem Informasi Manajemen Pernikahan*, SIMKAH). This programme was launched in tandem with the application of the personal identification number (*Nomor Induk Kependudukan*, NIK), introduced by the government in 2009.[71] This is also known as the electronic identity card (e-KTP). The SIMKAH uses the NIK as the main parametre by which to examine the validity of a person's private details. However, during the first years of its operation, the SIMKAH did not link up with the NIK database stored by the Ministry of Home Affairs. Nevertheless, it was already able to prevent any inaccurate scrutiny of the age of the bride. At the end of 2015, numerous regencies initiated the integration of the local civil administration database with the SIMKAH database managed by the KUA. It was an outcome of the regulation issued by the Minister of the Ministry of Home Affairs, which allows its civil registration bureaus to give the civil administration data access to relevant government institutions, including the KUA.

This cooperative model was later expanded on an even greater scale. At the end of 2017, the Ministry of Religious Affairs and the Ministry of Home Affairs officially signed a cooperation accord that ushered in the use of e-KTP in marriage registration nationwide. E-KTP has now become a compulsory document in marriage registration. The Ministry of Home Affairs now authorises the KUA of the Ministry of Religious Affairs throughout Indonesia to access civil documents and validate NIK stored in the administrative system run by the Bureau of Civil Administration. Conversely, the Ministry of Home Affairs is also entitled to access data on marriage registration managed by the Ministry of Religious Affairs. Of course, according to Anwar Saadi, the implementation of the use of e-KTP depends on the readiness of each KUA to undertake this task.[72]

That said, the integration of marriage registration into civil administration has had important consequences. Firstly, because nowadays, the KUA obliges them to submit an electronic identity card (e-KTP), it is no longer possible for both the brides and grooms to fiddle their ages using the legal proof issued by the village head. A legally eligible bride to register a marriage (16 years and older) but does not yet possess an identity card can no longer get away with just handing in a declaration from the village office. Instead, she has to submit a letter from the local civil administration bureau declaring that the NIK has been verified and the identity card is being processed. This procedure means there is no longer any room for backdating birthdates (*menuakan usia*) when applying to register a marriage.

---

71 *Peraturan Presiden* (the Presidential Regulation) 26/2009 *Tentang Penerapan Kartu Tanda Penduduk Berbasis Nomor Induk Kependudukan Secara Nasional* (on the implementation of the identity card on the basis of a national identity number).

72 "Pencatatan Nikah Hanya Menggunakan KTP Elektronik," accessed March 15, 2019, https://bimasislam.kemenag.go.id/post/berita/pencatatan-nikah-hanya-menggunakan-ktp-elektronik.

PEMERINTAH KABUPATEN PASURUAN

DINAS KEPENDUDUKAN DAN PENCATATAN SIPIL

Komplek Perkantoran Kabupaten Pasuruan, Jl. Raya Raci KM-9 Telp. (0343) 741919

BANGIL - PASURUAN

SURAT KETERANGAN

Nomor : 475/04586/424.066/2017

Yang bertanda tangan dibawah ini adalah :

Nama : Drs. SUNYONO, MM
NIP : 196002211981011003
Jabatan : Kepala Dinas Kependudukan dan Pencatatan Sipil Kabupaten Pasuruan
Alamat : Komplek Perkantoran Kabupaten Pasuruan, Jl. Raya Raci KM.9 Bangil - Pasuruan

Menerangkan bahwa :

NIK :
Nama :
Tempat/Tanggal Lahir : PASURUAN / 01-01-2000
Jenis Kelamin : PEREMPUAN
Alamat :
RT/RW :
Kel./Desa :
Kecamatan :
Agama : Islam
Status Perkawinan : Belum Kawin
Pekerjaan : Belum/Tidak Bekerja
Kewarganegaraan : WNI

Penduduk tersebut diatas benar-benar sudah melakukan perekaman KTP-el dan penduduk yang bersangkutan telah terdata dalam Database Kependudukan Kabupaten Pasuruan.

Demikian surat keterangan ini kami buat sebagai pengganti KTP-el, dipergunakan untuk kepentingan Pemilu, Pemilukada, Pilkades, Perbankan, Imigrasi, Kepolisian, Asuransi, BPJS, Pernikahan dan lain-lain, dan kepada yang berkepentingan agar menjadi maklum.

Surat Keterangan ini berlaku selama 6 (enam) bulan sejak diterbitkan.

Pasuruan, 17 January 2017

KEPALA DINAS KEPENDUDUKAN DAN
PENCATATAN SIPIL KABUPATEN PASURUAN

Drs. SUNYONO, MM
Pembina Utama Muda
NIP. 196002211981011003

FIGURE 6 Letter from the local bureau of civil administration, substituting identity cards

Secondly, when the bride is not legally allowed to register her marriage, primarily because her age is under 16 on the day of the marriage ceremony, the *modins* usually marry a couple informally for social reasons and postpone the registration. It means that one consequence of the modernisation of the marriage registration system is an increasing number of unregistered marriages and this problem still exists. My observations in a village in Sumbersari sub-district show that the registration of six out of forty-five marriages during 2017 was delayed because of the bride's age. On a more positive note, this delay in registration also suggests that people are inclined to register their marriage despite their limited legal literacy.

Villagers are less daunted, and it seems that marriage registration is easier and more negotiable. The great advantage is that the *modins* always find pragmatic solutions to different problems even though it appears that the implementation of the NIK has obviously failed in its goal of reducing births out of wedlock and eliminating underage marriage. Putting something on the statute books is not always cut and dried. The implementation is not as simple as it sounds. In a follow-up to integrating civil administration and marriage registration through the SIMKAH, the Ministry of Religious Affairs introduced a marriage card (*kartu nikah*) in November 2018. It is stipulated in the newest regulation on marriage registration, the Regulation of the Minister of Religion 20/2019. The Minister of Religious Affairs argued that the card is yet another offshoot of the SIMKAH. The card works like an identity card. The Ministry of Religious Affairs is keen to stress that the card is handy and can be used in multiple instances as a substitute for a marriage certificate. As it is equipped with a barcode, it is believed that the card will eliminate the forgery of a marriage certificate.

7 Conclusion

In Indonesia, the administration of Muslim marriages in the KUA can be a fundamental step in the direction of the bureaucratisation of Islam. The bureaucratisation of Islam refers to the process by which the state co-opts religion and centralises Islamic religious authority within its own institutions.[73] We see how state actors empower state-funded administrative bodies to shape Islamic discourses and regulate religious matters in the public sphere. The KUA

73 Ann Marie Wainscott, *Bureaucratizing Islam: Morocco and the War on Terror* (Cambridge: Cambridge University Press, 2017), 14; Müller, *The Bureaucratization of Islam and Its Socio-Legal Dimensions in Southeast Asia: Conceptual Contours of a Research Project*, 2.

is the Ministry of Religious Affairs' frontline agency to deal with these matters. However, for a number of years, as long as the KUA has existed, problems related to the position and the rights of formal and informal marriage functionaries as well as the administrative system have required considerable adjustment if they are to function adequately.

In its dealings with marriage, the KUA has to manage both the religious and administrative aspects of Muslims. Herein lies its dilemma. On the one hand, the KUA is supposed to exercise traditional religious authority when it comes to the religious side of marriage, while it has to function as a modern administrative bureau on the other. In other words, the KUA is a religious bureaucracy yet must perform as a public service office. The tension between the religious and the administrative aspects has generated significant complexities which have dogged it right up to the present.

The Ministry of Religious Affairs has attempted a series of reforms of the KUA over the last few years to sift out some of these complexities. These reforms have been introduced into numerous fields and include administrative fees, the positions of *penghulu*s and *modins*, their competencies, and the administrative system itself. Despite the solutions the reforms have offered, they have brought a number of problems in their wake. It seems as if one problem is solved, another one arises.

The first problem is related to the administration fee with which *penghulu*s have been confronted. It has led to the problem of alleged unlawful gratification. The lack of a specific legal procedure to regulate the administrative fee for a marriage ceremony outside the office (*bedolan*) even led to the prosecution of a *penghulu* in Kediri, East Java, in 2013. The Ministry of Religious Affairs has introduced various bureaucratic reforms to cope with this crisis. Among the decisions it has taken, the Ministry of Religious Affairs has made marriage registration free of charge. This policy was influenced by the Law of Civil Administration, which positioned marriage registration as a civil registration. The Law stipulates that each citizen has the right to obtain a *dokumen kependudukan* (civil document) free of charge. Because marriage certificates are deemed equivalent to other civil documents, Muslim marriage registration should cost nothing accordingly. Only people who wish to conclude *bedolan* are expected to pay extra to cover the costs incurred by *penghulu*s. This reform has meant that the KUA officials apparently tended to identify themselves as both civil registration and religious officials. However, it seems that the Ministry of Religious Affairs is still exigent in securing the religious nature of the KUA. It achieved this by restoring the position of *penghulu*s at the epicentre of the KUA. Now it turns out that only a *penghulu* can serve as the head of the KUA.

The second reform has occurred in two interconnected areas: the affirmation of the PPN as the only agency for marriage registration and the dismissal of the marriage registrar's assistant. The central government pushed its formal officials to monopolise the administration of marriage and, consequently, disregarded an important role played by informal religious leaders. The government argues that the practice of *modin*s sails close to the wind of corruption. However, I argue that the issue has to do with the uncertain legal status of the marriage registrar's assistant, which means the government is disobliged to pay them a salary.

In practice, the reform seems hard to change the position of informality. For local people, Muslim marriage is a religious ceremony that necessitates the authority of informal religious leaders, *modin*s, far more than the formal authorities, *penghulu*s. *Modin*s do not concern themselves solely with administrative matters, but are also involved in the religious sides of marriage. As has been the tradition, people tend to delegate any marriage administration to a *modin*. By doing so, villagers manage to achieve two goals simultaneously: sidestepping the administrative rigmarole and satisfying the requirements of religion. From a social point of view, the loss of their legal status as the marriage registrar's assistant does not affect their roles as *modin*s. As a result, these informal leaders cannot be replaced just like that.

The third kind of reform, integrating marriage registration into the civil administration, seems to have run into the same sorts of problems. The use of the NIK is unquestionably to avoid fraudulent changes in the ages of the couples. Yet, there is no guarantee that this will stop people's willingness to marry their children under the statutory marriageable age. In cases like this, the intervention of the *modin*s remains important. Neither the modern system nor the government officials are likely to be able to handle this situation adroitly. Confronted with a problem like this, the *modin*s will come up with a solution. Their most common solution is to perform a religious marriage with a delayed/retroactive registration. Although religious marriage literally does breach the law, the delay in registration does guarantee the legal status of the couples.

In the next chapters, I leave the discussion on the legal and bureaucratic reform of marriage administration in the KUA and turn my focus to look at the law in action. I try to understand how people deal with state law and negotiate their interests to comply with it. However, before plunging into this discussion, the following chapter presents the cultural context of the society in which I have done my research. This is to give a preliminary basis to help understand how Islamic marriage is practised and in what ways traditional social actors play roles.

PART 2

Legal Practice

CHAPTER 4

Understanding Pasuruan: Present-Day Islam and Cultural Life

1 Introduction

This book deals with the reform of the bureaucracy concerned with marriage and how it has affected the everyday legal practice of marriage in a rural society. It includes an analysis of the local practices and lived experiences of marriage in a Muslim community in a regency in the north-eastern part of East Java province: Pasuruan. This chapter offers an introduction that will help to understand the socio-economic history, the religious and cultural life, and the development of Islam in Pasuruan. It consists of three sections. It first sets the scene by delineating the historical development of Pasuruan, including the history of the Madurese migration and the historical development of Islam. Secondly, it addresses current cultural, religious, and political life. The last section centres on specific elements of the community in which I did my fieldwork.

2 Historical Context

According to the *Encyclopaedie van Nederlandsch-Indië*, the name Pasuruan derives from the Javanese word *suróh*, which means betel. The *Encyclopaedie* mentions the *kromo* (high) Javanese equivalent of the name, *pasedahan*, from the root *sedah*, which also means betel.[1] However, this name has gone out of use and the fact that Pasuruan was once a place where the betel (areca) palm grew in abundance has long since faded from people's memories. The alternative name of Pasuruan, Gembong (the name of a river dividing the town), which many Javanese used in the past, is also no longer used.

The district of Pasuruan is located around 65 kilometres southeast of Surabaya, the capital city of the province. Today Pasuruan is home to 1,501,798 Muslim people or 98 percent of the entire population. Around 15,612 (1%), a group of Hindus, most of whom live in the southern highlands around the

1 P.A. van der Lith and Joh. F. Snelleman, *Encyclopaedie van Nederlandsch-Indië*, vol. 3. (Amsterdam: KIT Royal Tropical Institute, 2010), 233.

 | DOI:10.1163/9789004516113_005

volcano Mount Bromo, constitute the second largest population.[2] Historically, it was not until the Mataram kingdom occupied the southern part of Surabaya in the 1600s that Pasuruan became an important town. After the advent of Mataram, Pasuruan was ruled by regents who were subordinates of the Mataram Sultanate in Central Java. The area surrounding Pasuruan was a frontier area of Mataram, especially in view of its close relationship with the "stubborn remnants of Hinduism in the easternmost corner of the island." Elson says it "served both as a field of combat and a redoubt for rebels."[3]

This section explains the history of Pasuruan, including the arrival of Madurese migrants, the socio-economic situation in the colonial period and the development of Islam, rounding off with the changes which occurred after the Proclamation of Independence and under the New Order era.

2.1 *Madurese Out-Migration to Pasuruan*

Pasuruan, and this is generally true of other areas located in the Eastern Salient of Java (*tapal kuda*), is home to people of Madurese descent. The historical ties between Madura and Pasuruan go back a long way to the thirteenth century, when Raden Wijaya, the founder of the Majapahit kingdom, agreed to grant Wiraraja, the Regent of Madura, the Eastern Salient of Java in gratitude for his support of the kingdom. Nevertheless, earlier literature suggests that both Javanese and Madurese were already conscious of belonging to the same cultural community. Husson categorises Madurese out-migration to East Java into six chronological orders. He claims that Madurese serfs first went to East Java in the thirteenth and fourteenth centuries to colonise agricultural land and support the Majapahit kingdom. This migration was partly the result of geographical factors such as scarcity of good soil, deforestation, and erosion on their own island.[4] This marks the first out-migration wave of Madurese to Java.

The second wave of migration took place between the sixteenth and nineteenth centuries. At the time, Madura was a source of soldiers for the powers fighting for supremacy in East Java. The military missions stimulated population movements. To take one example, the VOC recruited a thousand Madurese for the war against Blambangan in 1741. Madurese soldiers who had been

2 BPS Kab. Pasuruan, *Kabupaten Pasuruan Dalam Angka 2016* (Pasuruan: BPS Kab. Pasuruan, 2017).

3 R.E. Elson, "Sugar and Peasants: The Social Impact of the Western Sugar Industry on the Peasantry of the Pasuruan Area, East Java, from the Cultivation System to the Great Depression" (Monash University, 1979).

4 Laurence Husson, "Eight Centuries of Madurese Migration to East Java," *Asia and Pacific Migration Journal* 6, no. 1 (1997): 79.

involved in different battles in East Java remained there afterwards. If they did return to Madura, they brought back such glowing stories about the prospects in East Java that they motivated other Madurese to move there.[5] The third migration was an exodus of Madurese peasants between 1820 and 1850. During this period, Madura had the status of a free province under the 1745 agreement between the Regent of West Madura and the VOC, which stated that the Regent would be allowed to govern independently in return for an annual contribution of money and troops. This situation continued until the liquidation of the VOC in 1799 when Madura lost its special self-rule status, which had severe consequences for the locals. They had to pay crippling taxes and retributions, and therefore many left their island to begin a new life in East Java with their families.[6] The emigration disadvantaged the local agriculture in Madura in terms of the decrease in manpower during the planting and harvest seasons. The island was spun into an economic downturn, and its dependence on Java became more marked during this period.[7]

As mentioned before, the scarcity of good soil in Madura has been an enduring problem and has always formed a barrier to agricultural development. Agricultural harvests in the nineteenth century were far from enough to satisfy local needs. Some references indicate the widespread use of coolies and seasonal and permanent workers from Madura in East Java, particularly in Pasuruan, Besuki, Jember, Probolinggo, Bondowoso and Lumajang. These areas were the important cash-crop centres of the province. A report shows that in 1892, 40,000 Madurese migrated to East Java. The enormous demand for workers in East Java began when the Dutch East Indies government opened a whole series of plantations there between the 1830s and the 1870s. In addition to the very large-scale government project, enterprising individuals also set up their own private plantations. The establishment of these private plantations produced a rapid spurt in Madurese migration. Madura quickly became a reservoir of the manpower which was so vital to this development. For instance, Probolinggo experienced a 5.2 percent population increase in 1854, attributable to the arrival of Madurese. The expansion of the government plantation project and private enterprises meant that the cane-sugar industry of Java was the second largest in the world after Cuba.[8] This seasonal migration marked the fourth wave of migration which took place in the latter part of the nineteenth cen-

5 Ibid., 81–83.
6 Ibid., 84–85.
7 Ibid., 85.
8 Ulbe Bosma, "The Cultivation System (1830–1870) and Its Private Entrepreneurs on Colonial Java," *Journal of Southeast Asian Studies* 38, no. 2 (2007): 275–291.

tury. According to Husson,[9] with reference to Weddik, kinship ties meant that migrants from Sampang and Bangkalan chose to reside in Pasuruan. Quoting Van Nes, Elson reveals that, in the 1830s, demographically, Madurese constituted around 35 percent of Pasuruan residents, approximately 170,049 Javanese and 92,463 Madurese.[10]

The fifth round of migration occurred during the Japanese occupation (1942–1945). During this period, Madurese peasants suffered famine and poverty because of the continual worsening of the island's economy due to failed harvests and crippling taxation. A very large group of Madurese made their way to East Java on foot, travelling at night to avoid the sun, in their battle to survive, seeking to find food and work in Java.[11] The last wave of migration occurred between the 1950s and the 1960s and still continues today. Big cities in East Java have experienced a rapid rate of urbanisation as a consequence of natural population increase and migration from rural areas. The Madurese supplied the workforce, labourers, and coolies for the plantation around these cities. They also worked as shopkeepers of run food stalls (*warung*), became rickshaw-drivers (*tukang becak*) and fruit sellers. Internal solidarity among Madurese seems to play an important role in the group's economic situation.[12] Interestingly, the migratory influx has led to a more fluid social structure in Pasuruan. The Madurese who settled there were not really inclined to submit to the pretensions of Javanese aristocrats.[13]

2.2 *Colonial Occupation*

As I mentioned earlier, a huge wave of Madurese migrants arrived in Pasuruan during the nineteenth century, when the Dutch East Indies government set up a project encouraging the establishment of plantations and sugar factories. The Pasuruan area was first figured as an important area on the stage of Java's history when, in 1830, Governor-General Van den Bosch decreed that it was part of the cultivation system. This was a policy introduced by the Dutch government that imposed on the Javanese population the obligation to grow and make compulsory deliveries of coffee, sugar cane and other export products in exchange for crop payments.[14] The expansion of agricultural commodities

9 Husson, 'Eight centuries of Madurese migration to East Java,' p. 86.
10 Ibid., 85.
11 Ibid., 88–89.
12 Ibid., 90–92.
13 Robert W. Hefner, *The Political Economy of Mountain Java: An Interpretive History* (Berkeley: University of California Press, 1990), 195.
14 Fasseur Cornelis, "The Cultivation System and Its Impact on the Dutch Colonial Economy

required thousands of labourers and coolies. Although the Dutch introduced many commercial crops, the two most successful during the life of the system proved to be coffee and sugar.

At the height of the cultivation system, the labour force mobilised for government enterprises was coerced, and their sheer numbers were massive.[15] Meanwhile, the number of coffee trees planted grew significantly until eventually 70 percent of all Javanese families were involved in compulsory cultivation, and more than half of them worked with coffee. However, the payment for these products was not commensurate with the market value or with the efforts required by the planters. The value of the export product amounted to 11.3 million guilders in 1830 and rose to 66.1 million in 1840.[16] Although, as a consequence of its astonishing profitability, coffee remained a government monopoly longer than any other crop,[17] the northern littoral stretching from Pasuruan to Surabaya became Java's largest sugar-growing region. It would remain so for the duration of the cultivation system. Hence, it goes without saying, this system had a considerable impact on the economic and social life of the Pasuruan people. Nevertheless, in contrast to areas in Central Java, Pasuruan did not suffer under the cultivation system.[18] Certainly, the cultivation of sugar cane and the sugar industry offered prosperity to the native elites but did not have any considerable impact on ordinary people.[19]

In terms of the administrative development of the area, the Pasuruan regency was officially inaugurated in 1901. Besides sugar, the regency had centres of forestry and copper mining. The town of Pasuruan served as the capital of the regency. It was also made the capital of the present-day regencies of Probolinggo, Malang and Lumajang. As time passed, the economic position of the Pasuruan regency declined as a result of various factors. One of the most important was that the Gembong River, which divided the town, gradually silted up.[20] At the same time, in the early twentieth century, Surabaya Harbour

---

and the Indigenous Society in Nineteenth-Century Java," in *Two Colonial Empires. Comparative Studies in Overseas History*, ed. Bayly C.A. and Kolff D.H.A. (Dordrecht: Springer, 1986), 137–154; Melissa Christina van Bijsterveld, "Continuation and Change on Dutch Plantations in Indonesia" (Leiden University, 2018).

15 Hefner, *The Political Economy of Mountain Java: An Interpretive History*, 45.

16 Cornelis, "The Cultivation System and Its Impact on the Dutch Colonial Economy and the Indigenous Society in Nineteenth-Century Java."

17 Hefner, *The Political Economy of Mountain Java: An Interpretive History*, 43.

18 Ibid.

19 Dédé Oetomo, "The Chinese of Pasuruan: Their Language and Identity" (Australian National University, 1987).

20 Ibid., 16.

was expanded, and the Surabaya-Malang railway was opened. The opening of this railway somewhat undercut the importance of Pasuruan, and it slipped into an industrial decline. Much of its trade was diverted to Probolinggo. The capital of residency was transferred to Malang in 1930.[21]

2.3 *Pre-Independence*

The historical background of the orthodox understanding of Islam in the pre-independence era explains the rapid growth of Sarekat Islam (SI, Islamic Union) in Pasuruan[22] and later of the NU. SI was a party that grew out of an association of Muslim merchants who wanted to improve their economic interests to put them more on par with those of Chinese merchants in Java. It became a political party in the 1920s. Trying to trace the history of SI in Pasuruan is a difficult exercise because of the lack of sources. A representative of SI was quite active in his visits to those villages in Pasuruan with which he had personal and financial ties, and in them, he would set up a village religious leader as a sort of local organiser. Because of its configuration, SI attracted peasants and quickly became an organisation embraced by the peasants in their struggles against the infidel rulers and the *priyayi*, a social class comprising the elites and government officials. This idea of struggling against the rulers and social elites struck a profound chord among traditionalist Muslims. Another reason SI expanded its influence was that it slotted neatly into the wave of Islamic revivalism, which swept Java around the 1910s and shared the SI ideals of communal solidarity and belonging.[23]

The development of SI was interrupted by the onset of a severe economic crisis, popularly known as the Great Depression, in Indonesia during the 1930s. Although this Great Depression had a detrimental effect on the Pasuruan economy, it did not change the political face of Pasuruan very much. Under this calm surface, the NU quietly began to expand its influence.[24] It pursued a slightly different strategy to that of SI. It adopted a nonconfrontational strategy towards the rulers and, on the ground in the villages, encouraged rural religious teachers to promote its own style of religious platform. Students in *pesantren* (*santri*) were sent into areas of the countryside to organise *pengajian* (classes in

21 Ibid.

22 Harry J. Benda, "The Pattern of Administrative Reforms in the Closing Years of Dutch Rule in Indonesia," *The Journal of Asian Studies* 25, no. 4 (1966): 592.

23 Elson, "Sugar and Peasants: The Social Impact of the Western Sugar Industry on the Peasantry of the Pasuruan Area, East Java, from the Cultivation System to the Great Depression."

24 Hefner, *The Political Economy of Mountain Java: An Interpretive History*, 197.

Qur'an), thereby laying the groundwork for the establishment of a new chapter of the organisation. In short, its strategies were apolitical.[25] Its priorities have been not to provoke immediate anticolonial resistance but to concentrate on disseminating traditional Islam. By deploying this cautious approach, the NU won the hearts and minds of that section of the population which was still less 'Islamic,' succeeding in spreading its base to the southern highlands, even though the contest between Islam and Javanism (*kejawen*) in the highlands was still ongoing.[26]

The Dutch colonial rule was powerful enough to curb attempts to establish Indonesian sovereignty but was not strong enough to eliminate the Nationalist spirit. At that point, the Indonesians still did not have the power to compete with the colonial ruler and therefore needed outside help. Beginning in March 1942, the Japanese provided just this help by taking over Dutch power in Indonesia. Sadly, it was a false dawn, and Indonesians would soon have to face the reality of the hardship of Japanese rule: a scarcity of food, clothing and medicines as well as forced labour on a large scale. Pasuruan people remembered the Japanese occupation (1942 to 1945) as a difficult and frightening period.[27] The Japanese's policy towards Islam was virtually the reverse of that of the Dutch and exploited the old antipathy towards Christian rulers.

The Japanese authorities courted religious teachers in the villages and rewarded them by increasing their local power. In a nutshell, the effect of the Japanese policy was to expand the growth of the Islamic movement. In return, the Japanese were eager to obtain the aid of these religious leaders in the fight against the return of the former rulers.[28] Moreover, Japanese support was also crucial to the establishment of the Masyumi (*Majelis Syuro Muslimin Indonesia*), a federation of all Indonesian Muslim organisations, in which the NU's executives played important roles. The NU then became part of the government bureaucracy through its involvement in the *Shumubu*, the Japanese-created Office of Religious Affairs.[29] In the final months of the Japanese occupation, *Hizbullah*, a military arm of the Masyumi, launched an intensive campaign to win mass membership in Pasuruan. The resultant success guaranteed Muslim supremacy in lowland Pasuruan.[30] *Hizbullah* was potentially challenged by the

---

25 Harry J. Benda, *The Crescent and the Rising Sun: Indonesian Islam under the Japanese Occupation, 1942–1945* (Dordrecht: Foris Publications, 1983).

26 Hefner, *The Political Economy of Mountain Java: An Interpretive History*, 197.

27 Oetomo, "The Chinese of Pasuruan: Their Language and Identity," 14.

28 Benda, *The Crescent and the Rising Sun: Indonesian Islam under the Japanese Occupation, 1942–1945*.

29 Ibid.

30 Hefner, *The Political Economy of Mountain Java: An Interpretive History*, 198.

establishment of the Nationalist youth corps in 1944, Peta (*Pembela Tanah Air*, Defenders of the Homeland). However, Peta failed to significantly influence the Muslim communities in Pasuruan, which remained a firm NU bastion.

2.4 *Post-Independence and the New Order Era*

With the Proclamation of Independence in August 1945, the new state of the Republic of Indonesia came into being in the territory of the former Dutch East Indies. However, the dream of an independent Indonesian state was opposed by the former colonial power. At the end of the Second World War, the Dutch asserted their intention of regaining the colony with the support of their European allies. The war of attrition, popularly known by Indonesians as the Revolution, lasted for more than four years.[31] The Dutch organised a military expedition in 1946, but it failed to raise resistance in urban Pasuruan.[32] Nevertheless, in some ways, it did encourage a republican movement in the southern part to resist the infiltration of NU influence from the north. This movement caught the Islam-based organisations in Pasuruan at a disadvantage and led to the establishment of Nationalist dominance in the region following the war. However, greatly assisted by the vast development of *pesantren*, traditionalist Muslims did manage to preserve their entrenched socio-structural power.

A year earlier, in 1945, Indonesia had declared its Independence. Soon after Independence, the government sought to hold a legislative election. But, given the prevailing political instability, the election was not possible. In 1953, the government was able to pass a bill on elections which was enshrined as a law. It gave the right to vote to everybody over the age of eighteen or who had been married. The election campaign followed hard on the heels of the passing of the law. The first election was held in September 1955. In this general election, devout Muslims were drawn to the Masyumi and NU. In contrast, Nationalist Javanese chose to pursue their struggle through either PNI (*Partai Nasional Indonesia*, the Indonesian National Party) or PKI (*Partai Komunis Indonesia*, the Communist Party of Indonesia).[33] This division shaped the development of Islamisation in Pasuruan, which was very much bound up in the *aliran* (stream) pattern of party mobilisation. Political parties infiltrated rural areas canvassing votes. The NU enjoyed major success and won a significant number

31 Kevin W. Fogg, "Islam in Indonesia's Foreign Policy, 1945–1949," *Al-Jami'ah* 53, no. 2 (2015): 308.

32 Hefner, *The Political Economy of Mountain Java: An Interpretive History*, 198.

33 Justus M. van der Kroef, "Indonesia's First National Election: A Sociological Analysis," *The American Journal of Economics and Sociology* 16, no. 3 (1957): 238.

of seats (18.4%) in Parliament.[34] The Masyumi scored an even bigger win, as the runner-up, with 20.9 percent of the votes. Religion featured prominently in the political campaign.

Compared to other areas, the polarisation in Pasuruan was relatively simple: split between the NU-dominated northern lowlands and the Nationalist southern highlands, although the influence of the Masyumi in Pasuruan was inescapable. The NU was highly critical of the Masyumi, disagreeing with its modernist ideology. Nevertheless, the NU and Masyumi leaders met on common ground in their ideas about Communism. They identified communists with atheists. Although certain figures in the NU condemned the PKI as an anti-Islamic organisation, some NU leaders were less concerned about the communists than their modernist Muslim rivals.

In Pasuruan where religious issues have always loomed large, Islam has wielded a significant influence. Masyumi leaders and radical *kyai*s from the NU demanded that the traditional ritual practices in the highland south be outlawed. Their opposition came before the 1955 election when tensions escalated after a group of Muslim activists (linked to radical factions in the NU) occupied a famous upland *dhanyang* (a sacred place). Although overall, the Islamic political parties were disappointed with the result of the first election of 1955 on the national level, in Pasuruan itself, the election results confirmed the dominance of the NU, which enjoyed a significant win, 61 percent of the votes, in that election. Only Madura produced a more stunning result than Pasuruan.[35] This NU electoral victory in Pasuruan put the Pasuruan's Javanist highlanders in a tricky situation. The election results meant that the significant success of the Islam-based political parties posed a severe threat to their religious traditions.

Another development in the wake of the election was the growing influence of the PKI. The economic decline in Indonesia, which dogged the late 1950s and early 1960s, had a severe impact on inflation. The PKI took the opportunity presented by the deteriorating economic situation to expand its rural constituency. At the end of 1963, the PKI introduced a campaign to make the land reform enacted in the 1960 Agrarian Law a reality. The PKI mobilised farmers into 'unilateral actions' (*aksi sepihak*) to seize the land of large landowners and hold demonstrations in support of sharecropping. Unsurprisingly, this initiative provoked strong reactions from Muslim landlords.[36] East Java was the scene of some of the most violent confrontations between Muslims and communists.

34 Robert W. Hefner, "Islamizing Java? Religion and Politics in Rural East Java," *The Journal of Asian Studies* 46, no. 3 (1987): 550.

35 Hefner, *The Political Economy of Mountain Java: An Interpretive History*, 200.

36 Ibid., 201.

Tellingly, in lowland Pasuruan, the PKI failed to gain the support of the rural people as the power exerted by the *kyai*s proved too strong. Realising it was flogging a dead horse, the PKI soon focused its attention on the uplands.[37]

In the years 1965 to 1966, Indonesia experienced a dark chapter in its national history as large-scale killings, and civil unrest rocked the country. The killings generally targeted members of the PKI and its comrade organisations. The trouble began on the evening of 30 September 1965 when a group of militants who proclaimed themselves Soekarno's protectors executed six of Indonesia's top military generals allegedly to pre-empt a possible coup. However, Soekarno refused to associate himself with this movement. Now the cracks in the façade of his poor leadership begin to show. Major-General Soeharto, who at the time was the leader of Kostrad (*Komando Strategis Angkatan Darat*, Army Strategic Command), capitalised on the situation to claim control over the country. He deployed troops while propagating the idea that the movement's actions posed a danger to the nation. Masterminded by Soeharto and his military forces, propaganda associating the coup attempt with the PKI began to be disseminated.[38] The campaign was successful, convincing both Indonesian and international audiences that the murders were a PKI's attempt to undermine the government under President Soekarno. Nevertheless, the writing was on the wall, and public opinion began to shift against Soekarno, disturbed by his undisguised sympathy for the events of 30 September and his tolerance of communist elements.

Soeharto presented the campaign as a nationwide conspiracy to commit the mass murder of large segments of the population associated with the PKI. The army removed those top civilian and military leaders it thought were sympathetic to the PKI. By the end of October, the propagation of this conspiracy theory had easily won the support of Muslim leaders. These leaders, many of whom controlled large swathes of agrarian land, felt threatened by the PKI's efforts to speed up land reform. Furthermore, groups of devout Muslims joined in the purges against communists, arguing that it was their bounden duty to cleanse Indonesia of atheism. In March 1967, the Parliament stripped Soekarno of his remaining power and Soeharto was appointed as Acting President. In 1968, Soeharto was appointed to the first of his five-year terms as President. The term New Order was used to distinguish Soeharto's regime from Soekarno's Old Order.

---

37 Ibid., 202.

38 Jerome R. Bass, "The PKI and the Attempted Coup," *Journal of Southeast Asian Studies* 1, no. 1 (1970): 96–105.

During the New Order era, under the banner of Pancasila, the New Order attempted to control Islamic forces. Islamic political parties were weakened and merged into a single one in 1973 and, later, this new body was obliged to replace its Islamic foundation with Pancasila.[39] The philosophical foundation of the nation, ideologically Pancasila is not secular. Instead, it comprises five principles, the first of which is belief in One God. To reinforce this state ideology, a number of local governments initiated the idea of creating so-called Pancasila villages. Behind the concept lies the desire for people to have peaceful and prosperous lives and to strive for equality before the law. It was also meant to encourage citizens to make a strong commitment to practising their religious doctrine, particularly Islam. Consequently, it is not too farfetched to say that this idea was meant to be the New Order's strategy orchestrated to gain Muslim support. The Pasuruan government was also encouraged to establish these villages.[40] In its campaign, the central government stressed that commitment to the religious principle in Pancasila was the determinant in the application of the other principles. Therefore, the development of traditional Islamic schools (*pesantren*), which produced Islamic leaders, was considered consistent with the spirit of Pancasila.

Despite the success of this tactic, the New Order felt it necessary to establish another channel of communication with the Muslim community. In 1975, The MUI was established as a vehicle through which to mobilise support for its development policies from Muslims. In the 1990s, the New Order seemed to reach a turning point when it established the ICMI (*Ikatan Cendekiawan Muslim Se-Indonesia*, the Association of Indonesian Muslim Intellectuals). Some argued that the ICMI reflected the growing influence of Islam in the bureaucracy and the rise of a Muslim urban 'middle class.'[41] However, some others have claimed that it was an expression of the continuing Islamisation of daily life which had occurred in the 1970s and 1980s.[42] In Pasuruan, the trend towards the growing influence of Islam among the Muslim middle class did not seem to happen. *Pesantren* was not dislodged from its position as the key social institution that sustained the development of Islam in the area.

---

39 Martin van Bruinessen, "Islamic State or State Islam? Fifty Years of State-Islam Relations in Indonesia Hamburg: Abera-Verlag," in *Indonesien Am Ende Des 20. Jahrhunderts*, ed. Ingrid Wessel (Hamburg: Abera-Verlag, 1996), 19–34.

40 Pemda Kab Pasuruan, *The Present Day of Kab Pasuruan* (Pasaruan: Pemda Kab Pasuruan, 1974).

41 Robert W. Hefner, "Islam, State, and Civil Society: ICMI and the Struggle for the Indonesian Middle Class," *Indonesia* 56, no. October (1993): 32.

42 Bruinessen, "Islamic State or State Islam? Fifty Years of State-Islam Relations in Indonesia Hamburg: Abera-Verlag."

3 Cultural, Religious and Political Life

Islam, which came from the northern part of Central Java, penetrated this area in the first part of the sixteenth century.[43] As Islamisation took hold in this region, it led to the development of what is known as coastal Islam (*Islam pesisir*), and slowly but surely, it emerged as the centre of so-called traditionalist Islam.[44] The most fundamental feature of this type of Muslim community is its deep commitment to upholding religious traditions such as collectively reciting *dhikr* (remembrance of Allah, a series of devotional acts) dedicated to the dead and reciting prayers for the Prophet (*solawatan*) as well as deep-seated obedience to religious leaders.

The influence of Islam was reinforced by the expansion of traditional religious schools (*pesantren*) in the northern lowlands during the last half of the nineteenth century. These schools became centres of the propagation of traditional Islam. On a wider scale, they were also crucial to lowland politics and social structure. Marital ties connected wealthy families to *pesantren* teachers. Ordinary villagers were also expected to make gifts of money and land for religious teachers to support the running of the *pesantren*.[45]

Nevertheless, Hefner remarks that Pasuruan is one of the most heterogeneous regencies in Java[46] As I have already mentioned, *kejawen* holds sway in the south. At the same time, Islamic traditionalism predominated in the north. This Islamic orientation is not the preserve of certain social classes but spans them all. In this section, I wish to explain particular traits of the Pasuruan people who live in the northern lowlands, including their culture, religion, patron-client ties and politics.

3.1 *Cultural Life*

My personal acquaintance with this area began when I studied in an Islamic secondary school (*madrasah aliyah*) in the town of Jember in the late 1990s. I passed through this area on my way back and forth to my hometown, Sidoarjo. The character of the people living in this area was not so much different from the people living in Jember. The most distinctive feature of this community is

---

43 M.C. Ricklefs, *A History of Modern Indonesia* (Bloomington: Indiana University Press, 1981), 34.

44 M.C. Ricklefs, *Polarising Javanese Society: Islamic and Other Visions, c. 1830–1930* (Leiden: KITLV Press, 2007); Koentjaraningrat, *Javanese Culture* (Singapore: Oxford University Press, 1985), 318.

45 Hefner, *The Political Economy of Mountain Java: An Interpretive History*, 195.

46 Hefner, "Islamizing Java? Religion and Politics in Rural East Java," 533–554.

its language. By and large, the people speak in Madurese or, when they do speak in Javanese or Indonesian, they do so with a Madurese accent. As discussed earlier, the strong influence of Madurese culture in this area, and other eastern East Java parts in general, has a long historical trajectory. The emigration from Madura constituted a new diaspora in Java.[47] After an intense socio-cultural interaction with the natives of the eastern part of Java, a new-hybridised culture was formed called *pedalungan* or *orang campuran* (mixed people).[48] This new culture displays special characteristics: the use of local language, the pattern of economic activities, and political participation.[49] Another reference calls them *pendhalungan*. The term comes from the word *dhalung* in Javanese, which means a big pot of cooked rice. This area has become a melting pot of Javanese and Madurese cultures.[50] The society is identified with an agrarian culture, hard work, strong solidarity and great respect for Islamic leaders.

The other major sub-cultures of East Java are known as *arek* or *arekan* and *matraman*. I spent my childhood in Sidoarjo in which both language and culture are characterised as *arekan*. Geographically, *arekan* culture is located in the central part of East Java, stretching from Surabaya to the south coast of Malang regency. The term *arekan* itself comes from the Javanese word *arek*, which means children or young people. *Arekan* is associated with being 'modern' in terms of being open-minded, rational, well-educated, and easily adapting to new situations. From the religious point of view, if *pendhalungan* people are said to be very fervently attached to a traditional type of Islam and are identified by their great respect for Islamic leaders, *arekan* tends to practise Islamic traditionalism rather less assiduously. The third sub-culture, *matraman*, is situated in the western part of East Java, from the north to the south coast, bordering the province of Central Java. *Matraman* people still preserve a culture that has been inspired by the Mataram sultanate in Central Java. They are identified with their more subtle use of language, their respect for kingship and their embracing of the most refined values of Javanese cultures, such as their facility in the use of polite language in daily conversations. Local norms are set on the basis of patriarchy and hierarchy.[51]

---

47 Husson, "Eight Centuries of Madurese Migration to East Java."

48 Konstantinos Retsikas, "The Power Of The Senses: Ethnicity, History and Embodiment in East Java, Indonesia," *Indonesia and the Malay World* 35, no. 102 (2007): 970.

49 Retsikas, "The Power Of The Senses: Ethnicity, History and Embodiment in East Java, Indonesia"; Konstantinos Retsikas, *Becoming—An Anthropological Approach to Understandings of the Person in Java* (London: Anthem Press, 2012).

50 Christanto P. Raharjo, *Pendhalungan: Sebuah 'Periuk Besar' Masyarakat Multikultural* (presented in Jelajah Budaya 13 August, 2006), 3.

51 Mufidah Ch, "Complexities in Dealing With Gender Inequality: Muslim Women and

Besides the language marker, another indication of the *pendhalungan* community is the way people dress. Although they follow a similar traditional model of understanding Islam as in other places in East Java, the women in this area show distinct peculiarities in dressing. Embracing the Madurese culture, the young and old women wear *kebaya* (traditional Indonesian blouse), traditional hijab (*kerudung*) and *sarong* (a length of fabric wrapped and tied around the body at the waist) in bright, contrasting colours. The idea behind selecting such colours is that they reflect courage, openness and a certain straightforwardness. The men wear a loose black blouse with red and white stripes. The sharp stripes are meant to encourage the building of a strong character and fearlessness in facing challenges. The loose clothes indicate freedom and openness. This outfit is called *pesa'an*, and is worn on both formal occasions and in daily life. The women like to wear accessories and conspicuous jewellery. They can fashion it from either gold or silver and sometimes include unique motives. They wear jewellery to display social and economic status.[52]

3.2 *Religious Groups*

The regency of Pasuruan has long been one of the most important centres of Islamic traditionalism in Java. As a channel of traditionalist Muslim clerics, after its foundation, the NU quickly attained dominance in lowland political life. In the Indonesian religious landscape, a 'traditionalist' is someone who embraces one of the four Sunni schools of jurisprudence.[53] Islamic traditionalism is the main feature that distinguishes the NU from Muslim 'modernist' or 'reformist' organisations.[54] In addition to its adherence to traditional Islam, the NU has been forthright and quite active in promoting the role of a religious civil society. The NU criticised state power and became a vehicle for social cohesion among citizens in the 1980s and 1990s. The NU became a political party in the 1950s but was merged into the Partai Persatuan Pembangunan (PPP, the United Development Party) in 1973. Finally, at the NU Situbondo National Congress (*Muktamar*) in 1984, a group of its intellectuals and activists urged for a return to the *khittah* (guidelines) of 1926. This would have meant that the NU abandoned politics and reverted to being a purely religious and social organ-

---

Mosque-Based Social Services in East Java Indonesia," *Journal of Indonesian Islam* 11, no. 2 (2017): 459–488.

52 Etty Herawati, *Kain Dan Pakaian Tradisional Madura* (Jakarta: Dinas Museum dan Sejarah, Pemerintah DKI Jakarta, 1979).

53 Rumadi, *Islamic Post-Traditionalism in Indonesia* (Singapore: ISEAS-Yusof Ishak Institute, 2015), 23.

54 Faisal Ismail, "The Nahdlatul Ulama: Its Early History and Contribution to the Establishment of Indonesian State," *Journal of Indonesian Islam* 5, no. 2 (2011): 247–282.

isation.[55] However, since the collapse of the New Order, many NU leaders have dominated strategic positions in the central government bureaucracy, let alone in Pasuruan.

Within the NU itself, a diversity of religious tendencies is apparent. Some NU leaders in Pasuruan adhere strictly to classical *fiqh* doctrines when it comes to the relationship between religions, religious minorities and some particular issues within Islam, such as polygyny. They are quite critical of the central organizers of the NU who have promoted modern ideas of tolerance and pluralism. This critical group is anecdotally known as *NU Garis Lurus* (Straight Path NU). *Kyai*s who have limited education and live in *kampung* (village) are likely to be proponents of this group.

Despite this divide, the majority of NU leaders in Pasuruan prefer to cultivate an understanding of the middle path of Islam. They promote an idea called *Islam Nusantara* (Archipelago Islam), which represents the close interaction between Islam and local cultures. *Islam Nusantara* emphasises that to be a Muslim, one does not have to ignore national and local identities. Instead, both national and local identities can co-exist with an Islamic identity. The combination of the two can assist one to be a devout Muslim and a Nationalist at the same time. This 'progressive' line of the NU began to gain popularity among NU members when Abdurrahman Wahid chaired this organisation from 1984 to 1999. Wahid successfully led the NU in its adoption of values such as democracy and religious tolerance.[56]

The NU is not the only Islamic group active in Pasuruan. Although the Muhammadiyah and the Persis (*Persatuan Islam*, Islamic Union) also have a presence, they are less popular. Both organisations were inspired by the reformist movement inaugurated by Muhammad Abduh in the magazine *Tafsir Al-Manar*. The Muhammadiyah chose to follow a path that emphasises both religious and secular education and tolerance of other faiths. In contrast to the NU, the Muhammadiyah encourages its followers to use their own legal reasoning (*ijtihad*) rather than adhering to tradition. Adherence to legal decisions made by previous jurists (*taklid*) should be avoided. This religious idea is designated *pemurnian akidah* (purifying the faith).[57] As did the Muhammadiyah, Persis has evolved in the direction of reforming traditional Islamic practices.

55 Robin Bush, *Nahdlatul Ulama and the Struggle for Power within Islam and Politics in Indonesia* (Singapore: Institute of Southeast Asian Studies, 2009), 28.

56 Alexander R. Arifianto, *Islam Nusantara & Its Critics: The Rise of NU's Young Clerics* (Singapore: RSIS, 2017).

57 James Lowe Peacock, *Purifying the Faith: The Muhammadijah Movement in Indonesian Islam* (Chapel Hill: University of North Carolina Press, 1978).

It opposes the practice of kissing another person's hand as a sign of respect, a practice that remains part of the NU tradition.[58]

Furthermore, Bangil, the capital of Pasuruan, is home to the headquarters of Shiʿa Islam in Indonesia. The rapid development of this Islamic stream led to an anti-Shiʿa protest in 2007. The protest, mainly championed by older NU members, took place in front of the YAPI (*Yayasan Pesantren Islam*, the Foundation of Islamic School) in Bangil. The YAPI is a *pesantren* that belongs to Shiʿa Muslims. It was founded by Husein al-Habsy, an Indonesian of Arab descent, in 1976 and has expanded into an established educational institution covering primary to high school that welcomes students from Shiʿa and Sunni families. The same protest recurred in 2011. The attackers threw stones at a female *pesantren* of the Shiʿa community.

This action angered the youth wing of the NU, *Ansor*, which urged police to investigate the attack. This youth wing of the NU is genuinely concerned with the right to exist of religious minorities and is not in favour of the far-right wing of Islam. Other youth forums also showed their concern and organised a rally in front of the YAPI, claiming that the protection of diversity is enshrined in the national motto of *Bhinneka Tunggal Ika*.[59] This stand on the point of principle demonstrates that there is a tendency among the younger generation of the NU to embrace a more moderate understanding of Islam, one which encourages the protection of religious minorities.

Another recent development is that the right-wing Islamic organisation established in August 1998, the Islamic Defender Front (FPI, Front Pembela Islam), which is most strongly represented in the urban areas, has begun to gain influence in rural areas. From a theological point of view, it is not different to the NU and a number of local *kyai*s have even shown an interest in it. The FPI promotes the idea of *amar makruf nahi munkar* (commanding what is good and forbidding what is evil) and even allows the use of violence in its implementation. Its principal attraction to this idea is that the organisation perceives it as part of real *dakwah* (propagation). The FPI has become rather notorious for its paramilitary division, which carries out intensive raids on massage parlours, bars, karaoke venues, gambling centres and other evil places, especially during Ramadhan.[60]

---

58 Jeremy Menchik, *Islam and Democracy in Indonesia: Tolerance without Liberalism* (New York: Cambridge University Press, 2016).

59 Samsu Rizal Panggabean, "Policing Sectarian Conflict in Indonesia: The Case of Shiʿism," in *Religion, Law and Intolerance in Indonesia*, ed. Tim Lindsey and Helen Pausacker (London: Routledge, 2016), 280–281.

60 Helen Pausacker, "Pink or Blue Swing? Art, Pornography, Islamist and the Law in Reformasi

FIGURE 7 The traditional way of celebrating a birthday, calculated based on the Islamic lunar calendar. It involves the recitation of Quranic chapters led by a religious leader.

The relationship between the FPI and the NU is not always good. During the last few years, the local branches of the FPI and the local NU youth organisations have often been at loggerheads. In 2017 the tension intensified, resulting in an attack committed by a group of FPI members on a house that belonged to a member of *Ansor*. The attack was triggered by a misunderstanding about a Facebook post, believed to have humiliated the top FPI leader.[61] In mid-2017, the local FPI invited its top leader, Rizieq Syihab, to deliver a speech in the *tablig akbar* (great congregation). This sermon elicited a harsh reaction from the audience since he severely criticised the government and the leaders of the NU for not supporting the idea of assigning the Sharīʿa a formal place in the fabric of the nation.

Indonesia," in *Religion, Law and Intolerance in Indonesia*, ed. Tim Lindsey and Helen Pausacker (London: Routledge, 2016), 290.

61 Muhajir Arifin, "Gara-Gara Postingan Di Medsos, Ansor Dan FPI Pasuruan Bersitegang," *Detik.Com*, accessed October 14, 2018, https://news.detik.com/berita-jawa-timur/d-3495695/gara-gara-postingan-di-medsos-ansor-dan-fpi-pasuruan-bersitegang.

The traditional understanding of Islam as practised by the NU has influenced local people's social life in northern Pasuruan. Important phases of life, such as birth, marriage, birthdays and death, are celebrated and commemorated in a localised form of Islamic ritual. Beatty remarks that all rituals reflect the interests of orthodoxy in creating social harmony in the neighbourhood by recommending adjusting one's behaviour to unorthodox others.[62]

3.3 *Patron-Client Relations*

The growth of traditionalist Islam affects the relationship between the state, religious leaders and the Muslim people. The robust commitment to Islamic traditions and the strict obedience to religious leaders (*kyai*s) have complicated the relationship between religion and the state. Community-level politics operate on the basis of the patron-client ties which characterise the society in the easternmost part of East Javanese.[63] The bulk of these is manifested in informal institutions, for instance, *kyai*s and *santri* (people of *pesantren*). These Islamic institutions and religious leaders are two fundamental entities that maintain such power relations.[64] *Pesantren* serves as a centre in which knowledge of Islam is transferred to pupils (*santri*) and *kyai*s are reproduced.[65] *Pesantren* is not only considered to be the guardian of traditionalist Islam as a whole, but become part of both religious and socio-cultural institutions in which *kyai*s are the main actors.[66] They preserve the chain of traditionalist Islam within the structure of intellectual and social networks, to which marriage and kinship make a considerable contribution. Both *pesantren* and *kyai*s co-maintain an entity that is known as *santri* culture,[67] which entails a mixture

---

62 Andrew Beatty, *Varieties of Javanese Religion: An Anthropological Account* (Cambridge: Cambridge University Press, 1999), 155–157.

63 Phillip Drake, *Indonesia and the Politics of Disaster: Power and Representation in Indonesia's Mud Volcano* (New York: Routledge, 2016), 5.

64 Dhofier, *The Pesantren Tradition: The Role of the Kyai in the Maintenance of Traditional Islam in Java*; Robert W. Hefner, "Reimagined Community: A Social History of Muslim Education in Pasuruan, East Java," in *Asian Visions of Authority: Religion and the Modern States of East and Southeast Asi*, ed. Charles F. Keyes, Laurel Kendall, and Helen Hardacre (Honolulu: University of Hawaii Press, 1994), 75–95.

65 Azyumardi Azra, Dina Afrianty, and Robert W. Hefner, "Pesantren and Madrasa: Muslim Schools and National Ideals in Indonesia," in *Schooling Islam: The Culture and Politics of Modern Muslim Education*, ed. Robert W. Hefner and Muhammad Qasim Zaman (Princeton: Princeton University Press, 2010), 174.

66 Ronald Alan Lukens-Bull, "A Peaceful Jihad: Javanese Islamic Education and Religious Identity Construction" (Arizona State University, 1997), 5; Hiroko Horikoshi, *Kiai Dan Perubahan Sosial* (Jakarta: P3M, 1987), 114.

67 Yanwar Pribadi, "Religious Networks in Madura: Pesantren, Nahdlatul Ulama, and Kiai as the Core of Santri Culture," *Al-Jami'ah: Journal of Islamic Studies* 51, no. 1 (2013): 1–32.

of Javanese and Islamic cultures.[68] To put it simply, the religious orientation of traditionalist Islam is imbued with the people's devotion to a strict observance of Islamic principles and their intensive performance of religious rituals[69] and is inextricably identified with the core position of *pesantren* and *kyais* (religious leaders). These religious leaders are the main actors in the social relations[70] that uphold not only religious authorities through Islamic scholarship but also strongly define social and political roles. The relationship between them and local people is embodied in a patron-client tie.

After more than half a century, the time has come to re-assess Clifford Geertz's important 1960 work on Javanese *kyai*s, which has been a basis for further studies about their changing position in the complexity of social transformations in Indonesia. He argues, instead of being alienated from the pressures of nationalism and Islamic modernism, *kyai*s transformed themselves into a kind of cultural broker for a different sort of interest. *Kyai*s have played a significant role in transmitting Islam to ordinary people and occupied a focal position within the traditional social structure. They have also managed to carve themselves out and play a new social role that has offered them the possibility to enhance their social power and prestige.[71] The political role of *kyai*s has been most conspicuous in their function as a mediator of the political issues concerning nationalism for the villagers surrounding them. Mansurnoor remarks *kyai*s are, and always will be, embedded in the socio-political and religious lives of Muslims. He emphasises their roles in maintaining the balance between their attachment to religious tenets and the local setting in which they operate.[72] The critical role played by *kyai*s can take a variety of forms as either *kyai pesantren* or *kyai tarekat* (Sufi orders). As suggested by Turmudi, as a group, *kyai*s have striven either to make the existing social order compatible with religious ideals or to mould these religious ideals to be compatible with the existing order.[73]

68 Zamakhsyari Dhofier, "Kinship and Marriage among the Javanese Kyai," *Indonesia* 29 (1980): 47–58.

69 Ibid., 50.

70 Lukens-Bull, "A Peaceful Jihad: Javanese Islamic Education and Religious Identity Construction," 5; Horikoshi, *Kiai Dan Perubahan Sosial*, 114.

71 Clifford Geertz, "The Javanese Kijaji: The Changing Role of a Cultural Broker," *Comparative Studies in Society and History* 2, no. 2 (1960): 230.

72 Iik Arifin Mansurnoor, *Islam in an Indonesian World: Ulama of Madura* (Yogyakarta: Gadjah Mada University Press, 1990).

73 Endang Turmudi, *Struggling for the Umma: Changing Leadership Roles of Kiai in Jombang, East Java* (Canberra: ANU E Press, 2006).

Patronage is also a part of formal institutions, especially when religious leaders enter politics and the state bureaucracy. This tendency is incontrovertible when we look at the reality in Pasuruan in the last decade. Furthermore, *kyai*s are commonly wealthy landowners, and therefore part of the social elite.[74] The local people in Pasuruan are heavily dependent on *kyai*s socially and, even more importantly, in all matters related to religious normativity. For instance, they come to *kyai*s to ask for blessings and prayers or seek advice on an appropriate name for their offspring or the date of a marriage ceremony. It is only the *kyai*s who have the authority to interpret the Sharīʿa. In any interpretation of marriage and familial matters, rather than state regulations, it is Sharīʿa, as embodied in *fiqh*, which is taken as the authoritative norm in the management of their daily lives, with a helping hand from the influence of local traditions.

How the state deals with religious issues remains an important topic of public debate in present-day Indonesia. The following short sketch illuminates how traditionalist Islam interacts with, or at least contests, the state in the Pasuruan context. It was at the end of the Islamic holy month of Ramadhan in mid-September 2008 when a tragedy hit the town of Pasuruan. Thousands of people, many of whom were mothers between the ages of forty and sixty, went to the private home of the famous and wealthy Saychon family. They descended on the house upon hearing news about an alms distribution that had spread like wildfire a few days before. In the early morning, they gathered in front of the gates in the hope of collecting the sum of Rp. 40,0000 ($3.07) in a cash donation. This distribution is supposed to be an annual tradition observed by that family. Unfortunately, the cash delivery turned into a deadly stampede. The women in front fought to scream as they were pushed from behind in the crowd. More than twenty people were crushed to death. Called to account, a Saychon son, Faruq, was named by the police as a suspect as he was the coordinator of this distribution. The local criminal court decided to sentence Faruq to three years' imprisonment, indicting him with negligence causing death.[75]

Unhappily that year, the Saychon family had not chosen a charitable institution to distribute the alms as had been its custom since the 1980s. Among many reasons was that the family did not want to delegate its long-established identity as a philanthropist to other agencies. The Saychon family thought it important to maintain its social standing as a donor, showing solidarity with the poor. Another version has it that, by holding such a self-managed distri-

---

74 Dhofier, "Kinship and Marriage among the Javanese Kyai."

75 Tempo.co, "Trauma 'Zakat Maut', Haji Syaichon Salurkan Zakat Ke Badan Amil," *TEMPO Interaktif*, last modified 2009, accessed June 15, 2017, https://m.tempo.co/read/news/2009/09/07/151196632/trauma-zakat-maut-haji-syaichon-salurkan-zakat-ke-badan-amil.

FIGURE 8 Each family adopts its own respected *kyais* whose photos are hung on the wall in the front room.

bution, family members were more confident that the funds would reach the intended recipients, as it was dubious about the trustworthiness of existing private and state-run charitable institutions.

Not unnaturally, the tragic incident gave rise to religious debates about the legal status of the direct distribution of almsgiving. The head of the BAZNAS (*Badan Amil Zakat Nasional*, the National Almsgiving Body), Didin Hafiduddin, was harsh in his criticism. He stated that direct distribution is not an Islamic tradition, but owes far more to feudal tradition. Nevertheless, he did not deny that there was a problem with social trust in government almsgiving agencies.[76] Taking a different tack, Hasyim Muzadi, the general head of the NU, was reluctant to accept the impermissibility of such private distributions. In his view, the path the Syaichon family chose was genuinely good, but the negligence shown during the distribution was of legal matter subject to police investigation.[77]

76 Tempo.co, "Tebar Zakat Ala Haji Syaikhon Tak Sesuai Quran," *TEMPO Interaktif*, last modified 2008, accessed June 15, 2017, https://nasional.tempo.co/read/news/2008/09/16/058135727/tebar-zakat-ala-haji-syaikhon-tak-sesuai-quran.

77 Tempo.co, "Pembagian Zakat Haji Syaikhon Fikri Tidak Haram," *TEMPO Interaktif*, last modified 2008, accessed June 15, 2017, https://m.tempo.co/read/news/2008/09/16/058135791/pembagian-zakat-haji-syaikhon-fikri-tidak-haram.

This case reveals several interesting social aspects. Undeniably individuals with higher socio-economic status have the right/duty to employ their resources to provide protection and benefits to persons of lower status who reciprocate this gesture by owing obedience to their patron.[78] However, if their social status is to be preserved, this initiative should be undertaken privately, eschewing the involvement of the state agencies. The rationale is that, whenever the state sees an opportunity, it will try to usurp the mechanisms sustaining these patron-client relations.

3.4 *Political Sphere*

The scholarly discussion has linked politics in East Java to *politik aliran* (stream politics). First proposed by Clifford Geertz, this is a political force that was built on deeply rooted streams present in socio-religious communities. Scholars have argued that the first democratic election in 1999 reflected the old pattern of *politik aliran*. Despite the complex multi-party system available in Indonesia, electoral competition in East Java has unquestionably been dominated by two major *aliran*-oriented parties: the Partai Kebangkitan Bangsa (PKB, The National Awakening Party), the NU-based political party, which broadly represents the traditionalist *santri* community, and the PDI Perjuangan which tends to attract the ballot-papers of the *abangan* (Muslims practising syncretic Islam) voters. As times have changed, some scholars argue that the intense competition between individual candidates, publicly known as *perang figure* (war of personalities), has challenged the old *politik aliran*. These political candidates have not only managed to win votes from their traditional communities but are now increasingly looking beyond the old *aliran* identities. *Aliran* remains central to political life. Yet, current social changes have meant that *politik aliran* has lost a lot of its significance.[79] The latest development has led to the rise of 'new clientelism' in which patron-client relations within *aliran* are weakening (*dealiranisasi*) and are being replaced by more open arrangements.[80]

During the four general elections held in Pasuruan since 1999, the PKB has won the most votes on the regency level. In the 2009 election, fifteen out of the fifty seats or 30 percent of the local members of Parliament were from the

78 James C. Scott, "Patron-Clients Politics and Political Change in Southeast Asia," *The American Political Science Review* 66, no. 1 (1972): 92.

79 Andreas Ufen, "From Aliran to Dealignment: Political Parties in Post-Suharto Indonesia," *South East Asia Research* 16, no. 1 (2008): 5–41.

80 Rubaidi, "East Java: New Clientalism and the Fading of Aliran Politics," in *Electoral Dynamics in Indonesia: Money Politics, Patronage and Clientelism at the Grassroots*, ed. Edward Aspinall and Mada Sukmajati (Singapore: NUS Press, 2016), 277.

PKB. In the 2014 election, the PKB suffered a dramatic decline, gaining only twelve parliamentary seats or 24 percent. Second in the race were the nationalist parties, namely PDI Perjuangan and Partai Gerindra, each with seven seats. Despite this decline, the PKB has succeeded in having one of its representatives appointed as the Parliament leader. Not only this, the current Regent, Irsyad Yusuf, who was a PKB member of the Parliament in the previous term, is an overarching icon of the triumph of both the PKB and NU. In the 2018 election for a new Regent, none of the political parties proposed candidates to stand against him. He, supported by Gus Mujib Imron, the leader of the renowned Pesantren Al-Yasini, put himself up as the only single candidate (*calon tunggal*).

4 Social Life in Sumbersari

This section explores some particular aspects of the area in which I have been conducting my fieldwork. Sumbersari is a pseudonym of a sub-district. It is composed of seventeen villages in which the majority of the people, especially in the southern part, speak Madurese. Only those living in the north, bordering the town of Bangil, speak Javanese. Now, in spite of speaking in Madurese, all the local residents identify themselves as Javanese.

According to Retsikas, this kind of area is characterised by an interesting idea of the endless transformation from one culture, Madurese, to another culture, Javanese, which he calls becoming. Local people tend to describe the major character trait of the Javanese as the quality of *halus* (refinement), while the Madurese side is perceived as *kasar* (rough-and-ready).[81] Anthropologists have said that among Javanese people, to 'behave as a Javanese' means 'to conduct him/herself with urbanity.' In everyday life, a person is said to be Javanese if his or her daily behaviour mirrors the ideal of *sejatining becik*, which means aspiring to a character based on *pituduh* (acting advisedly) in the Javanese tradition. Conversely, somebody is said to be not Javanese if his or her daily way of life fails to reflect the good values embodied in Javanese culture.[82] Under these circumstances, Madurese try to become 'Javanese.' Despite their best intentions, this does not alter the negative stereotype of Madurese in circulation among the Javanese. Some Javanese still think that Madurese migrants are reluctant

---

81 Retsikas, *Becoming—An Anthropological Approach to Understandings of the Person in Java*, xiv.

82 Ayu Sutarto, "Becoming a True Javanese: A Javanese View of Attempts at Javanisation," *Indonesia and the Malay World* 34, no. 98 (2006): 41.

to integrate into Javanese society. Husson argues that Madurese are "the victims of a deep-seated prejudice which pictures them as coarse and brutal."[83] The situation is not improved by the fact that they tend to resist exogamy and favour self-segregated residence.[84]

Sumbersari, as is common in Maduro-Javanese areas, has to contend with an array of social problems, chief among them poverty[85] and a tendency not to participate in formal education. This avoidance of the established formal educational system has made *pesantren* a central institution. *Pesantren* offers an alternative educational institution that is perceived to be adequate to fulfil their needs as it inculcates in students not only the knowledge they require to function in society but also instils religion and character-building in them. In the following, I seek to explore two major elements in Sumbersari.

4.1 *Economy and Education*

Based on the 2015 official record, Sumbersari has around 63,635 residents, with a birth rate of 1.49 percent per year. The majority of the people of Sumbersari work as farmers and labourers (*kerja serabutan*). 70 percent of the economic resources of the villagers is generated by the agricultural sector. The rate of unemployment is fairly high. Although the land, 50 percent of which is rice fields, is generally fertile, the crops cultivated do not make any significant amount of money. The smaller area of the land is given over to dry cultivation (*tegal*), on which the people plant rice here during the rainy season. However, as this is impossible in the dry season, they plant maize, mango trees and tuberose flowers. When adverse weather conditions mean that the going gets tough, the farmers raise cattle and goats. The majority of women do not earn money outside the household. They sometimes do work at home embroidering the costume worn by women during Islamic prayers (*mukena*) but this generates only a very low income.

Participation in the formal education of people aged ten and older is generally low. 28 percent of them (or about 17,799 persons) have only completed primary school and have not continued to a higher level. This percentage decreases significantly at junior and senior high school levels. Only 6,171 people (9.7%) have a first-level secondary school certificate, while a mere 4,146 (6.5%) have finished senior secondary school. Nevertheless, it should be noted that these figures relate to secular education. This society pays great attention to

83 Husson, "Eight Centuries of Madurese Migration to East Java," 91.

84 Ibid., 92.

85 Gerben Nooteboom, *Forgotten People: Poverty, Risk and Social Security in Indonesia, the Case of the Madurese* (Leiden/Boston: Brill, 2015).

their children's religious education in various Islamic education institutions, ranging from small-scale *pesantren* to very large ones. Hence, their participation in informal *pesantren* education appears to be the best explanation of why the number on to the last two levels of formal education is so low. It must also be said that, though youngsters are increasingly going on to higher education (university), their number is still very small, 0.6 percent.[86]

At the level of the Pasuruan regency, the number of formal Islamic schools is lower than that of formal public schools. However, coming down to the Sumbersari sub-district, Islamic schools appear to be as important as their public counterparts. Even at the level of middle school, Islamic schools are dominant. Leaving that aside, what is evident on both district and sub-district levels is that informal schools, *pesantren* and *madrasah diniyah*, are the most common educational institutions in the area. Its curriculum spans the primary to the high school level. As mentioned above, the high number of *madrasah diniyah* on the primary (ūlā) level indicates the locals' concern about equipping their children with adequate knowledge of and skills related to their religion from an early age.

Quite aware of the situation, the local government has recently drawn up a policy designed to support the importance of *madrasah diniyah*. In 2016, the *Bupati* issued Regulation 21/2016 which obliges Muslim pupils in the primary and junior high schools to attend *madrasah diniyah* for at least two hours in the afternoon.[87] Article 4 of the Regulation states that, as an informal school, the purpose of the *madrasah diniyah* is to expand children's capacity so as to form them into pious and well-behaved persons. The regulation also urges people to support the operation of *madrasah diniyah* financially.

4.2 Pesantren *Atmosphere*

Sumbersari is nowadays home to nearly thirty *pesantren* or about 10 percent of all the *pesantren* in Pasuruan. Based on statistical records, in 2014 there were 320 *pesantren* in Pasuruan alone. All the *pesantren* run *madrasah diniyah*, while some also run formal Islamic schools. However, not all *madrasah diniyah* belong to *pesantren*. Consequently, the number of *madrasah diniyah* far exceeds the number of *pesantren*.[88] *Pesantren* represent a discourse of what

86 BPS Kab. Pasuruan, *Kecamatan Rembang Dalam Angka 2015* (Pasuruan: BPS Kab. Pasuruan, 2015), 46–48.

87 Peraturan Bupati Pasuruan (Regent's Regulation of Pasuruan) No. 21 of 2016 On the Obligation to Study in a *Madrasah Diniyah*.

88 BPS Kab. Pasuruan, *Kecamatan Rembang Dalam Angka 2015*, 54.

it is to be a devout Javanese Muslim.[89] For people living in the lowlands, *pesantren* education is considered to be an important factor in shaping their children's lives. Commensurate with this mindset, the ideal pattern is that female teenagers study in *pesantren* after completing primary school. Middle-class religious families want their daughters to study in major *pesantren*, which are renowned for their long-established tradition of training Islamic subjects.

Parents send their daughters to *pesantren* to equip them with a good understanding of Islam to assist them in their future. They are firmly convinced that *pesantren* will give a guarantee of the inculcation and protection of female morality. To ensure the system works properly, *pesantren* education generally adopts the concept of educational segregation, keeping male and female pupils separated.[90] Although they are happy for their daughters to participate in this, for women in particular general education is still perceived as less important than religious education. This is because women are supposed to work in the home and raise children. The general line of thinking is that women do not need a good educational foundation to carry out these tasks. Local people seem to ignore the fact that a mother has more influence on educating children than a father. They refer these jobs to *dapur* (kitchen), *sumur* (well) and *kasur* (bed). Confirming this assertion, the general pattern shows that female students in informal *pesantren* are significantly higher than male students. To give an example, Pesantren Miftahul Ulum in Krajan village has around 600 female students and just 30 male students who board (*mukim*) in its dormitories (*pondok*).

Here is a review of how central *pesantren* provide informal Islamic education. In mid-March 2017, I met Alfi from Sumbersari, a female student at a local Islamic university. I was eventually invited to visit her house and was introduced to Gus Raibin, her forty-seven-year-old father, who serves as an *imam*, leader of a small mosque (*langgar*), and her mother. In spite of its strong commitment to Islamic normativity, this family appears to present a notable exception. Their daughter is the only one, among other religious family members, who has reached a university education. Nearly all the women of Alfi's age are already married and busy with their children. I was curious about how local people generally view the relationship between religion and education. They explained to me:

89 Muhammad Latif Fauzi, "Traditional Islam in Javanese Society: The Roles of Kyai and Pesantren in Preserving Islamic Tradition and Negotiating Modernity," *Journal of Indonesian Islam* 6, no. 1 (2012): 125–144.

90 Eka Srimulyani, *Women from Traditional Islamic Educational Institutions in Indonesia: Negotiating Public Spaces* (Amsterdam: Amsterdam University Press, 2012), 118.

> Sumbersari is different. Religion is the prime instrument in preserving morality. Girls are encouraged not to obtain a fully rounded education (*sekolah tinggi*). This is nothing to do with the lack of financial resources. People do not comprehend the contribution made to life by (secular) education. When women are assumed to become housewives, why spend much money on schooling? Furthermore, they believe that vocational high school only provides students with the skills required to work in a factory. There is a stereotype it is morally improper for a devout woman to do menial work.

However, the winds of change are coming, and in the last decade, parents have been increasingly insistent that their children acquire not only a good understanding of Islam, but also acquire general knowledge and practical skills. Consequently, *pesantren* has been expanding curricula to respond to these new aspirations. In my fieldwork, I have found that over the last few years, a number of *pesantren* in Sumbersari have been attempting to reduce the gap between religious and secular education. This is coincident with the development on the national level, which has shown a growing tendency for Islamic schools to be more open to change. In 2009, Pesantren Al-Ikhlas set up a vocational school (*sekolah menengah kejuruan*). Likewise, some years ago, in addition to the informal *madrasah diniyah*, Pesantren Roudlotunnajah expanded its range of formal schools. It opened an Islamic junior high school (*madrasah tsanawiyah*) that educates students in both Islamic and secular subjects. Since the opening of this school, this *pesantren* has enjoyed a considerable increase in the number of students, although not all of them are boarders. This all suggests that parents are now aware that having a diploma in formal education is the touchstone to a much better life future for their children.[91]

Sumbersari itself does not have many major *pesantren*. The number of students who board in many of them generally numbers between 20 and 100. Only a few of them have more than 200 students. The majority of the students are local, but a few come from neighbouring areas and places in Madura. The majority of *pesantren* in Sumbersari have been established by *kyai*s linked by ties of descent, marriage, and education, forming an Islamic linkage that extends across eastern Java and Madura.[92] Many of them are graduates of the respectable Pesantren Sidogiri in Pasuruan. For this reason, numerous

91 This is based on my interviews with the leader of this *pesantren*.

92 Hefner, "Reimagined Community: A Social History of Muslim Education in Pasuruan, East Java."

madrasah diniyah in Sumbersari are official branches (*ranting*) of the Pesantren Sidogiri's Madrasah Miftahul Ulum (MMU) which has been going since the 1930s. The MMU runs *madrasah diniyah* on four levels: *isti'dadiyah* (preparatory), *ibtida'iyah* (basic), *tsanawiyah* (middle) and *aliyah* (high). These *madrasah* at the *ranting* level teach the same curriculum, subjects and references which are taught in the MMU headquarters.

Among East Javanese Muslim traditionalists, Pesantren Sidogiri enjoys the reputation of being the most distinguished and important centre for studying the classical books (*kitab*) on *fiqh* used by the Shāfiʿī school. Among the references taught are *Matn al-ghāya wa al-taqrīb* by the Baṣra jurist Abū Shujāʿ al-Iṣfahānī (d. 1197) and its commentary *Fatḥ al-qarīb al-mujīb* by Muḥammad Ibn al-Qāsim al-Ghazzī (d. 1512) and those produced by the Malībarī family such as *Fatḥ al-muʿīn bi sharḥ qurrat al-ʿayn* by Zayn al-Dīn al-Malībarī (d. 1579).[93] Pupils on the *aliyah* level are taught using *fiqh* sources from a comparative perspective. Its alumni network is well maintained, joined together in an association called *Ikatan Alumni Santri Sidogiri* (IASS, the Association of the Sidogiri Alumni). This network, encompassing district representatives throughout East Java, regularly holds a *bahtsul masail* forum in response to the need to find solutions to everyday religious problems.

5 Conclusion

This chapter has offered a brief description of the historical context and the current developments in Islam and other fields in Pasuruan. Pasuruan is a regency in East Java province inhabited by a majority of Muslim communities that generally show a tendency towards practising the traditional Islam[94] encouraged by the NU. This religious orientation draws strength from the fact that many Pasuruan residents have historical roots in the island of Madura. For many centuries, Pasuruan has been the destination of Madurese migrants. Their migration indeed gathered strength because of the job opportunities offered by the sugar-plantation project in the nineteenth century. The migrants

93 Martin van Bruinessen, "Kitab Kuning: Books in Arabic Script Used in the Pesantren Milieu, Comments on a New Collection in the KITLV Library," *Bijdragen Tot de Taal-, Land- en Volkenkunde* 146, no. 2 (1990): 244–246; Scott C. Lucas, "Justifying Gender Inequality in the Shāfiʿī Law School: Two Case Studies of Muslim Legal Reasoning," *Journal of the American Oriental Society* 129, no. 2 (2009): 242.

94 Dhofier, *The Pesantren Tradition: The Role of the Kyai in the Maintenance of Traditional Islam in Java*, xix.

have acculturated with the Javanese, a mingling which led to a distinct sub-culture called *pedalungan* or *pendhalungan*. This community is established on the basis of patron-client relationships in which *kyai*s or the leaders of *pesantren* act as the patron.

The influence of Islam in Pasuruan was strongly reinforced by the expansion of traditional religious schools (*pesantren*) in the northern lowlands during the last half of the nineteenth century and the early part of the twentieth century. These schools served as centres for the propagation of traditional Islam. Although the influence of the NU is predominant, Pasuruan is home to different Muslim groups. These include modernist organisations such as the Muhammadiyah and Persis, albeit their influence is less intense. In addition to Sunni Islam, followers of Shiʿi Islam can also be found in Pasuruan. Although they have a centre for their religious education, their existence sometimes provokes harsh opposition from the local people.

The development of traditionalist Islam in Pasuruan constantly affects the relationship between the state, religious leaders and the Muslim community. The commitment to practising Islamic traditions and the strongly inculcated obedience to *kyai*s have complicated the relationship between religion and the state. Community-level politics operate based upon the patron-client ties which characterise the eastern part of East Javanese society in general. This social configuration appears to have infiltrated and influenced political life. Since 1999 in Pasuruan, PKB, an NU-based political party, has been the winning party on the regency level in the last four general elections. Furthermore, Irsyad Yusuf, the current Regent who is an ex-member of the PKB faction in parliament, can be considered an overarching icon of the triumph of the NU.

The political and social situation in Pasuruan is not significantly different from that in other areas in the eastern part of East Java. Areas such as Probolinggo, Lumajang and Jember also have a big number of Madurese migrants who have evolved into a *pendhalungan* community. Nevertheless, Pasuruan does have its own idiosyncrasies which set it apart. Firstly, Pasuruan is geographically close to the capital city of Surabaya. The most obvious consequence of this proximity is the presence of a huge industrial complex in Pasuruan. On the bright side, the industrial development in this area has provided an ample range of job opportunities for the local youth. After finishing high school, there is a tendency for young people to want to make money as factory workers rather than go to university. Secondly, Pasuruan borders areas with an *arekan* sub-culture. As I mentioned earlier, the *arekan* sub-culture is considered 'modern.' A local anecdote says that *pendhalungan* people are deemed modern after they have adopted the Javanese *arekan* sub-culture, speak Javanese or go to state schools. Thirdly, in its southern part, Pasuruan is home to Mount Bromo, the centre of a non-Islamic movement, making Pasuruan one of the most heterogeneous regencies in Java.

Sumbersari, where I have been doing my fieldwork, can be identified as an agrarian society. Agriculture contributes 70 percent of the economic resources of the villagers. Sumbersari has to contend with an array of social problems, chief among them poverty and a tendency not to participate in formal education. This avoidance of the established formal educational system has made either *pesantren* or *madrasah diniyah* a central institution. *Pesantren* offers an alternative educational institution that is perceived to be adequate to fulfil their needs as it inculcates in students the knowledge they require to function in society and instils religion and character-building in them. However, the winds of change are coming in the last decade. *Pesantren* has been expanding curricula to respond to a new aspiration, i.e., providing general knowledge and practical skills. This is coincident with the development on the national level, which has shown a growing tendency for Islamic schools to be more open to change.

The next chapter focuses on marriage practices in a village in Pasuruan. It tries to understand the entanglement of local norms and the roles of local actors, namely *kyai*s (religious leaders) and *pengarep* (voluntary traditional matchmakers) in the everyday practice of marriage. It specifically questions in what ways the social structure of traditionalist Islam influences the practice of marriage in the community of Sumbersari in Pasuruan. Significantly, it also includes an analysis of the roles of the individual agencies of the couples in shaping a marriage.

CHAPTER 5

Performing Marriage: The Influences of Cultural and Islamic Norms

1 Introduction

In Muslim societies, marriage is a legal act, an exchange of a contract regulated by a code of law rooted in religious precepts. In social practice, it is imbued with a variety of local norms and influenced by the diversity of local actors throughout the Muslim world.[1] This chapter examines how these norms and actors interact with each other to shape these marriage practices. It aims to broaden our understanding of the entanglement of different norms governing marriage and the roles of the actors involved in everyday marriage practice in a village. This chapter seeks to answer the following questions: What do locals consider the fundamental norms which constitute a marriage? In what ways do individuals negotiate with these norms? To what extent do local actors such as *kyai*s (traditional religious leaders) and *pengarep* (marriage intermediaries) become involved? What are their orientations? What changes have taken place?

The material in this chapter is the fruit of my fieldwork in Sumbersari, a religious sub-district in rural eastern East Java. As mentioned in the previous chapter, at first glance Sumbersari society looks fairly homogenous. First and foremost, its strong attachment can simply identify it to a certain form of Islam, generally referred to as 'traditionalist Islam,'[2] characterised as '*santri* culture.'[3] Nevertheless, despite its homogeneity in terms of Islamic orientation and practices, contemporary Sumbersari presents an interesting spectacle of heterogeneity in marriage practices. For this reason, this chapter offers some narratives

1 Ali, "Marriage in Classical Islamic Jurisprudence: A Survey of Doctrines"; Alami, *The Marriage Contract in Islamic Law in the Shari'ah and Personal Status Laws of Egypt and Morocco.*

2 Dhofier, *The Pesantren Tradition: The Role of the Kyai in the Maintenance of Traditional Islam in Java*; M. Bambang Pranowo, "Pesantren, Traditional Islam in Contemporary Rural Java: The Case of the Tegal Rejo Pesantren," in *Islam in the Indonesian Social Context*, ed. M.C. Ricklefs (Clayton: Monash University Centre of Southeast Asian Studies, 1991), 39–56; Mun'im Sirry, "The Public Expression of Traditional Islam: The Pesantren and Civil Society in Post-Suharto Indonesia," *The Muslim World* 100, no. 1 (2010): 60–77.

3 Dhofier, "Kinship and Marriage among the Javanese Kyai"; Pribadi, "Religious Networks in Madura: Pesantren, Nahdlatul Ulama, and Kiai as the Core of Santri Culture."

 | DOI:10.1163/9789004516113_006

that reveal the complicated relationship between the norms, the agency of the actors involved and the social structure.

Below, I commence with an overview of the intermixture of Islamic and cultural norms in Sumbersari. To illustrate this, I present a brief sketch of how a young man dealt with localised norms and the social actors that impacted the social process prior to his marriage, namely finding a potential spouse. His experience leads me to an overview of the broader spectrum of social life in Sumbersari. Here, I identify issues that are key to marriage practices: the centrality of informal Islamic education compared to other institutions and economic life. The next section seeks to demonstrate the ways in which the complicated relationship between social actors determines the virtues of an ideal spouse.

2 Presenting Munir-Ulfa

Munir was a twenty-nine-year-old married man when I first met him in early 2017. Wearing *sarong* and a fake (*tiruan*) jersey of an English football club, he welcomed me to the house in which he lives. The house is not his own but belongs to his parents-in-law, which is in line with the still common uxorilocal tradition, requiring that, after marriage, a husband lives in the bride's house. My local female collaborator, a classmate of Munir's wife, introduced me to his family when they studied in the same *pesantren* during the period 2006 to 2012. I expected to have an initial glimpse of the allegedly popular practice of *nikah sirri* (unregistered marriage). Interestingly, Munir tried to convince me that this custom has begun to decrease, although he did mention some of his female neighbours whose (re)marriages had been concluded without the presence of official registration. We then suddenly moved on to a very personal talk about his life trajectories up to the moment of his marriage.

Munir graduated from a local junior Islamic high school (*madrasah tsanawiyah*) in 2002. Munir has been studying various Islamic subjects, ranging from *'aqīda* (theology), *fiqh* (jurisprudence), *akhlāq* (ethics) to *naḥw* (Arabic grammar). He is fairly familiar with the classical *fiqh* doctrines like those documented in 'yellow' Islamic treatises (*kitab kuning*).[4] After graduating from junior high school (*sekolah menengah pertama*), for a number of reasons, Munir decided not to continue his studies, despite the fact he was assured of his

4 Bruinessen, "Kitab Kuning: Books in Arabic Script Used in the Pesantren Milieu, Comments on a New Collection in the KITLV Library," 227.

parents' support. One important hindrance was his problem in making sense of what higher formal education could contribute to his life. Acquiring a thorough understanding of Islamic matters has seemed to him to be more important. Munir explained in more detail:

> The expectation of those who study at senior high school is to find a job in a factory. This idea does not appeal to me. You must follow strict rules, especially those dictating the working hours. This severely curtails your flexibility. What if one of your family falls ill and you need to accompany him/her to a medical centre? [In a factory] You have to submit a letter asking for permission to do so. That is too awkward. My younger brother, who has just received a letter of acceptance from the factory, has decided not to take up the offer. He prefers to run a street stall.

For three years, Munir was employed as a teaching assistant (*guru bantu*) at the *madrasah ibtidaiyah* in which he studied. After the holy month of Ramadhan 2006, Munir chose to follow his uncle and head to Jakarta, the capital city. After working in Jakarta as a builder's labourer, he moved to Subang (West Java), working in a small restaurant (*warung*) owned by a man from Malang, East Java. From there, he moved on to other cities in East Java, first Jember and later Surabaya. While he was in Surabaya, he was happy as he was able to manage to visit his parents in his home village once every two weeks. However, in mid-2010, he decided to leave his job because he needed to take care of his father, who was growing older and weaker.

Meanwhile, his father was worried about his son's future family life. At twenty-three, Munir was still not married. Villagers generally consider a bachelor of this age to be rather too old to marry, especially as he was in a position to support a family.[5] Aware of his predicament, Kholil, their neighbour, offered to help him seek a suitable wife. The former was thinking of a close relative of his in his natal village, who had a daughter called Ulfa. At that time, she was fifteen and studying in a renowned *pesantren* in a suburb of Pasuruan. Munir and his parents accepted Kholil's offer. Subsequently, Kholil visited Ulfa's parents, conveying to them that a man would approach them with a proposal asking their daughter to be his wife. Kholil played the role of a marriage broker, referred to locally as a *pengarep*. A *pengarep* is commonly perceived to be undertaking a worthy mission because he or she facilitates communication between the two

5 Geertz, *The Javanese Family: A Study of Kinship and Socialization*, 56.

families concerned.[6] This social process is what local people refer to as *ngen-angen* (literally winds, spreading the word).

Ulfa was the only daughter in her family. Her parents were happy to receive the proposal. Neither Ulfa nor Munir was known to one another before. Ulfa's parents eagerly anticipated Munir's visit. This visiting stage, called *namu* in Javanese, signifies a kind of preliminary negotiation.[7] Culturally speaking, the parents' agreement to the man's visit implies their approval to take their daughter as a wife. Following the approval of Ulfa's parents, Munir visited her house accompanied by the *pengarep*. In traditional Javanese society, this stage is called *nontoni* (viewing).[8] The purpose of the visit is to give both the prospective husband and the girl a chance to see each other. In this *nontoni* stage, Ulfa did not join the meeting. Instead, she was asked to serve guests a cup of coffee, bringing it from the kitchen to the front room. It was this very short encounter that enabled them to see each other. Munir made up his mind to marry Ulfa. Religious considerations, particularly the idea of the purity (*kesucian*) of a girl,[9] were a fundamental reason for his decision. Ulfa was studying in a *pesantren* which Munir, and local people in general, assumed would strictly guard the sexual morality of its pupils. Ulfa was then engaged (*neket*).

Ulfa's parents chose her prospective husband. Ulfa depended on her parents to decide the worth of her potential spouse, so as she might enjoy a blessed life together. The marriage proposal was accepted, but the marriage contract was suspended until she had completed her studies. In some cases, when there is a big age gap between the bride and the groom, parents marry their daughters directly. However, after the initial introduction, the prospective groom and bride generally have a chance to meet in private, yet under supervision. This was not the case with Ulfa and Munir, because Ulfa returned to the *pesantren*. They could not really be said to have had a proper courtship period involving a series of private meetings. During the waiting period prior to the wedding, her parents occasionally invited Munir to join them in a visit to give money (*ngirim*, Javanese) to Ulfa in the *pesantren*. The locals jocularly refer to

6 Anke Niehof, *Women and Fertility in Madura (Indonesia)* (Leiden: Instituut voor Culturele Antropologie en Sociologie der Niet-Westerse Volken, 1985), 115.

7 Geertz, *The Javanese Family: A Study of Kinship and Socialization*, 62.

8 Smith-Hefner, "The New Muslim Romance: Changing Patterns of Courtship and Marriage Among Educated Javanese Youth," 446.

9 Middle-class rural women in numerous parts of the world also have the tendency to accept patriarchal norms of honour and purity. See Santi Rozario, "Islamic Piety against the Family: From 'Traditional' to 'Pure' Islam," *Contemporary Islam* 5, no. 3 (2011): 285–308; Smith-Hefner, "The New Muslim Romance: Changing Patterns of Courtship and Marriage Among Educated Javanese Youth," 453.

the man's participation as *ngredit* (paying off a loan). A young man needs to become involved in this process to build his reputation as a good person with his potential parents-in-law and socialise with their extended families.

Munir's ideas of his future spouse's expectations give a strong hint of the significance of norms constraining women's sexuality imposed by *pesantren*. The *pesantren* education of a girl is important since it symbolises purity. Over the centuries, Islamic norms on marriage have been an inseparable part of people's daily lives and have become embedded in the customary social system. In the process, the division between the two has somehow blurred. Like so many other aspects of Javanese society, when referring to early scholarly works on cultural norms (*adat*), it is difficult to identify which belong exclusively to Islam and derive from the pre-existing tradition prior to the coming of Islam.

Clifford Geertz, referring to Mohamed Koesnoe, stressed the significance of the notion of propriety in any discussion about *adat*. He states: *Adat* is constructed as "the form of life of the Indonesian people as founded in their sense of propriety."[10] Therefore, Bowen has underlined that the term law cannot be used to exemplify the complicated norms surrounding marriage and other matrimonial matters. In rural settings, legal matters are usually bound up with older people, religious commitment, and a sense of propriety.[11] In the next section, we shall see how the sense of propriety operates in everyday practice and how local actors, such as *pengarep*, are key figures in the implementation of this strategy.

3 *Pengarep* and Cultural Norms

This section elucidates the role of a *pengarep* and examines the influence of different local norms on the social processes set in the train prior to marriage. These norms are dependent on which social category a family belongs to. Each narrative that follows represents one of these social classes. While the first story exemplifies a lower-class family, the second story reveals the process in middle-class families.

3.1 *Kulsum's Arranged Marriage*

This is the story of the marital experiences of Kulsum. When I met Kulsum in early 2007, she was thirty-one and was married to her second husband. Her first

10 Clifford Geertz, "Local Knowledge: Fact and Law in Comparative Perspective," in *Local Knowledge: Further Essays in Interpretive Anthropology* (New York: Basic Books, 1983), 210.

11 Bowen, *Islam, Law, and Equality in Indonesia: An Anthropology of Public Reasoning*, 18.

marriage had been concluded in 2001, a couple of months after she graduated from an Islamic junior high school (*madrasah tsanawiyah*). Kulsum was raised in a religious family and claimed to be the only girl in the village at the time who had enjoyed any formal schooling. However, she did not pursue her education to a higher level and was eventually married off. She told me the following:

> My father insisted that I keep studying. He accompanied me when I handed in a registration form at a *madrasah aliyah* in the centre of Sumbersari. My older sister had said *binek noapah asekola, monduk beih rapah* (a woman does not need to take secular education, studying in *pesantren* is enough). Unfortunately, not long after, our beloved father was fatally injured in an accident. It was a destiny which changed my life dramatically.

The father died in the accident. Sometime after the accident, Kulsum was married to a man from the same village. The family's decision to marry her was unquestionably a direct consequence of her father's death. No one in the household was able to assume his mantle of providing financial support for her education. Kulsum had no other options available to her, as she succinctly said *neser reng tuah* (out of consideration for the parents). She did not make any verbal declaration giving her consent, but simply acquiesced in the marriage arrangement. Her only recourse was to register her thoughts by remaining silent (Javanese, *manut*). Certain Shāfiʿī jurists have deemed that the silence of an unmarried woman can be taken as her consent.

Kulsum had reached the age of puberty when she was married. After the wedding, Kulsum was considered to be legally an adult and, therefore, competent to manage her marital life. The marriage was assumed to set the seal on her maturity. Hildred Geertz has remarked that marriage is an important rite of passage, a pivotal moment, that marks the transition from childhood to adulthood[12] through the constitution of a new family unit of father-mother-children in a cycle of rites of passage set out in Van Gennep's framework.[13] Adulthood

---

12 Geertz, *The Javanese Family: A Study of Kinship and Socialization.*

13 Van Gennep designated the ritual ceremonial patterns which mark an individual's transitions in his/her life as rites of passage. The concept of "liminality" was introduced to indicate the time in which people are teetering on the threshold of entering a new phase in their lives. Rites of passage include rites of separation, transition, and incorporation. Marriage is part of the rite of incorporation, while rites of separation are most apparent in funeral ceremonies. Meanwhile, transition rites are found in the rituals surrounding betrothal and pregnancy. Arnold van Gennep, *The Rites of Passage* (London: Routledge & Kegan Paul, 1960), 11.

here denotes the stage at which women are considered capable of managing their own household affairs. The latter is congruent with the notion of *rushd* (legal capacity to contract or financial competency) in the classical *fiqh* doctrine. There is no exact demarcation line that determines the age of *rushd* of a woman, but it does crucially involve reliance on the opinion of the *walī*. Some classical jurists, the Mālikī in particular, decree that marriage is an essential requirement for a woman to have financial competence.[14]

In fact, Kulsum began a family with very little knowledge about either sex or household management. Islamic marriage is a contract of exchange that involves a set of rights and obligations incumbent upon each party. Kulsum had an obligation to submit to her husband because, reciprocally, she was assumed to have the right to maintenance. Under the umbrella of a marriage contract, she moved from her birth family to come under her husband's protection. After marriage, Kulsum requested her husband and his family allow her to remain close to her mother. This was granted as she and her husband went to live in a house next door to her natal family's dwelling.

The marriage, unfortunately, survived less than two years. She admitted that her husband was rude and disrespectful. When she encountered a problem with her husband, she lost no time complaining about this to her mother. Moreover, her views about his bad behaviour were confirmed by remarks like *mak kerreng lakennah be'en jeh* (What a rude man your husband is) made by her older sister. It was suggested to Kulsum that she ask for a divorce from her husband. He granted her an out-of-court *talak* (pronouncement of divorce), witnessed by a religious leader and her family. Despite the social stigma of being a divorcée, Kulsum decided not to remarry. She preferred to continue her studies in the equivalent of a senior high school (*kejar paket C*) and participated in social activities. Only ten years later, in 2012, did she seek and obtain a legal validation of the divorce after lodging a divorce petition (*cerai gugat*) with the regional Islamic court. The divorce certificate enabled her to remarry legally.

3.2 *Marriages in Middle-Class Family: Fahim and Her Sister*

Ibu Fatimah is a descendant of a local *kyai* whose family has played a respected role in the development of Islam in her village. Her first marriage ended in divorce. She then remarried to a man from a *pesantren* family and gave birth

---

14 Nayel Badareen, "Identity and Authority: Changes in the Process of Debates over the Islamic Marriage Contract among Contemporary Muslim-Arab Intellectuals" (PhD Dissertation. The University of Arizona, 2014), 58.

to two daughters. The first daughter, Fahim (now 22 years), studied in a *pesantren* in Pasuruan. After finishing the first two years, at the age of fifteen, she was unexpectedly brought home to be married off to a man whom she had never even met before. Fahim was raised in a conservative family with the doctrine that a good daughter should never say no to her parents was inculcated in her. She was not allowed any room to negotiate and was married at the end of 2010. The very reason the parents wanted her to get married was, unquestionably, the man's social background and his competency in knowledge of Islam. Her husband had studied in a prestigious *pesantren* in the town. His current activities are still affiliated with that *pesantren.* Initial communications between the two families were mediated by a *pengarep* who was Ibu Fatimah's neighbour.

Fahim marriage was not the end of the story. In 2016, her younger sister, Anis (16 years), was subjected to the same experience. Ibu Fatimah was impressed by the personality of one of the teachers at a *madrasah diniyah* near her house. Mahmud, the teacher, was believed to be well mannered and skilled in reciting the Quran (*pintar ngaji*). Somehow or other it reached Mahmud's ears that Ibu Fatimah wished to make him her son-in-law. It all began when Anis suffered a small accident in the *pesantren* in which she was studying. She had to return home to receive intensive medical treatment. Mahmud visited her and Ibu Fatimah rejoiced in the happy accident which gave Mahmud the chance to become better acquainted with her daughter. Unaware of any ulterior motive, Anis had no suspicion that this initial step would lead to her being married off. Not long afterwards, Mahmud came with his family to propose to her (*lamaran*). Her father agreed to the proposal as long as the marriage could be postponed for two years after Anis had finished her study. Unfortunately, the father passed away a year later. Anis ended up marrying Mahmud a couple of months after her father's death.

3.3 Pengarep *and Its Important Role*

In a society like that of southern Sumbersari whose culture is heavily permeated by influences from Madura, marriage is generally thought to be the prerogative of families. Obedience to one's parents, particularly the father, is the most important norm. This cultural norm is enshrined in a well-known Madurese dictum *bhuppa' bhabhu' ghuru rato* (father, mother, teacher, and formal leader, respectively). However, although the power over the household belongs to male authority, the marriage pattern tends to be uxorilocal. A husband moves to live with his wife's family after marriage, especially when he does not own his own house. This custom means that it is relatively easy for a woman to get the protection and support of her natal family.

Both the cases exemplify the practice of arranged marriage. In a nutshell, it is a form of marital union in which the parents, usually the fathers, choose appropriate spouses for their daughters or sons. This pattern tends to be even stronger and more frequent when the female spouse is young, and the male is much older. Sumbersari people refer to this type of marriage arrangement as *ajuddhuagi* (married-off). This local term implies not only the decision about the choice of a spouse, but also the decision about the timing of the marriage is firmly in the hands of the parents. Furthermore, the arrangement is found whatever the type of marriage, registered or unregistered. However, any decision to register is dependent upon multiple factors, such as whether or not the girl is of an age to enter into a legal marriage and the presence of a legal document in the case of remarriage.

Nilan argues that marriage among middle-class families is influenced by the two-pronged values of faith and family. However, faith is generally considered less important than family.[15] Furthermore, in different Asian contexts, the practice of arranged marriage is also justified by the juxtaposition of the ideologies of family honour and shame.[16] Local people usually opt for an arranged marriage, seeing it as a manifestation of control and an ability to preserve social honour. As was Ibu Fatimah, parents of a certain class in Sumbersari are concerned about ensuring that their daughters marry a suitable man. For this reason, girls' mobility is subject to stringent control. The concept of who constitutes a possible husband is primarily based on the man's religious orientation and estimates of his moral capital. When a man, versed in religion, comes to ask their daughter, there is a feeling of afraid that the man will be married to another woman (*takok ekalak oreng*, Madurese) if they do not soon accept the marriage proposal. Wealth and social standing do not count as highly as the notion of good manners.

In the East Javanese context, Beatty has revealed that understanding the social sentiments helps us recognise the roles of the undercurrents of emotions beyond the purview of the family but still within the context of a community. Emotions such as shame, reluctance and respect construct societal relationships in which the concept of *apik* (goodness), in opposition to ugly (*elek*), plays an ineluctable part.[17] The most visible embodiment of the notion of *apik* in the

15 Pam Nilan, "Youth Transitions to Urban, Middle-Class Marriage in Indonesia: Faith, Family and Finances," *Journal of Youth Studies* 11, no. 1 (2008): 65–82.

16 Santi Rozario, "Islamic Marriage: A Haven in an Uncertain World," *Culture and Religion* 13, no. March 2015 (2012): 159–175.

17 Andrew Beatty, "Feeling Your Way in Java: An Essay on Society and Emotion," *Ethnos: Journal of Anthropology* 70, no. 1 (2005): 53–78.

everyday practice of marriage is best revealed in the selection of a potential spouse. The scales are tipped by the emphasis placed on the degree of religious behaviour and moral character (*oreng bhagus*, a good man), without the consideration that this could be superficial behaviour. Identity as a *santri* is highly preferable. If someone presents a girl's parents with a young man with this qualification, the latter will not decline the proposal. They believe in Islamic doctrine, based on the Prophetic tradition, which gives religion (*lidīnihā*) precedence over everything else when selecting a spouse.[18]

My fieldwork materials suggest that the financial resources of the groom frequently trail in as the least consideration. However, we cannot ignore that pragmatic considerations about the potential husband's social background and economic circumstances do not escape the parents' attention. Therefore, despite the prominence given to the concept of *apik*, the economic motivations of a woman and her family sometimes seem to offer the best reason to explain her decision to marry. The ideal situation is when the husband plays the role of breadwinner, and the wife acts as the financial manager of the household.[19]

The concept of *apik* in marriage also infiltrated ideas about sexuality. It has to do with the notion of a woman's chastity. Chastity is culturally deemed an essential symbol of family honour. Local people express this in the word *praban* (maiden or virgin),[20] which specifies the ideal condition of a possible wife. A social mechanism that prevents women from publicly indulging in interaction with unrelated members of the opposite sex imposes it. They labelled those who breach this mechanism incapable of self-discipline (*ta' tao thenka*). Likewise, when he chose Ulfa, Munir confessed that Ulfa's purity (*kesucian*) was the principal reason for his choice.

Moreover, it is impossible to reduce marriage to a simple, Islam-based contract legitimating sexual intercourse between the bride and the groom.[21] It is just one part of a wide spectrum of social contexts. Hallaq has described the position of Islamic marriage as the cornerstone of communal harmony.[22]

---

18 One Prophetic tradition relevant to this issue is recorded in Islamic books, such as *Bulūgh al-marām*: "*Tunkaḥ al-mar'atu li'arba'in, lidīnihā, linasabihā, lijamālihā, wa limālihā.*" This means that "marry a woman for the intensity of her religious devotion, kin reputation, beauty and wealth." Aḥmad ibn 'Alī Ibn Ḥajar al-'Asqalānī, *Bulūgh al-marām min adillat al-aḥkām* (Riyadh: Maktaba al-Rushd, 2005), 350.

19 Not confined to, this principle also applies to other cultures. See Nurul Ilmi Idrus, *Gender Relations in an Indonesian Society: Bugis Practices of Sexuality and Marriage* (Leiden: Brill, 2016), 82.

20 Niehof, *Women and Fertility in Madura (Indonesia)*, 107.

21 Ali, "Marriage in Classical Islamic Jurisprudence: A Survey of Doctrines," 12.

22 Hallaq, *Sharī'a: Theory, Practice, Transformations*, 271.

Looking at the issue more pragmatically, it is worth noting that numerous marriages in my research site have involved marriage partners from the same family. A marriage acts to strengthen familial relationships and land ownership. Described as *mapolong tolang* (collecting the scattered bones),[23] on a down-to-earth level, this kind of marriage is intended to preserve the property of a family from depredations by outsiders (*oreng lowar*).[24]

Another aspect of the influence of the local culture on marriage is the age of marriage. Sumbersari locals consider that nineteen is too late for women to embark on matrimony. Without a doubt, the significance of marriage for women is bound up with the concepts of marriageability and saleability. Society perceives an unmarried adult woman to be an unsaleable maiden or old spinster (*perawan tua*). Meanwhile, men are not tarred with this saleability stereotype when they remain unwed. Instead, the people in a circle around a bachelor will make fun of him, taunting him with being *tak bengal* (timid), *banci* (effeminate) or other allusions to sexual potency.[25]

Kulsum's marriage, and her divorce, underline the local notion of *juddhu* (*jodoh*, Indonesian; divine destiny). Related to a spouse, *juddhu* has to do with the principle of *mompong* (good fortune). Parents, not necessarily the father, are more committed to the concept of *mompong bedheh se mentah* (feeling fortunate that a male is proposing marriage). The application of the principle of enjoying good fortune is justified by the Islamic ideas which circulate among the local people. Kyai Hidayat, a respected *kyai* of southern Sumbersari, argued that a woman should not accept anyone but a religiously committed man who has good character. He referred to a *ḥadīth* (sayings of the Prophet Muhammad) narrated by al-Tirmidhī (d. 892), stating that if there should come to a father to marry (his daughter) one who is religiously committed and of good character, he is pleased, then he should marry her to the man. If he does not, there will be tribulation (*fitnah*) in the land and widespread corruption.[26]

The notions of *mompong* and *apik* have proved to be decisive factors in determining the selection of a spouse. Besides these ideas, the role of the *pengarep* appears important to facilitate the implementation of these notions. As in Munir's case, he conveyed his proposal of marriage to the girl's parents through the offices of a *pengarep*. A *pengarep* is usually a family member or a

---

23 Mansurnoor, *Islam in an Indonesian World: Ulama of Madura*, 84.

24 A. Latief Wiyata, *Carok: Konflik Kekerasan Dan Harga Diri Orang Madura* (Yogyakarta: LKiS, 2002), 58.

25 Idrus, *Gender Relations in an Indonesian Society: Bugis Practices of Sexuality and Marriage*, 82.

26 Abī ʿĪsā al-Tirmidhī, *Jāmiʿ al-tirmidhī* (Riyadh: Bayt al-Afkār al-Dawliyya, 1999), 192.

close neighbour who performs the role of brokering marriage between the two families concerned. Although this brokerage is undertaken voluntarily, once the role is assumed, a *pengarep* is responsible for finding a suitable wife for a young man. The *pengarep* will do his/her best to answer her parents' requirements. Whatever the answer is, acceptance or rejection, the *pengarep* will communicate it to the man or his parents. Some people still believe that rejecting the first marriage proposal for their daughter is a social solecism. There is a local belief that it can lead to *sangkal* (karma), the daughter to whom the proposal has been made will be doomed to remain a spinster. Based on Niehof's research findings in Madura in the 1980s, the concept of *sangkal* articulates concern about a girl's marriage prospects which contributes significantly to the perpetuation of the custom of early marriage.[27]

The role of a *pengarep* is essential in many ways, particularly when women's mobility and social interaction between the genders are strictly controlled. Gus Raibin, my key informant, indicated that, upon receiving an affirmative answer from the girls' parents through the *pengarep*, the man's family has the confidence to organise a betrothal (*peneket*). In other words, the presence of a *pengarep* might curtail the risk of embarrassment to the man's parents should the proposal be rejected. It underscores that the local notion of shame encompasses not only controlling a girl's sexuality but also upholding the family's dignity. In the case of remarriage, the function of *pengarep* is also important. When a divorcée or widow is approaching the end of the prescribed period before a new marriage can occur (*ʿidda*), it is considered acceptable for a *pengarep* to approach her to deliver a new marriage proposal.

A *pengarep* also plays a role in remarriage. Although her divorce had not been legally recognised by the state, the community regarded Kulsum as a divorcée. Hence, she was often requested to welcome male guests in search of a prospective wife. A *pengarep* was the intermediary who introduced them to Kulsum. On some occasions, her own brother-in-law assumed this role. Kulsum had great difficulty in coming to terms with this reality, although she could understand why her close relatives were undisturbed by these proceedings. Her brother-in-law's principal motivation was to help Kulsum improve her situation in life. Although the situation caused her to feel uncomfortable, she did her best to negotiate her attitude towards this long-standing local tradition. They made an agreed compromise: *la kadung dennak jek dus nodusin, temmonen beih lah tak usa terrosagi* (when a guest already shows up, just greet him; there is no need to take it seriously).

27 Anke Niehof, *Women and Fertility in Madura (Indonesia)* (Leiden: Instituut voor Culturele Antropologie en Sociologie der Niet-Westerse Volken, 1985), 109.

4 *Kyai*: Seeking Religious 'Middle Ground'

This section elucidates the roles of religious leaders (*kyai*s) in managing the problems of marriage and sexuality. The case I analyse stems from the experiences of Kyai Karim, a prominent *kyai* in Sumbersari, when he was faced with the problem of having to deal with a polygynous marriage. This case throws interesting light on his socio-political position. He is not just an ordinary religious leader who runs a *pesantren*. He is much more than this as he is counted among the top leaders in both social and semi-governmental Islamic organisations. For instance, he is the head of the sub-district level of the Indonesian Council of Ulama and is one of the advisory chairmen of the regional chapter of the NU. His role has demonstrated that his grasp of how different legal systems operate is indisputable in both these positions. Importantly, the locals recognise him as a religious leader whose understanding of Islam is not influenced by old-fashioned ideas (*kolot*) and is open (*terbuka*) to the modernising world. The case recounted below shows beyond doubt that he was able to maintain his authority as a *kyai*, that is, as he claimed, he assumed responsibility for taking charge of morality and was able to challenge the state law. Fealy and Bush have remarked that 'ulama' find themselves subject to competing pressures exerted by the society and the state.[28] My research has shown that 'ulama' are constantly challenged when confronted with the real problems in society, which in fact require a non-state settlement but demand compliance with the state law. What follows is the narrative.

4.1 *A Polygyny Case*

A few years ago, a man, Rudi, and a woman, Nana, arrived at Kyai Karim's *pesantren*. Rudi confessed that he had had a love affair (*pacaran*) with Nana, whose age was around twenty-five, for a few years. Rudi even claimed to have rented Nana a house so that he could indulge in intimate relations with her all the time more easily. Kyai Karim argued that Rudi's word intimate relations expressed was a pseudo term to refer to having extramarital sex, known locally colloquially as *kumpul kebo* (living together without being married). Kyai Karim showed no hesitation in urging them to undergo a marriage ceremony to legitimise (*menghalalkan*) their relationship. Then the cat was out of the bag. The problem was in fact not as straightforward as he had expected. Rudi was a civil

28 Greg Fealy and Robin Bush, "The Political Decline of Traditional Ulama in Indonesia," *Asian Journal of Social Science* 42, no. 5 (2014): 536–560.

servant and was already married to another wife. It is important to note that a male civil servant in Indonesia is prohibited from entering into a polygynous marriage without the permission of his superior (*pejabat*).[29] Kyai Karim was in a dilemma. As a religious leader, he was bound by the doctrine in classical Islamic law inspired by the fear that extramarital sex makes it obligatory for a man to marry. Meanwhile, under state law, the permission of the first wife is required.

To cut a long story short, according to Islam, he married them as he believed this was the only way to rescue the couple from living in sin (*kumpul kebo*). For Rudi, it was a polygynous marriage. After the conclusion of the marriage ceremony, Kyai Karim asked the couple to sign a letter declaring that they had been religiously married. This letter was in place of a marriage certificate. The letter mentions the names of the couples, the witness and the religious leader who solemnised the marriage. Kyai Karim urged Nana to tolerate her position as a second wife in unofficial polygyny. However, Rudi found it hard to maintain good relations with Nana, especially when Nana demanded legal certainty over her status as a wife. When Rudi failed to comply with Nana's demands, she decided to report their informal marital union to the man's supervisor, taking the signed informal marriage letter with her as proof. Soon this polygynous marriage was the talk of the town.

A prominent official from Rudi's office met Kyai Karim to make sure that Nana's complaint was soundly based. Should this prove to be the case, her husband could be subject to legal sanctions for entering into a marriage that counted as non-procedural polygyny. The official alleged that Kyai Karim had married them illegally, accusing him of 'selling' the marriage ceremony. Kyai Karim was highly offended and, in return, blamed the official for being incapable of controlling his staff's morality. He then challenged the official with a set of questions set out in the following conversation.

Kyai Karim	Would you mind telling me what your current rank is?
Official	Echelon 3
Kyai Karim	When you go away on official business do you ever meet a woman whom you want to date? What do you do then?
Official	Yes, this is no more than typically male behaviour.

29 This prohibition is enshrined in Government Regulation no. 45/1990 jo. Government Regulation no. 10/1983 on the permission for marriage and divorce of civil servants. See O'Shaughnessy, *Gender, State and Social Power in Contemporary Indonesia: Divorce and Marriage Law*, 34.

Kyai Karim	Well now, you have finally mentioned that phrase "typically male." Do you want to 'buy' or to marry? I actually cannot accept polygyny because it is difficult to do justice to all the wives involved. But, if you do not marry, you are simply fornicating. Please do not complicate the problem, but find the best solution.
Official	Yes, *Kyai*, (this is tricky) so how should I go about it?
Kyai Karim	This situation obliges you to return to religious rules. You are supposed to respect not only state regulations but also religious teaching. The second should weigh more heavily.

This conversation shows that Kyai Karim resorted to Sharīʿa in his search for the solution to this problem of *kumpul kebo*, which he assumed to be a consequence of the obstruction generated by state law. He argued that Sharīʿa played an important role in safeguarding a person's religious life in this situation. However, he hastened to underline that religion should not be taken lightly as a broom to sweep up sins. In fact, when a couple has already sunk (*terperosok*) into moral turpitude, and the state law can no longer provide a solution, the religious authorities cannot just abandon them to a moral limbo. He stated:

> Polygyny is very casuistic. From an ordinary point of view, no wife can accept her husband taking another wife. I have a daughter. I shall never agree that her husband enters into other marriages. But, in the case in which a man finds himself morally obliged (*terpaksa*) to indulge in polygyny, he has no escape although his decision will not be accepted by society. God has indicated that polygyny is difficult. It can only be resorted to in exceptional circumstances like preventing illicit sex.

4.2 *Legal Reasoning and Thinking Outside the* Madhhab

The expanding corpus of literature has enhanced our insights into the complicated relationship between social norms and legal practice,[30] in which Sharīʿa continues to act as an independent normative system. Cammack et al. have argued that control over marriage practice is played out in a contested arena in which different social actors seek to exercise their power.[31] Importantly, con-

30 Bowen, *Islam, Law, and Equality in Indonesia: An Anthropology of Public Reasoning*, 8; Sally Engle Merry, "Law, Culture, and Cultural Appropriation," *Yale Journal of Law & the Humanities* 10, no. 2 (1998): 575–603.

31 Cammack, Young, and Heaton, "Legislating Social Change in an Islamic Society: Indonesia's Marriage Law."

temporary public debates about Islam and social change in Indonesia indicate that Sharīʿa has been challenging the legal concept of marriage introduced by the state, which has complicated or does not allow procedures permissible according to Sharīʿa. Examining the law-making process, Cammack argues that, despite the failure to impose the compulsory enforcement of Sharīʿa on the adherents of Islam, Muslims have successfully defended traditional Islamic norms against ongoing legislative efforts to change the substance of Islamic marriage law.[32]

What has been happening in contemporary social practice? Based on his research on social relations in a West Javanese regency, Stijn van Huis suggests that the modernisation of the law of marriage-related matters has harmed the authority of ʿulamaʾ. In their efforts to safeguard their authority, they have been compelled to create a competing legal order and challenge Islamic courts' authority in respect of judicial divorce.[33] Also, in the West Javanese context, Grijns and Horii have pinpointed the dilemmas and compromises which epitomise the contending norms on marriage and sexuality on the societal level. They emphasise that the influence of the conservative interpretation of Islam in controlling morality leads to the continuing practice of child marriage.[34] In the localised context of religious Lombok, Platt puts forward a convincing case for arguing that the state law on marriage has been unsuccessful in superseding the so-called community-based law in the form of localised Islam and *adat*. In other words, social acceptance has prevailed over state-based legitimacy. Legal processes in Islamic courts do not always generate significant outcomes for defining the legal status of a wife.[35]

The case cited above reveals that Kyai Karim's reasoning about Islamic marriage crystallises in the notion of safeguarding Sharīʿa. This entails at least two aspects: legalising (sexual) relations and avoiding harm (sinful acts). However, the way Kyai Karim has been coping with this particular instance of polygyny deserves close attention, in particular making a detailed examination of the legal reasoning he used. In the interviews, Kyai Karim stated: "*Saya mengambil garis tengah pada kasus yang terjadi. Kalau mau disiplin ya pakai Syafiʿī*" (I took a middle ground to resolve the case. If you are religiously disciplined, you are

32 Cammack, "Islamic Law in Indonesia's New Order."

33 van Huis, "Islamic Courts and Women's Divorce Rights in Indonesia: The Cases of Cianjur and Bulukumba," 139.

34 Grijns and Horii, "Child Marriage in a Village in West Java (Indonesia): Compromises between Legal Obligations and Religious Concerns."

35 Platt, *Marriage, Gender and Islam in Indonesia: Women Negotiating Informal Marriage, Divorce and Desire*, 36.

bound to follow the Shāfiʿī). Despite the supremacy of the Shāfiʿī *madhhab* in the area, he was clearly admitting that the Shāfiʿī way had not yet produced a suitable model for settling this sort of problem. Therefore, he underscored the notion of the middle ground. In his choice, he was stressing that this was not a typical case and therefore demanded an alternative legal settlement.

What he meant by 'middle ground' was moving away from the Shāfiʿī School to another *madhhab* in his search for a solution. One problem which loomed large was that the woman came to him accompanied by no one but her man/husband. It was not clear whether she had already obtained the consent of her familial *walī* (*wali nasab*). In an ordinary situation, the *wali nasab* is allowed to delegate his role of marriage guardian to another person. This process is known as *tawkil wali*. In addition to a *walī*, three aspects are required to be present in the conclusion of a marriage contract, i.e., the bride and the groom, the proposal and acceptance (*ījāb* and *qabūl*) and the pronouncement of the marriage contract (*ṣīgha*). Besides these most dominant factors, Muslim jurists have been locked in a dispute about other aspects, namely the dowry (*mahr*), witnesses (*shuhadāʾ*) and the marriage guardian (*walī*). In the view of Shāfiʿī and Mālikī jurists, all these have to be present. Only the Ḥanafī jurists argue that a marriage without the consent of a *walī* can be valid.[36] Interestingly, behind his decision to take the middle ground by Kyai Karim lies a particular stream of legal reasoning. His argument was constructed on the basis of a principle that "if there is a danger that the woman might become mired in immorality (*fasād*), the judge has the right to marry her to a man of her own social status (*kufu'*)." This principle is founded on *ḥadīth* no. 1879, narrated by Aisha, from the collections of Ibn Mājah, which says, "Any woman whose marriage is not arranged by her guardian, her marriage is invalid, her marriage is invalid, her marriage is invalid. If (the man) has had intercourse with her, then the *mahr* belongs to her in return for his intimacy with her. And, if there is any dispute, then the ruler is the guardian of the one who does not have a guardian."[37]

This case of illegal polygyny resonates with the notion of the internal plurality of a law. Salim quotes Menski's concept of 'a quadrangle of law,' which has been essential to the further development of the triangle of law introduced by earlier scholars.[38] An important factor in his model is not just that he reiterates the four elements of law (state, religion, society and international), but

36 Susan A. Spectorsky, *Women in Classical Islamic Law: A Survey of the Sources* (Leiden/Boston: Brill, 2010).

37 Muḥammad ibn Yazīd Ibn Mājah, *English Translation of Sunan Ibn Majah with Commentary*, translated by Nasiruddin al-Khattab, Vol. 3 (Riyadh: Darussalam, 2007), 78.

38 Salim, *Contemporary Islamic Law in Indonesia: Shariʿah and Legal Pluralism*, 25–26.

the factor which he terms 'plurality of pluralities.' It means that each element of law has internal plurality too. This concept is very relevant in an examination of Kyai Karim's actions. By saying that he had "not only adhered to the state law but also religious teaching," he showed a tendency to position the state law and Sharīʿa in juxtaposition to each other. In his solution, Kyai Karim settled the case by exploiting the internal plurality of legal opinions in Islamic jurisprudence. He produced creative legal reasoning in his attempt to shape his decision in accordance with Islamic law. In his juggling of the different legal practices, he was aware that strict reliance on a particular *madhhab* was out of the question. Bowen's remark exemplifies his dilemma that Islam needs to reshape its response in a variety of contexts is very apposite. In Kyai Karim's opinion, a Muslim scholar has to engage in legal reasoning, thinking outside the *madhhab*, considering the reinterpretation of Islamic norms, and incorporating *adat* into law.[39]

5 *Menghalalkan*: Marriage to Legalise Relationship

In this section, I present two case studies to demonstrate the fact that ideas about marriage practices are changing. An examination of the individual experiences of newly wed girls shows that Sumbersari society is witnessing a diversity of forms in the increase in women's individual autonomy. Thanks to improved access to formal education and greater job opportunities for high-school graduates, girls now have far more room to exercise their agency in choosing their partners. Social mobility is emerging as a driving factor in changing outlooks on marriage and sexuality. Nevertheless, as shown in the first case, the *fiqh*-based concept of the authority of a marriage guardian is still paramount in defining a girl's sexual morality.

5.1 *The Girl Loves, the Guardian Decides*

In February 2017, my local collaborator took me to visit Aini's family. Aini, a twenty-one-year-old woman, was married in September 2011. After finishing Islamic primary school (*madrasah ibtidaiyah*), Aini studied in a prominent *pesantren* in a suburban area. Although the majority of *pesantren* have established *madrasah* with a graded-class system, not all of them have adopted a curriculum of general education. She preferred this *pesantren* because it runs a *madrasah* that combines both religious and secular subjects, adhering to the

39 Bowen, *Sharīʿa, State, and Social Norms in France and Indonesia.*

state curriculum. Unfortunately, she only managed to survive in this *pesantren* for a couple of months. She returned home and was sent to a local *pesantren* close to her village. This was also not a success. My collaborator said that Aini had wanted to study in a formal Islamic school instead of in a *pesantren*. Eventually, she obtained permission from her parents to continue at a *madrasah tsanawiyah* in the sub-district centre. Compared to her other classmates, she was older and looked more mature. Her parents were not really happy with this situation, not least because Aini could interact not only with her fellow female students but also with male ones in that school.

In the meantime, a young man, Ulum, fell in love with Aini. Ulum is three years older. He had graduated from the same school but by this time was in the second year of vocational high school (*sekolah menengah kejuruan*). Aini reciprocated his feelings. She said they pursued a *pacaran* (courtship) but never met in private (*kencan*). It was not long before Ulum proposed that she marry him but said that he was prepared to wait until after she completed her schooling. Quite unexpectedly, as far as Aini was concerned, Ulum's parents suddenly came to see her parents, proposing that she be Ulum's wife. The proposal took her parents by surprise, even though this situation is not unique to their tradition. Aini's parents happened to be aware that their daughter already had a special relationship with a young man. The parents were in a dilemma. The fact that the children were already emotionally attached loomed very large in their minds. Adding to the confusion was the custom that rejecting a marriage proposal is morally humiliating in the eyes of their society. There was a fear that their children would become too intimately involved and might bring some form of social dishonour to the family. The father decided to accept the proposal and allow his young daughter to become engaged. A couple of months later she married and stopped school because the school refused to accept a married student.

A graduate of a *pesantren*, she now spends her days at home as a housewife, raising a three-year-old daughter. I talked to her about her experiences. In a subdued voice, Aini expressed her sadness about dropping out of secondary school. But this did not mean that she was not happy. When I asked if she was pleased with the marriage, she smiled and acknowledged that she was married to a man of her own choice. She admitted that she was glad that the *pesantren* had taught her the values of *ikhlas* (sincerity) and *syukur* (gratitude). In this instance, Ulum and Aini were already acquainted with each other. Although the marriage ceremony was thrust upon them too fast, Aini was happy to be able to marry the man of her choice.

Koentjaraningrat remarks that the *santri* religious system provides the individual with a basic feeling of security through its concept of an intensively personal relationship with God.[40] This observation still seems pertinent to Aini's situation. I asked her opinion about her marriage being arranged by her parents and she responded as follows: "We had been developing the feeling of closeness (*dekat*) for a couple of months. Perhaps you could call it *pacaran*, but it was not the usual sort. The two of us never met together alone. *Pacaran* is really restrictive, but *kencan* (meeting in private) is considered out of the question and taboo." Again, Islamic marriage is not perceived merely as a contractual tie. For Muslims in Sumbersari or elsewhere, for that matter, marriage serves more as an act of worship (*ibadah*) which, according to the Prophetic tradition, completes one half of one's religion. It unites the physical (*lahir*) and spiritual (*batin*) forces which lead to a husband and a wife committing themselves to each other body and soul for the sake of God.

In Aini's case, it was unimportant to her that her parents should have sought her approval when the marriage proposal from Ulum's family was accepted. Aini, therefore, never expressed her agreement or rejection of the parent's decision. Even had she refused in view of the traditions of her society, as her guardian, her father would have exercised his right to coerce her into marriage. Fathers, or other male guardians, play a decisive role in controlling their daughters' behaviour[41] and determining the validity of a marriage contract.[42] The 1974 Indonesian Marriage Law requires the consent of both spouses. Both the bride and the groom are required to sign a letter of consent (*surat persetujuan mempelai* or N3 form) to be submitted to the marriage registration office as one of the obligatory documents to be handed over before a marriage ceremony can be registered.

Despite the decision made by her father, Aini's marriage reveals an ambivalence that necessarily suggests the evolution of sexual norms in a traditional community. Aini herself found her spouse, but her father decided the timing of the marriage. The younger generation in Sumbersari is showing a greater tendency to choose their own husbands and wives, but even so, the timing of the ceremony is not always up to them. During the last decade, as a result of increased access to and the extended duration of formal education, schools have been increasingly providing a space for the younger generation to meet

---

40 Koentjaraningrat, "Family and Religion in Indonesia," *East Asian Cultural Studies* 13, no. 1/4 (1974): 67.

41 Ann Black, Hossein Esmaeili, and Nadirsyah Hosen, *Modern Perspectives on Islamic Law* (Cheltenham: Edward Elgar Publishing, 2013), 129.

42 Muhammad Khalid Masud, "Gender Equality and the Doctrine of Wilāya," in *Gender and Equality in Muslim Family Law: Justice and Ethics in the Islamic Legal Tradition*, ed. Ziba Mir-Hosseini et al. (London: I.B. Tauris, 2013), 12.

prospective partners. Girls and boys are not separated in schools or classrooms, allowing them the freedom to interact with each other. As a consequence, young people, especially girls, are becoming more exposed to the notion of mutual love (*la padeh senneng*). This idea of mutual love has recently become more instrumental in shaping local marriage behaviour; the sexuality of the young is no longer a familial affair.

Aini's mutual love demonstrates that a woman's increasing autonomy in the choice of marriage spouse does not necessarily result in a more egalitarian view of gender relations in a family. When I asked about her understanding of gender relations in Islam and how this affected her marital life, she believed that a devout Muslim wife ideally acknowledges her husband's leadership and accepts his sexual advances.[43] This outlook is still a strong reflection of the conservative understanding of gender relations in Islam, disseminated in *pesantren*. Only a small number of *pesantren* proposed a newer idea of gender equality.[44]

In their views of what makes a marital relationship, Aini and other students in *pesantren* are familiar with *'Uqūd al-lujayn fī bayān ḥuqūq al-zawjayn* by Muḥammad ibnʿ Umar al-Nawāwī (AD 1813–1898), a textbook which claims to uphold patriarchal ideas of gender relations.[45] The book is not part of regular curricula but is usually read during Ramadan when people come to listen to it voluntarily. There are four chapters in the book. The first two chapters address the rights and obligations of wife and husband in a family. The first chapter sets out a husband's obligations towards his wife, namely treating her well, providing a livelihood and dower, as well as guiding her through the maze of rituals and wifely obedience to the husband. The second chapter describes a wife's obligations to her husband, including taking good care of him, submitting her body to him, staying at home while the husband is away, and keeping intimate parts of the body (*aurat*) covered at all times.

Another book popular among the *pesantren* community is *Qurrat al-ʾuyūn bi-sharḥ naẓm ibn Yāmūn fī adāb al-nikāḥ* by Muḥammad al-Tihāmī which

43 Nina Hoel and Sa'diyya Shaikh, "Sex as Ibadah: Religion, Gender, and Subjectivity among South African Muslim Women," *Journal of Feminist Studies in Religion* 29, no. 1 (2013): 69–91.

44 Bianca J. Smith and Mark Woodward, "Introduction. Decolonizing Islam and Muslim Feminism," in *Gender and Power in Indonesian Islam: Leaders, Feminists, Sufis and Pesantren Selves*, ed. Bianca J. Smith and Mark Woodward (London and New York: Routledge, 2014), 10; Husein Muhammad, *Fiqh Perempuan: Refleksi Kiai Atas Wacana Agama Dan Gender* (Yogyakarta: LKiS, 2001).

45 Muḥammad ibnʿUmar al-Nawāwī, *'Uqūd al-lujayn fī bayān ḥuqūq al-zawjayn* (al-Qāhira, 1919).

FIGURE 9 Aini is embroidering embellishments for Islamic dresses.

deals with sexual morality. This book encourages the importance of marriage as a means to preserve morality and establish a lineage. It also addresses a number of issues related to ethics related to sexual relations, such as reciting prayers, keeping the body clean and the proper times and places in which to have sexual intercourse.

Now, Aini stays at home, doing the housework and taking care of the children. Nevertheless, while her husband is working outside the house, she can use her free time in the morning to undertake some sort of economic activity which could generate a small amount of money. She, as do other neighbouring mothers, embroiders embellishments for Islamic dresses. The money she makes is enough to give her small daughter some pocket money (*uang jajan*).

5.2 *Marry Me! Marriage and Religious Piety*

In the first months of 2007, I made the acquaintance of Iin's family. Socially, it can be considered middle-class. The father works in a private factory and the mother runs a small greengrocery stall (*warung sayur*). Iin was twenty-one when I first met her. She had never boarded in a *pesantren*, but had attended Islamic state schools instead. As is a common practice in her circles, she had extended her studies of Islam at an informal *madrasah diniyah* just across the way from her house. After completing *madrasah aliyah* (Islamic senior high school) in 2014, she decided not to continue her studies but to join the workforce. Her mother told me that Iin had been encouraged to continue her studies at university, but the prospect had not tempted her. Iin began by working in a restaurant in the town of Bangil where she met a young man, Alim, at the end of 2015. He is three years older than Iin and is originally from her neighbouring village. He has been working as a factory hand in the industrial centre known as PIER (Pasuruan Industrial Estate Rembang), in which hundreds of major transnational companies operate.

As of September 2015, they have been in a serious relationship. In contrast to Aini, because Iin worked outside the home, she had ample opportunities to meet Alim privately. Because of her situation, Iin acknowledged that she did not want to have a long period of courtship with Alim. Reasons derived from sexuality, public morality, and certainty (*kepastian*) appear to have shaped her outlook. She believed that Alim was the man of her destiny (*juddhu*) but she feared that their relationship would not end in marriage. She, therefore, asked Alim to marry her as soon as possible. In April 2016, Alim's family came to Iin's parents to formalise the betrothal (*lamaran*) which would signify Iin's status as an engaged woman. After this Iin left her job, saying that she needed to prepare for a wedding in August, a few months after.

Iin articulated her ideas on marriage as follows:

> I thank God that my parents allowed me to marry a man of my own choice. I hope God blesses us in this marriage. This marriage will safeguard me from [the perils of] pre-marital sex. I just want to be a good wife to him and a good mother to my children. We don't have to worry about how we are going to feed our family. If our intentions are good, God will help us.

The brief sketch of Iin's marriage reflects the changing attitudes towards marriage among young local Muslim females in Sumbersari. It seems obvious that the dominant power of the older generation in the choice of marriage partners and the timing of the marriage is now gradually being offset by the girls' agency. A girl's consent to marriage has been emerging as an important factor. The Marriage Law, article 7 (1), stipulates girls can consent to marriage from the age of sixteen, while for boys, the age of consent is nineteen. However, the Law does make an exception for Muslims by stating that the permission of an Islamic court can serve as a legal basis for marrying girls and boys under sixteen and nineteen, respectively. Their consent to the marriage is dependent upon the consent of their male guardians if they are under the age of twenty-one. This means that the individual autonomy of the girls is only really acknowledged if they are already older than twenty-one.

Furthermore, Iin's views on what marriage means to her have been formulated with Islamic doctrines on sexuality and morality in mind. She proposed an array of arguments related to sexuality, saying that, for instance, marriage would preclude damaging interaction (*pergaulan rusak*) and ease her concerns about premarital sex. Marriage was the only way open to her to make their sexual relationship lawful (*menghalalkan hubungan*). Of course, this was not the only reason. Playing a big part in her thoughts were the ideas of founding a lineage (*namba ketoronan*) and complying properly with worship (*nyampornaagi ibedeh*). Many *ḥadīths* state this value: marriage completes one half of one's religion; it is part of *Sunna* (practices of the Prophet); one of the three persons entitled to the help of the Almighty is he or she who marries with a vision of preserving his or her chastity. These ideas have always featured prominently in the chapters on marriage in the classical *fiqh* treatises and have been a constitutive element of the worldview of Muslims whom the *pesantren* culture has deeply influenced.

Muslim feminists have explicitly encouraged the interpretation of sexuality and sexual interaction enshrined in the Islamic texts, as an essential part of individual experience and as the cultivation of spiritual awareness.[46] In spite of framing marriage as a means to avoid sinful acts, it is also indisputably regarded as an expression of piety.[47] Over the past two decades, marriage as a step on the right road towards piety has been encouraged as a way to cultivate a pious self among Muslims who have not enjoyed an education in traditional Islamic institutions.[48] Scholars connect this phenomenon to the rise of religious piety in this secular world. Recent trends in the anthropological study of Islam suggest that modernisation does not necessarily result in secularisation or religious desacralisation.[49] Instead, it gives rise to the proliferation of multiple modernities.[50] This change has generated an increasing demand for the re-advancement of religious and traditional institutions in a whole gamut of temporal sectors.[51]

46 N. Hoel, "Engaging Islamic Sexual Ethics: Intimacy, Pleasure and Sacrality," *Sexualities* 18, no. 1–2 (2015): 84.

47 Asma Barlas, *"Believing Women" in Islam: Unreading Patriarchal Interpretations of the Qur'an* (Austin, TX: University of Texas Press, 2002), 153.

48 Rozario, "Islamic Piety against the Family: From 'Traditional' to 'Pure' Islam"; Rachel Rinaldo, *Mobilizing Piety: Islam and Feminism in Indonesia* (New York: Oxford University Press, 2013).

49 Peter L. Berger, "The Desecularization of the World: A Global Overview," in *The Desecularization of the World: Resurgent Religion and World Politics*, ed. Peter L. Berger (Washington: Ethics and Public Policy Center, 1999), 11.

50 Timothy P. Daniels, "Introduction: Sharia Dynamics and the Anthropology of Islam," in *Sharia Dynamics: Islamic Law and Sociopolitical Processes*, ed. Timothy P. Daniels (Cham: Springer International Publishing, 2017), 14.

51 Kalanges, *Religious Liberty in Western and Islamic Law: Toward a World Legal Tradition*, 4.

Religious piety is also closely related to individual agency. Smith-Hefner, for instance, has underscored the changes among the urban, educated young Javanese Muslims who have been influenced by the rise in the awareness of individual autonomy and the expansion of their own increasing agency. Even the agency of women has been expanding and opening up a range of possibilities. This has allowed them to navigate their own actions in their quest to find different solutions as long as these sustain their ideals of a better life. In this respect, Schielke has underscored that "Muslims' engagement with their religion is neither the outcome of blind adherence, nor the result of coercion, but an active and dynamic process of engagement with ideals of good life and personhood."[52]

6 Conclusion

In this chapter, I have discussed the ways people in religious Sumbersari mould the practices associated with marriage. Despite the homogenous tradition of Islam in the area, the narratives indicate the internal heterogeneity of the relationship between the agency of the actors involved, cultural norms and prevailing social structure in their selection of whom to marry. I suggest that, in all social categories, the ideas of an ideal spouse are conceptualised within the set of localised ideals of chastity (*kesucian*), correct behaviour (*apik*) and good fortune (*mompong*). These notions culminate in the identity of what it is to be a *santri*. As we have seen, these values are certainly present in the case of Munir and Ulfa. In their pre-marriage process, we are given to understand that the *pesantren* was an important factor in the maintenance of the *fiqh*-based orientation towards marriage. In other words, being a *santri* signifies the purity of a girl and her high moral principles. In Sumbersari, the implementation of these ideas in marriage and remarriage is still dependent on the roles of the *pengarep* (traditional marriage broker) and *kyai*s (religious leaders), although the role of the latter might be superseded.

Assuming the role in facilitating the communication between the two families concerned, the *pengarep* are very important to families noted for their religiosity and those whose daughters have been educated in *pesantren*. *Pengarep* help to protect the reputation of the family and preserve social honour. Their role is not only confined to the first marriage. Instead, remarriage has become

52 Samuli Schielke, "Second Thoughts about the Anthropology of Islam, or How to Make Sense of Grand Schemes in Everyday Life," *ZMO Working Papers*, no. 2 (2010): 5.

an arena in which *pengarep* exercise their influence too. As shown in the case of Kulsum, who is from a lower-class family, we see how cultural norms such as *mompong*, *juddhu* and *apik* are also intertwined with religious rationales. Kulsum's out-of-court divorce suggests the overriding importance of social acceptance compared to formal legal recognition. Likewise, practices among middle-class families also show the importance of this role. Fahim was married-off after a *pengarep* visited her parents. Her husband is a *santri* from a middle-class family and, therefore, a good catch. People were very much afraid that the man would be married to another woman (*mompong*) if the marriage proposal was not accepted. This same reasoning applied in the case of Fahim's sister.

Another key actor in any marriage is *kyai*s. *Kyai*s are important in resolving the legal issues which intersect with religion-related sexual morality. They maintain their roles in the production of an Islam-based legal norm that exercises control over sexual morality, which sometimes clashes with the state legal norm. In addition, divergent opinions in traditional *fiqh* doctrines have been essential to the construction of legal reasoning, which ties in with people's interests. The ability to exercise legal reasoning has become a fundamental instrument by which *kyai*s can maintain their legitimate authority in society. Because of the involvement of *kyai*s, marriage has been, and is still, an effective tool by which to tackle the problems of religious morality and female sexuality.

Increasing participation in formal education and the rise in women's mobility have challenged these tried and tested practices.[53] Formal schools now provide a space in which young people can meet prospective partners. Mutual love is becoming more important. Because they now have more room to exercise agency in the selection of a possible spouse, the role played by *pengarep* is a diminishing one. Nevertheless, for girls, finding a beloved partner is still not a crucial factor in deciding when they marry. In many cases, the decision of the timing of marriage is still firmly subject to the parents' authority because they are still the people supposed to exercise control over their daughter's sexual morality. Parents usually refer to this obligation in terms of preserving the social honour of a family. Even when women are able to articulate their consent to a marriage, they still need to depend on religiously inspired principles to make sense of their choices.

In Pasuruan a woman who divorces informally (out of court) and wants to remarry will experience no problem in finding a *kyai* willing to marry her to a

---

53 Gavin Jones, "Which Indonesian Women Marry Youngest, and Why?," *Journal of Southeast Asian Studies* 32, no. 1 (2001): 67–78.

new spouse, despite the absence of a marriage certificate, an attitude found in other parts of Indonesia too, like in Cianjur, West Java.[54] This suggests that religious norms still prevail over other legal norms, especially in remarriage. Furthermore, with the help of their traditional stalwarts, the *kyai* and *pengarep*, the villagers in Pasuruan are managing to continue to observe their community-based legal system, thereby forestalling the heavy involvement of state institutions.[55] Platt has underlined the dominant influence of community-based law, which saps the efficacy of the Marriage Law.[56] The narratives in this chapter have revealed some of the dilemmas and compromises that must be made on different levels in society due to the diversity of values in marriage and family.

In the next chapter, I will analyse the relationship between the state official functionary in charge of marriage registration (*penghulu*s) and their informal village counterparts (*modin*s), so long embedded in villagers' marriage ceremonies. The chapter adopts the concept of 'state-in-society' approach. It will also present an attempt to investigate the ways local people negotiate their own interests when dealing with a regulation of the marriage fee newly introduced by the government.

---

54 van Huis, "Islamic Courts and Women's Divorce Rights in Indonesia: The Cases of Cianjur and Bulukumba," 271.

55 Grijns and Horii, "Child Marriage in a Village in West Java (Indonesia): Compromises between Legal Obligations and Religious Concerns," 12.

56 Platt, *Marriage, Gender and Islam in Indonesia: Women Negotiating Informal Marriage, Divorce and Desire*, 149.

CHAPTER 6

Registering Marriage: The Relationship between *Penghulus* and *Modins*

> *"Ancaman saya begini: Saya turun jabatan atau buku nikahnya saya coret. Saya tidak mau instansi pemerintah dilecehkan."*
>
> This is my warning: I resign, or I cross out the marriage certificate. I do not want a government institution humiliated.
>
> PAK YUSUF, the head of a KUA office in Pasuruan

1 Introduction

It was at the end of January 2017. I stopped my motorcycle as I passed the Sumbersari grand mosque in Pasuruan. I cast my eye over a green building next to the mosque. The building looked dirty, and the front garden was untidy, but the entrance gates stood open. A small signboard reading 'Kantor Urusan Agama' still hung on the fence. The leaves of a mango tree in the corner of the garden dropped down over some parts of the signboard. I was hesitant but finally approached a young man sitting at a *warung* (food stall) directly opposite the mosque. I asked him if that building was the KUA office[1] for which I was searching. The young man told me that the building had been unoccupied for months. The office had in fact been moved a couple of hundred metres to the south, taking over a building belonging to the sub-district branch of the NU.

The following day, I visited the office and met its highest official, Pak Yusuf,[2] the head of the KUA, who simultaneously serves as the Pegawai Pencatat Nikah (PPN, the official marriage registrar). His position is socially acknowledged as the equivalent of a *penghulu* or a *naib*. Pak Yusuf briefly explained that they had had to move because the major parts of the old building needed renovation. He

1 The KUA is a state body at the sub-district (*kecamatan*) level which is responsible for the administration of Muslim marriages.

2 All names are pseudonyms.

 | DOI:10.1163/9789004516113_007

said that the Ministry of Religious Affairs' Provincial Office had approved a proposal for reconstruction. However, he did not know much about the cadastral history of the land as he had only been the head of this KUA since October 2014. He resides in an area close to Surabaya, the capital city of the province of East Java, which involves a journey of one hour by motorcycle to reach the office. On those days on which the number of marriage ceremonies[3] rises, he has to spend the night in the office to attend the ceremonies held early in the morning the next day. During my fieldwork, he often invited me to be his guest at the office too. I was very happy to accept his offer as it also enabled me to have extensive chats with Pak Rohmat, one of the local officials whose house is just a few dozen metres from the office.

Pak Rohmat is a non-tenured employee (*pegawai honorer*) who has been affiliated with the KUA for more than twenty years. He explained that, ever since the KUA was inaugurated in 1961, it had rented the house next to the mosque. In the early 1990s, the government had allocated land near the sub-district health centre for the construction of a new KUA office. Some local religious elites who knew about it fiercely opposed the plan. They argued that the KUA, whose task is to deal with Islamic affairs, was ideally situated alongside a mosque. In the end, the government cancelled the construction project. Later, after the intervention of religious leaders, the owner of the (rented) house was prepared to exchange his property for the allocated land. Since then, the house has been government property, even though the exchange was carried out unofficially. As a local villager, Pak Rohmat has been assigned to cooperate with village authorities to finalise its legal status. He is happy to take on this assignment, arguing, "it's the source of my income."

This narrative gives a very good impression of how informal religious leaders exercise their power in the (re)making of a state institution.[4] The resistance to the construction of a new building makes it quite clear that a state institution cannot really be isolated from its social context. Referring to similar situations, Davis argues that "informality is both a mirror and a determinant of the state's formal reach."[5] Moreover, it is also obvious that, in the perception of the religious leaders, the KUA is more than a formal institution involved in

3 To avoid misunderstanding, herein marriage ceremony refers to *akad nikah* or *ijab kabul*, the stage at which the woman's guardian in marriage offers the bride to the groom who then declares his acceptance.

4 Adam White, "Introduction. A State-in-Society Agenda," in *The Everyday Life of the State: A State-In-Society Approach*, ed. Adam White (Seattle: University of Washington Press, 2013), 1–12.

5 D.E. Davis, "Informality and State Theory: Some Concluding Remarks," *Current Sociology* 65, no. 2 (2017): 317.

the administration of marriage. Rather, the KUA officials, not least the *penghulus*, who deal specifically with marriage, are also assumed to possess religious authority. This perception is based on the reasoning that the task of the *penghulus* is to conduct a marriage ceremony according to Islamic norms or, at least, to validate that a marriage ceremony has been performed in accordance with Islamic rules and can therefore be legally registered.

This chapter examines the fact that a state agency like the KUA is unlikely to be detached from the social forces with which it engages.[6] Klinken and Barker have emphasised the importance of "the study of the state in relation to the broader social context in which it is embedded."[7] Bearing this in mind, I would like to draw attention to a wider debate about the state in society. Hence the emphasis in this chapter lies on the ways *penghulus* negotiate their authority in a society in which the influence of informal religious authorities is dominant. It elucidates how the KUA and its officials on the subdistrict level shape and implement the rules on marriage registration and analyses how they interact with the different actors in the local society.

On the basis of my observations of the everyday practice of the KUA in my research field, I suggest that, given their situation, the KUA officials have to negotiate their authority in a variety of contexts. They personally considered that, for the sake of stability, it was important to enhance their good relationship with religious leaders and local elites. It seems that officials like Pak Rohmat, who is a local villager, play an important role in bridging relations between the KUA and the local elites, including *modins*. Moreover, considering the principle of the 'dual validity' of Muslim marriages, that is, the legal obligation of marriage registration and the religious nature of the marriage ceremony, the flexibility of KUA officers in interpreting and implementing the rules is the key to the success of implementing state-imposed marriage registration.

Unquestionably, the relationship between the religious and administrative aspects of marriage places *penghulus* on the horns of a dilemma. This quandary is not a recent phenomenon. When we trace the history of *penghulus* at the beginning of the colonial era, we find this problem crops up time and again. Researchers have argued that, long before Independence, state-promoted *penghulus* found themselves poised at a crossroads between the

6 Christian Lund, "Rule and Rupture: State Formation through the Production of Property and Citizenship," *Development and Change* 47, no. 6 (2016): 1199–1228.

7 Gerry van Klinken and Joshua Barker, "Introduction: State in Society in Indonesia," in *State of Authority: The State in Society in Indonesia*, ed. Gerry van Klinken and Joshua Barker (Ithaca, NY: Cornell University, 2009), 5.

interests of Muslim leaders and those of the colonial government.[8] It has been the fate of *penghulus* to be stereotyped by religious leaders as people whose Islamic education left much to be desired.[9] Discussing their contemporary, delicate balancing act, Nurlaelawati has remarked that the KUA officials, including *penghulus*, show an inclination to co-operate with 'ulama', tending to position themselves as 'ulama' rather than as state officials. Examining their role in divorce, she found that *penghulus* have assumed an intermediary role between the 'ulama' and the Islamic courts. Even more interesting is that, as she suggests, the KUA officials in particular areas adopt an ambivalent position towards judicial divorce when they go ahead with the marriage registration of a husband and a wife who claim to have been in divorce but fail to present a divorce certificate.[10]

This chapter asks a fundamental question: In what ways do *penghulus* maintain their authority? This resonates with other questions, such as: What language do they use in their struggle for power in society? What is people's attitude towards them? What roles do *modins* play? How can we explain from observing the everyday interaction between people, *modins* and *penghulus*? By posing these questions, this chapter aims to scrutinise the (political) position of *penghulus* and the KUA officials in society at large. It then addresses the matter of how *penghulus* seek influence in navigating the recent introduction of marriage in accordance with state laws.

This chapter is composed of six sections. Following this introduction, I briefly elaborate on the foundational framework on which this chapter stands. The next section seeks to elucidate the social context in which the state is supposed to exercise its legal authority. From here, I address the presence of state institutions to introduce them into the core discussion. This section involves examining the different attitudes of KUA officials. Later, I expand my discussion of the image with an analysis of the recent trend in marriage registrations. The sixth section examines the interaction between *penghulus* and the entrenched social forces in the making of marriage practice.

---

8 Hisyam, *Caught between Three Fires: The Javanese Pangulu under the Dutch Colonial Administration, 1882–1942*.

9 Ibid.

10 Nurlaelawati, *Modernization, Tradition and Identity: The Kompilasi Hukum Islam and Legal Practice in the Indonesian Religious Courts*, 189.

2 Marriage Registration and the State-in-Society Approach

Pak Yusuf's words which begin this chapter, indicate that the state's legal authority over marriage is never free of challenges. Marriage has been, and still is, subject to competing authorities.[11] To extrapolate the complicated position of state officials like Pak Yusuf in society and their relationship with informal authorities,[12] this chapter borrows the conceptual framework of the 'state-in-society.'[13] By and large, this approach has been developed in response to the fact that the authority of the state principally shaped the modern world through the implementation of the force of its formal rules. However, in practice how these rules are determined by "those who are supposed to enforce them" and by "those who are supposed to obey them" is not cut and dried.[14] This situation inescapably gives rise to a wide range of competing authorities and discourses. Given the circumstances, it seems impossible to avoid the necessity of examining the compound relationship between the authority of the state and everyday social actors to comprehend their multiple narratives and political activities as reciprocal processes which constitute one another. The relationship between them is seen as a dialectical process.

This 'state-in-society' approach leads to a new, distinctive definition of the state. It revisits the concept proposed by earlier scholars like Max Weber, who conceptualised the state based on its institutional nature as a powerful organisation that allows it to resort to coercion.[15] This longstanding understanding of the state is encapsulated in Weber's commonly cited definition "a state is a human community that (successfully) claims the *monopoly of the legitimate use of physical force* within a given territory."[16] At the core of this definition lies the notion of domination by the means of physical force within the borders of the state's territory. Migdal has seen this domination as neither centred nor

---

11 Scott, "Social Norms and the Legal Regulation of Marriage," 1903.

12 Recent studies of the state and society have considered informality an analytical point of departure for theorizing governance, citizenship and social order. Davis, "Informality and State Theory: Some Concluding Remarks."

13 Among others, Joel Migdal is one of the leading scholars on the subject. His book "State in Society" published in 2001 has been fundamental in providing insightful viewpoints to deal with the enquiry into the making and the remaking of the state in the face of social realities. See Joel S. Migdal, *State in Society: Studying How States and Societies Transform and Constitute One Another* (Cambridge: Cambridge University Press, 2001).

14 White, "Introduction. A State-in-Society Agenda," 3.

15 Migdal, *State in Society: Studying How States and Societies Transform and Constitute One Another*, 111.

16 Weber, "Politics as a Vocation," 78.

single, exclusively occupied by a formal organisation. Instead, he has come up with the idea of "society's multiple arenas of domination and opposition."[17] He also suggests that the state is a power that "embodies an ongoing dynamic, a changing set of aims" as the consequence of the engagement of social forces.[18]

In the study of Islamic law and society, this 'state-in-society' approach necessarily brings me back to a number of works that have suggested the so-called cultural shape of state activity. One is the seminal work by Rosen on the practices of the *qadi* in the context of Islamic law and Moroccan social and cultural life.[19] After examining the local Sharīʿa court records (*sijill*) in the town of Sefrou, Morocco, he found that the oaths sworn and the use of professional witnesses are not based on the exact reality; they are the outcome of the *qadi*'s personal construction which is constructed through a process of negotiation. This effort is made to establish the judicial facts, making it possible for the *qadi* to make decisions.

Migdal offers a dual-aspect definition of the state. He states: "The state is a field of power marked by the use and threat of violence and shaped by (1) *the image of a coherent, controlling organisation in a territory, which is a representation of the people bounded by that territory*, and (2) *the actual practices of its multiple parts*."[20] The first aspect, the state's image, assumes the state as a dominant and autonomous entity that controls the direction taken by the given society. This is also bound up with how the state has become an integral part of everyday social relations. It explains why it continues to exercise a certain form of authority.[21] The second aspect, the practice, connects with the ways the state's image is either reinforced or weakened by its own officials and societal agencies. In short, it focuses on the variety of practices that influence the sharp demarcation between the state and society.[22] It allows us to see how different actors negotiate state authority.

Using this framework, I perceive Muslim marriage registration as a political activity that inevitably involves interaction between the state agent and everyday societal agencies. My starting point is an examination of the devel-

---

17 Migdal, *State in Society: Studying How States and Societies Transform and Constitute One Another*, 99.

18 Ibid., 112.

19 Lawrence Rosen, *The Anthropology of Justice: Law as Culture in Islamic Society* (Cambridge: Cambridge University Press, 1989).

20 Migdal, *State in Society: Studying How States and Societies Transform and Constitute One Another*, 15–16.

21 White, "Introduction. A State-in-Society Agenda," 13.

22 Migdal, *State in Society: Studying How States and Societies Transform and Constitute One Another*, 20.

opment of registered marriage. I move on to analyse the practice of *penghulus* and the KUA, paying particular attention to the image portrayed. In my construction of this image, I analyse the internal dynamics within the KUA to understand how *penghulus* maintain the credibility of the KUA. I focus on the recent trends in the performance of the marriage ceremony and marriage registration which provide the arena in which different authorities continue to contest.

3 Building an Internal Synergy

This section analyses the behaviour of KUA officials and their interaction in the everyday running of the KUA. However, before going further, it is important to explain positions in the KUA. The positions in the KUA can be divided into three categories, namely the head, *penghulus*, and the administrative staff. In the KUA Sumbersari, these positions are occupied by four persons: two are civil servants, while the other two are non-tenured local positions. The office itself occupies a two-floor building. The ground floor consists of one big hall and four small rooms. The hall houses two desks, one in the front and one at the back, separated by an old sofa suite and armchairs in the middle.

The principal civil servant is Pak Zaki. He occupies the front desk, the registration counter. Previously Pak Zaki was a teacher in a state Islamic school in the town Bangil. In 2014, he decided to leave the school to become a KUA official. "I wanted to feel more relaxed in my new position," Pak Zaki said. He is responsible for keeping *buku register* (registration book). This book contains the personal details of the brides and the grooms, the date of registration, the proposed date of the marriage ceremony, the bride's guardian and where the marriage ceremony will take place. Perhaps he is right when he says that his new occupation is less hectic than his previous job but, in the process of marriage administration, Pak Zaki's desk lies at the heart of all the procedures. On a practical level, he is the one who verifies the accuracy of the data (name, age and the guardian of the bride).

Pak Yusuf, the head, occupies the back table. He began his career as a civil servant in the KUA in Pasuruan in 1985. Since then, he has been continuously employed as a KUA official, moving from one office to another across the region. He is neither the product of an Islamic university nor did he graduate from a *pesantren*. Instead, he attended a vocational high school (*sekolah menengah kejuruan*) in the 1970s and later studied economics, obtaining Sarjana Ekonomi's degree (SE, BA in Economics). In the past, it was possible for an administrative official like him qualified to be promoted to the rank of a structural official (*pejabat struktural*). Pak Yusuf achieved this at the end of 2004. In this position, Pak Yusuf fulfils the duties of a marriage registrar (PPN, Pegawai Pencatat Nikah).

In the past, the head of a KUA was not always a *penghulu*, although a *penghulu* could also hold a structural position (*jabatan struktural*) as the head of a KUA. In Pak Yusuf's case, he is the head but is not a *penghulu*. Nevertheless, because the office does not have its own *penghulu*s, he automatically assumes the function of a *penghulu*. This kind of situation can sometimes lead to problems if the head of a KUA is not well versed in the religious competencies expected of him by society. This is the reason the government has changed the regulation governing the position of the head of the KUA. Currently, the head of the KUA must be a *penghulu*.

The fact that Pak Yusuf has to act as a *penghulu* has emerged as a crucial issue in Sumbersari. Local people have problematised his educational background because he had never attended an Islamic school. Pak Yusuf has also not been adequately educated in Arabic. Importantly, particular societies, as in Sumbersari, demand the use of Arabic as well as that of the local language in the performance of a marriage ceremony, including the marriage sermon (*khutbah nikah*), the offer (*ijab*) and its acceptance (*kabul*). The people believe that the use of Arabic imbues the marriage ceremony with an additional blessing. This demand definitely requires that *penghulu*s possess well-honed skills in reciting Quranic texts or proficiency (*fasih*) in reciting prayers in Arabic. Therefore, it is quite common for local people to ask a *modin* or another religious leader to conduct the ceremony rather than a *penghulu*.

Some wooden-framed posters hang on the wall near Pak Zaki. At the top, a big poster announces the regulations determining the mechanism of the marriage registration fee, which stresses the difference between *nikah di KUA* (marriage in the KUA) and *nikah di luar KUA* (marriage outside the KUA). Beneath it, a poster reproduces a *ḥadīth* on the roles of the marriage guardian and witnesses in a marriage contract. This *ḥadīth* says *lā nikāḥa illā biwaliyyin wa shāhiday 'adlin* (no marriage except with a guardian and two non-discredited witnesses). It also contains a description of who can be a guardian and that they can come only from the paternal side. If the bride's father is absent, there are still twenty guardians eligible to replace him, ranging from grandfather to the oldest son of a paternal great-uncle.

A couple of metres from Pak Zaki's desk is the room in which the two non-tenured officials do their work. Their position is commonly called *sukwan*, derived from the word *sukarelawan* (voluntary). They are local natives, Pak Rohmat and Pak Hamid. Pak Rohmat's principal task is organising the marriage documents. As his house is close to the office, he has the duty of handling the

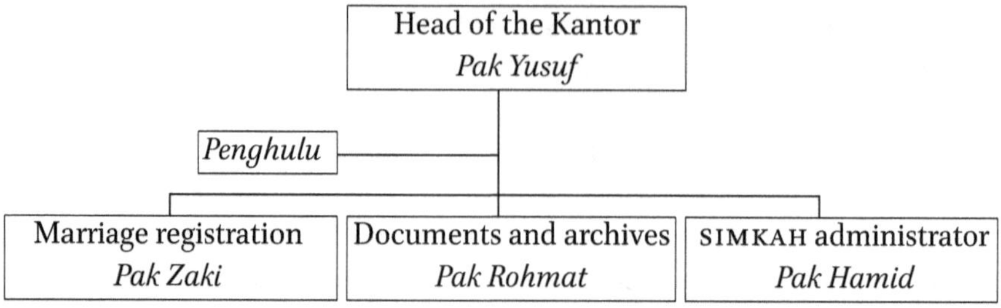

FIGURE 10 The structure of the KUA Sumbersari

day-to-day running of the KUA. Every morning, before office hours, he opens the door and cleans the floor. In the evening, he comes back to the office to make sure that everything is secure. Pak Rohmat is also responsible for recording the personal details of couples wishing to marry in the *buku bantu register* (back-up registration book). The difference between this book and the *buku register* is the column that mentions the number of copies of marriage certificates (*kutipan akta nikah*) given to married couples. Pak Rohmat also takes charge of writing their details down in the *buku nikah*, which each couple receives. The one with a green cover is for the wife (*buku nikah istri*), while the red-brick cover is for the husband (*buku nikah suami*). Pak Hamid's work is to manage electronic data. Since 2013, the data of husbands and wives have been collected electronically. The system is called SIMKAH (Sistem Informasi Manajemen Nikah).

Both Pak Rohmat and Pak Hamid are from families widely respected in religious circles and have played a considerable role in the development of the institution. In 1992, after finishing senior high school, Pak Rohmat took his older brother's position, who had just been promoted in the civil service rankings. Currently, his brother is serving as a *penghulu* in another sub-district. When he took over his brother's position, Pak Rohmat shared the same ambition, to be a civil servant. Therefore, some years ago, he took a bachelor's degree in Islamic education, which he hoped would accelerate his promotion. However, so far, this promotion has eluded him. Pak Hamid is a local villager who is a graduate of a prominent *pesantren* in the town which has not adopted secular education. Local people regard him more as an Islamic teacher (*ustadz*) than an official in a state institution. He heads an informal Islamic school (*madrasah diniyah*) in a *pesantren* that belongs to his uncle, one of the top leaders of the local branch of the NU. As his hands are full of these activities, he does not work at the KUA full time. Pertinently, his uncle has the authority to permit the use of the building as a temporary headquarters of the KUA. Moreover, his father is reported to have made the land barter transaction feasible in the past.

FIGURE 11 The head of KUA talks to a villager.

We can easily identify the difference between civil servants and non-tenured officials in their everyday performance, which essentially underlines their formal and semi-formal positions. Pak Zaki and Pak Yusuf dress more formally, in a white long-sleeved shirt on certain days, with an official badge pinned on their left breast. In addition, Pak Yusuf always wears a typically Islamic cap (*kopyah*). It seems that the *kopyah* says something about his state-sanctioned authority on Islamic matters. Pak Rohmat and Pak Hamid tend to dress more informally.

Although Pak Rohmat and Pak Hamid do not have permanent appointments, their position is important. Firstly, as said, their families are genealogically linked with religious elites in the area. Secondly, as locals, they share close emotional ties with the *modin*s. The majority of them are graduates of *pesantren*. There is an overwhelming tradition in the area that a marriage ceremony, particularly the couple's first marriage, should always be performed by a *modin*. In this position, the *modin* does not just organise the administrative documents required for the registration, he is in charge of the whole process. Thirdly, Pak Yusuf tends to assign one of his local officials to represent him in the informal monthly meetings between the *modin*s and village officials if he is unable to attend.

Meanwhile, as a civil servant whose job is to run the registration desk Pak Zaki feels bound to observe state regulations. He argues that he just implements the procedure as these have been committed to paper. Quite often, *modins* lodge complaints about him, alleging that he has been *terlalu ketat* (too rigorous) and *mempersulit* (makes matters more complicated than they are). This is a very common reaction when Pak Zaki insists that the couples turn up for the *rafak* (document verification). The *modins* are chary about *rafak* for several reasons. One objection is that either the bride or the groom is still a boarder in a *pesantren* or works out of town. Another reason is that the couple has not yet signed the marriage consent form. When this happens, a *modin* usually approaches Pak Rohmat to discuss the situation, hoping that he will help convince Pak Zaki that everything will turn out alright. Pak Zaki's principal concern is that: "*If an official from the* Kantor Kementerian Agama Kabupaten *conducts an audit and finds an irregularity; it is not their* (modins') *responsibility. We get the blame instead.*" Therefore, on certain occasions, the PPN, Pak Yusuf, has to resolve the impasse stating: "*Up to you,* modin. *If you do not want to follow our rules, please don't bother to work with us!*"

This explanation reveals a variety of issues, ranging from social forces in operation behind the local officials to the manoeuvres of *modins*, which inhibit the everyday practice of the KUA. Pak Yusuf is aware of this situation and needs to exercise his authority, albeit playing his power trump card very carefully. As the PPN, he is unquestionably a state representative, but as a *penghulu*, he tends to present himself in his guise as a religious authority. Pak Yusuf gives the local officials leeway to bridge the communications gap between the KUA and the local people. Meanwhile, Pak Zaki tends to position himself as the guardian of the state rules. Together these attitudes have been an important factor in co-shaping the everyday image of the KUA as an institution dealing with Islamic affairs and a state body in charge of marriage administration.

4 Registering Marriages and Remarriages

As far as marriage practices in East Javanese villages are concerned, when the two families have agreed on the date of the marriage ceremony, the girl's father approaches a *modin* to ask for the latter's help in arranging the marriage ceremony. At this point, I should explain that people usually go to *modins* for the first marriage. If it is not the first marriage for one of the couples, there is no guarantee that *modins* will feel obliged to participate in the process. The father-*modin* interaction represents the initial process in the implementation of the state law on marriage. In the Sumbersari setting, I observed a conversation between a father and a *modin* which ran as follows:

Father	Pak Haji, I am going to marry my daughter. How much is it to buy (obtain) a marriage certificate?
Modin	Praise be to Allah! Your daughter has found her future husband. I wish her a blessed relationship in this world and the Hereafter. The marriage certificate is not something to be bought but has to do with marriage registration which requires some conditions to be met. Firstly, the age of marriage: for women, this is sixteen and for men nineteen. Secondly, you have to hand in a family card, an identity card and a school diploma.
Father	Yes, they are all present and correct.
Modin	Are you going to handle the registration yourself or ask me to do it?
Father	I want you to handle it, Pak *Modin*, including the marriage ceremony.
Modin	If this is what you want, it will cost (a certain amount), covering the preparation of all the documents, transport costs and the marriage ceremony.

This conversation clearly shows that the villagers generally perceive marriage registration in terms of "buying a marriage certificate." They argue this is because they have to spend a certain amount of money to obtain it. The *modin* usually tells them that it is not a matter of buying a letter but registering a marriage. This misperception is not only prevalent in the matter of marriage registration. It also crops up in judicial divorce. The locals use the phrase *melleh talak ka hakim* (buying a divorce from the religious judges). Some people refer to it as *melleh kartu koning* (buying a yellow card) because the divorce certificate for a wife has yellow decorations on it.

Despite the local perception of marriage registration as buying a marriage certificate, when we look at the figures for marriages registered, it appears that this step has become an increasingly important part of local marriage practice. I talked to many *modin*s and they generally confirmed that marriage registration is already being perceived as a requirement by the local people. One of them said: "*It has changed now. Nearly all marriages are registered at the* KUA." With a Muslim population of 61,650, the Sumbersari sub-district has around 500–550 registered marriages a year. In the Pasuruan regency with Muslim population of 1,604,325 in 2015, the number of marriages was around 14,150 a year. The highest number of marriages in the most densely populated sub-district, Gempol, with a Muslim population of 199,272, was 1,308 per year. The lowest

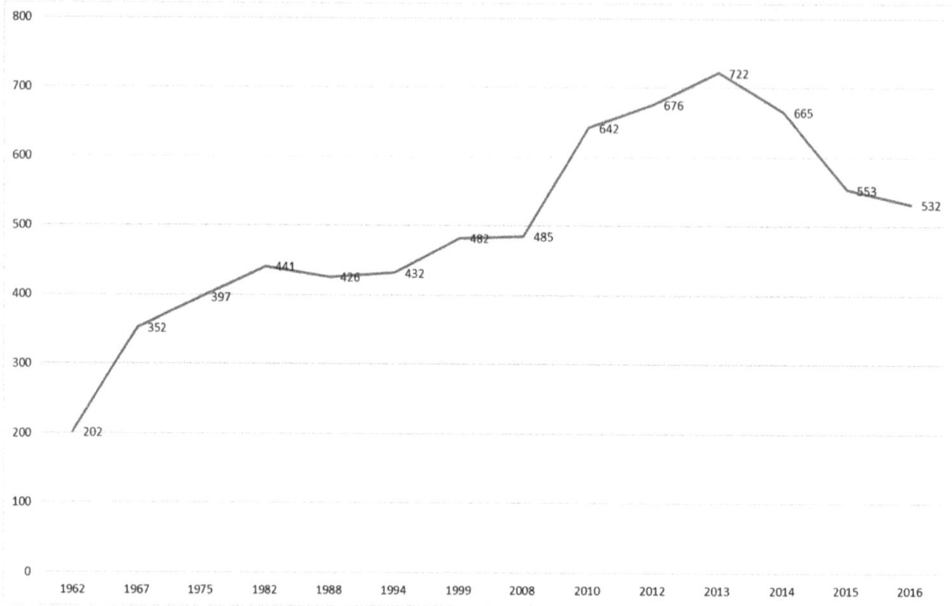

FIGURE 12 Registered marriages in the KUA Sumbersari

number, amounting to ninety-nine marriages a year, was found in the Tosari sub-district, in which the Muslim population is 5,625.[23]

My materials from the records of the KUA Sumbersari show that there was an increase in marriage in 2010 compared to previous years. In 2008, the number of registered marriages was around 485, and it escalated to 642 in 2010. Unfortunately, I have not been able to collect enough data to explain this escalation. However, if I might speculate on the basis of the information which I collected from *modins*, a number of factors were involved. Firstly, ever-married couples tend to register their remarriages. Secondly, people are more aware that many incentives, such as government subsidies or access to bank loans, are easier to obtain if they can produce a marriage certificate. Thirdly, both parents find it important to list their names on their child's birth certificates. What follows is the figure of registered marriage from the 1960s up to the present.

This chart shows that since 2015 there has been a tendency towards a decline in marriage registration. When I consulted this matter with the officials of the KUA, they argued that neither a decrease in marriages nor a rise in unregistered marriages caused the decline. Social mobility seems to have been the major factor in instigating this change. In distinction to the past, when marriages

23 BPS Kab. Pasuruan, *Kabupaten Pasuruan Dalam Angka 2016*, 232.

generally involved only local people, the younger generation now has ample opportunities to establish cross-cultural families. This assertion is endorsed by the introductory letter (*surat pengantar*) by the local KUA so that a groom can register his marriage at the KUA with which the bride is affiliated.

People's attitudes towards the importance of marriage registration no longer apply just to first marriages. They now extend to remarriages. The number of remarriages, in which one or both spouses is a *janda* (an ever-married woman) or a *duda* (an ever-married man), constitutes nearly one-quarter of the total number of marriages.[24] In the year 2015, there were 124 remarriages out of 553 marriages or 22 percent. Meanwhile, in the year 2016, there were 122 remarriages out of 532 marriages or 23 percent. This figure also suggests that there has been an increase in people's awareness about seeking a judicial divorce from an Islamic court. Based on the records from Islamic courts in 2015, the number of divorces registered at the KUA Sumbersari was 104. Twenty-three were divorces initiated by husbands (*cerai talak*), while the remaining eighty-one were requested by wives (*cerai gugat*). Here, the ratio of divorce was 19 percent compared to the number of marriages in the same year. From the above figure, I assume that both the KUA and the Islamic courts have increasingly shaped people's attitudes about dealing with marital matters. This finding corroborates earlier studies that have shed light on the growth of divorce cases in Indonesian Islamic courts over the last decade.[25]

5 Twofold *Akad Nikah* and *Ta'kīd al-Nikāḥ*

People's changing attitudes towards marriage registration, discussed in the previous section, underscore the optimism felt about the effective functioning of the state as a body that wields legal authority. Does this mean that people are now more inclined to surrender their religious affairs to a state agent? If so, to what extent does it affect the roles of traditional leaders? With reference to Law 22/1946 on the Registration of Islamic Marriage, Divorce and Reconciliation, Article 6 of the Compilation of Islamic Law states that a marriage ceremony must be held in front of and under the supervision of a marriage registrar

24 The KUA administration and the civil registration in Indonesia differentiate between *janda mati* (widow) and *janda cerai* (divorced woman) and between a *duda mati* (widower) and *duda cerai* (divorced man).

25 Nurlaelawati, "Muslim Women in Indonesian Religious Courts: Reform, Strategies, and Pronouncement of Divorce"; Mohamad Abdun Nasir, "Islamic Law and Paradox of Domination and Resistance," *Asian Journal of Social Science* 44, no. 1–2 (2016): 78–103.

(PPN). However, going back to the statement at the beginning of this article, it is obvious that Pak Yusuf was proclaiming the state-bestowed power to legalise Muslim marriage. He even uttered some threats to stress this authority. This situation leads me to inquire about what has happened to the state-society relationship lurking behind marriage registration.

Sometime in May 2017, a family in a Pasuruan village whose daughter was about to wed held a *walimah*. A *walimah* is a festive meal organised at the bridegroom's house to make a public announcement of the forthcoming marriage ceremony (*akad nikah*). It is usually held in the morning where relatives, neighbours and respected figures in the village are invited. The groom and a few of his family members also attend. The program commences with the recitation of *mawlid* (prayers for the Prophet) and prayers and usually concludes with an *akad nikah* ceremony. Two weeks earlier, when the bride's father had visited Haji Misbah, a *modin* in the village, to arrange the marriage ceremony, he decided to register it as a *nikah kantor*, marriage at the KUA office. Haji Misbah asked the father about who would serve as the *munakkiḥ* (a person to whom the marriage guardian delegates his authority to marry off his daughter), stating the following:

> I told the father that the obligation to marry a woman is the responsibility of the *wali*. It is much better if the *wali* undertakes this duty personally. However, he can delegate it to another suitable person if he prefers. However, it is thought vulgar for the *wali* to delegate it to the *modin* and, moreover, the *wali* is still obliged to be present at the marriage ceremony.

In a nutshell, the *walimah* was held on the same day as the *akad nikah* scheduled by the KUA. In the meantime, the father had been persuaded by his family to include the *akad nikah* during the *walimah*, following the usual pattern. It was said: "*Mumpung Gus Akib rawuh, dinikahno sekalian ae*" (Better to marry them now while Gus Akib is present). Gus Akib is a prominent religious leader whom the bride's family consults about Islam and other matters. Living as they do in the *pesantren* tradition, the locals still believe in the concept of *barakah* (blessing), a quality which is revealed in the performance of good religious acts by people.[26] Their ideal is a marriage ceremony blessed by the intermediation

26 In Sufism, one can receive God's blessing through the intermediary of a holy man such as a saint or a *murshid*. Within the *pesantren* tradition, students are supposed to respect their teachers not only in the classroom but also in all aspects of life. Failure to pay respect can cause the loss of the *barakah* of the teacher. See Martin van Bruinessen, *Tarekat Naqsyabandiyah Di Indonesia* (Bandung: Mizan, 1992), 215; Dhofier, *The Pesantren Tradition: The Role of the Kyai in the Maintenance of Traditional Islam in Java*, 61–62.

of Gus Akib. Hence the father raised the situation with Haji Misbah, the *modin*, who was among the guests at the *walimah*. Haji Misbah had no objection and permitted the *akad nikah* to take place. Nevertheless, he still insisted that *akad nikah* would also occur at the KUA a few hours later. This solution has led to a circumstance called *akad nikah dua kali* (twofold marriage ceremonies).

A religious leader like Gus Akib, who was willing to conduct a religious marriage ceremony, is probably the exception rather than the rule. Gus Akib is a village-level religious leader. Some religious leaders who enjoy a high reputation usually refuse to marry couples.[27] They usually suggest the family hold the ceremony at the KUA. These religious leaders are well aware of the consequences of a marriage which has not been properly registered. They tend to support the authority of *penghulu*s and the KUA and perceive both the marriage ceremony and the registration as an inseparable process.

The practice of *akad nikah dua kali* was the reason Pak Yusuf spoke so harshly. This practice is growing in the wake of the new policy drawn up by the central government in 2014 delineating a stricter boundary between marriage in the office (*nikah kantor*) and marriage outside the office (publicly known as *nikah bedolan*).[28] The basic principle at stake here is that the marriage ceremony is held at the KUA office. This complies with article 21 point (1) of the Regulation on the Registration of Muslim Marriages.[29] Interestingly, point (2) covers the rules to be applied when, with the PPN's agreement, a bride proposes her marriage be solemnised outside the KUA office. Now, the differentiation between *nikah* at the KUA and outside the KUA has been clarified by the introduction of a scale of multiple tariffs. Those who perform *nikah kantor* are charged Rp. 0. Meanwhile, the couple's family must pay more, Rp. 600,000 (approximately 40 US dollars) if they want to conclude a marriage ceremony outside the office or working hours. Before 2014, there was no difference between the two.

It was originally proposed that the marriage be conducted as a *nikah kantor*, but in practice involves both *nikah bedolan* and *nikah kantor*. The *nikah bedolan* is carried out without the attendance of a *penghulu*, while a *nikah kantor* is carried out at the KUA purely and simply to acquire state recogni-

---

27 This is according to Pak Syukron, a *modin* in Sumbersari.

28 Peraturan Pemerintah (Government Regulation) No. 48 Tahun 2014 tentang Perubahan atas Peraturan Pemerintah Nomor 47 Tahun 2004 tentang Tarif atas Jenis Penerimaan Negara Bukan Pajak yang Berlaku pada Departemen Agama (on the Revision of the Government Regulation No. 47/2004 on the non-tax revenue of the Department of Religious Affairs).

29 PMA No. 11/2007 on Pencatatan Nikah (Marriage Registration).

tion. Both ceremonies are sometimes performed on the same day. The issue seems to revolve around money. However, judging by the aforementioned story, it also has to do with more essential issues such as the marriage ceremony itself and the meaning people attach to it. Importantly, in *nikah kantor*, local people tend to delegate the role of marriage guardianship to a *modin*, not a *penghulu*. This situation also explains why *modin* still survive. The role they play meets religious-cum-administrative interests.

This section has demonstrated how *penghulu*s negotiate their authority as they navigate the pressures exerted by various forces: the state, local tradition, and their own interests. By drafting the new regulation, it seems that the state is seeking to increase its power of intervention in marriage. The campaign for *nikah kantor* actually began some years ago. In its implementation, the central government has made significant efforts to enhance the status of KUA offices, transforming them into 'ideal houses' in which to hold a marriage ceremony, renaming it *balai nikah* (marriage house). In the Sumbersari setting, the first floor of the office consists of an open hall that functions as the *balai nikah* in which marriage ceremonies are concluded. The existence of a *balai nikah* is becoming increasingly important, irrespective of the fact that the majority of them still provide less than adequate facilities. Therefore, the central government has spent a considerable amount of its budget on the Ministry of Religious Affairs to renovate hundreds of KUA buildings throughout Indonesia.[30]

Certainly, the differentiation between *nikah kantor* and *nikah bedolan* was not an issue in the past because there was no differentiation in the tariff. My observations in Sumbersari show that about 95 percent of marriage ceremonies prior to 2014 were conducted outside the office. By 2017, this situation had changed dramatically, and the rate of *nikah bedolan* was now 24 percent of 531 marriages. This pattern is not typical only of Pasuruan villages, it is also emerging in other areas, although the decline is not as significant as in Pasuruan. Let us look at the detailed figures of a KUA in an urban community in the town of Jember, East Java.[31] In 2013, the ratio of *nikah bedolan* was 92 percent of all marriages (730 of 799). It declined in the two years after. In 2014, *nikah bedolan* represented 598 of 792 (76%), while in 2015, they were 439 of 746 (59%). It climbed a little bit in 2016 (64%) and 2017 (76%), although the rise is still far below that of 2013.

---

30 Kemenag, "Tiga Tahun Jokowi-JK: Kemenag Pemrakarsa Dan Investor Terbesar SBSN," accessed May 7, 2018, https://kemenag.go.id/berita/read/505984/tiga-tahun-jokowi-jk--kemenag-pemrakarsa-dan-investor-terbesar-sbsn.

31 This data is calculated from the SIMKAH record which I obtained from a colleague of mine who is a *penghulu* at that KUA.

In a situation similar to that in Jember, in Yogyakarta the difference in the tariff has not exerted a significant influence. The rate of *nikah bedolan* remains high, at approximately 85 percent. A number of factors underlie this situation. Firstly, in the general perception of the people in Yogyakarta the state *penghulus* are religious officials with adequate knowledge of Islam. Therefore, they have no qualms about submitting all marriage matters to him. In many cases, *penghulus* lead the marriage ceremony and serve as the *munakkiḥ*. Secondly, the tariff for *nikah bedolan* is not really important to them. Thirdly, they tend to hold *nikah bedolan* because they invite their relatives, neighbours, and colleagues to witness the ceremony. Fourthly, in their quest for greater social recognition, some families hold the marriage ceremony in prestigious locations, hotels or halls. When catering to these interests, there is no reason not to invite a *penghulu*. Nevertheless, a small number of them do choose to have *nikah kantor*. Their reason is usually that they do not want to deal with the complexities in the official documents.[32]

The application of the new tariff has indeed elicited different reactions from members of society. Haji Misbah argued: "*The problem is that the difference is very big; Rp. 600,000 is a significant amount for villagers.*" Throughout the years 2004–2013, marriage administration costed Rp. 30,000 for either *nikah kantor* or *nikah bedolan*. If they opted for the assistance of a *modin*, people spent around Rp. 350,000. The above story shows that the brides' families generally preferred an *akad nikah* to be part of a *walimah*. This arrangement offered at least two benefits: the participation of other villagers and the involvement of an honoured, religious leader. It also backs up the assertion that a marriage ceremony has emerged as a fundamental arena in which religious leaders can exercise their authority.

As is commonly found in Muslim communities across the nation, a marriage ceremony merges both religious and social activities.[33] It echoes the general opinion of Muslim scholars who state that Islamic marriage is an embodiment of the elements of a civil contract, spiritual practice and worship of the divine.[34] This strongly suggests that an Islamic marriage is not merely a matter which falls into the category of *muʿamala* (civil contract), that is, pronouncing a contract of *ijab* (offer) made by the woman's guardian (*wali*), *qabul* (acceptance) by the man and the payment of dowry (*mahr*). It is undeniably a contract but has expanded its dimension to that of an *ʿibada* (ritual act) in which norm-

32 This is summarized from my interview with Pak Nasrudin, a *penghulu* in Yogyakarta, August 2019.

33 Mir-Hosseini, *Marriage on Trial: Islamic Family Law in Iran and Morocco.*

34 Nichols, "Religion, Family Law, and Competing Norms," 197.

ative and traditional elements of religion are engaged.[35] Therefore, in social practice, we see the marriage ceremony interwoven with religious rituals,[36] including the recitation of verses from the Quran, *sholawat* (prayers for blessings on the Prophet) and *tahlil* (prayers for the ancestors). I have witnessed many similar rituals in Pasuruan villages. In certain communities, particular days, like Friday *Pon*,[37] are believed to be especially auspicious for a marriage ceremony.

I discussed this issue with a local religious leader, Kyai Karim. He argued that it is understandable that people tend to conclude a marriage ceremony at home. His major concern revolved around the religious capacity of *penghulu*s. Religious leaders generally perceive *penghulu*s to be 'ulama', whereas, in fact, Pak Yusuf has never been trained in an Islamic institution. Kyai Karim was critical of the government for making it too easy to promote its functionaries to the position of *penghulu*s. Another point that he disparaged was that the facilities in the KUA are not yet up to standard (*pantas*) for conducting a marriage ceremony. He stressed both the bride and the groom must be treated with respect (*dimulyakan*) but, on certain busy days, they have to queue like people lining up for a dole of *raskin* (*beras miskin*, rice for the poor). Kyai Karim also made the point:

> I have heard public rumours that the *penghulu* is less than competent. His lack of skill in reciting *ayat* (Quranic verses) and *doa* (prayers) tends to get on people's nerves. People certainly think twice about involving him in a marriage ceremony. Marriage is a sacred ceremony. It is an *ibadah*. Like *sholat*, if you do not recite Surah Al-Fatihah, the principal element in *sholat*, properly, your *sholat* is unacceptable.

This criticism seems to represent a view commonly held among the villagers. They see *akad nikah* as a crucial stage that should be conducted under the guidance of a prominent religious leader, quite close to the problem of obtaining *barokah* (blessing). Hence, when organising a marriage ceremony, people usually ask a *kyai* they respect to lead the marriage ceremony. When they choose to have a *nikah kantor*, parents occasionally bring their chosen *munakkiḥ* to the office. In some peculiar circumstances, there have been families who had felt they had to perform a second *akad nikah* at home because they were dubious

35 Mir-Hosseini, "Marriage."
36 Black, Esmaeili, and Hosen, *Modern Perspectives on Islamic Law*, 114.
37 *Pon* is one of the five-day *pasaran* (marketplace) cycle in the Javanese calendar.

FIGURE 13 *Akad nikah* in the office, led by an informal *modin*

about the validity of the earlier *akad nikah* at the office. Consequently, *akad nikah dua kali* can be held both at home than the office or vice-versa.

The existence of *akad nikah dua kali* quite irrefutably demonstrates the state's attempt to control marriage has not been an overwhelming success. This development has indeed been an affront for Pak Yusuf, who is on the frontline of Muslim marriage registration. One of my informants, Pak Usman, a high-ranking official in the Ministry of Religious Affairs' District Office, acknowledged that people in Pasuruan villages still place great reliance (*ketergantungan*) on *kyai*s, and this dependence lies at the heart of the skewed relationship between state *penghulu*s and religious leaders.[38] Pak Yusuf is well aware that the forces of informal religious authority are challenging him. His discomfort prompts him to speak more on the state's behalf rather than think about perceiving himself as a religious authority. He uses his statements to underline his authority to bestow state recognition of religious marriage as the means to negotiate. Here is an example:

38 Interview with Pak Usman, the head of the Section on Islamic guidance of the Pasuruan Office of Religious Affairs, February 2017.

> I do not like them holding a traditional marriage ceremony at home and later having another marriage ceremony at the KUA. I usually ask the witnesses whether or not they are already married. If the answer is in the affirmative, I say: If it's a marriage certificate you're after, just ask your *kyai!*

The *modin* Haji Misbah, who serves as the intermediary between the state and people, also finds himself in a quandary. He has suggested using the concept he calls *ta'kīd al-nikāḥ* (officiating a marriage) for the second marriage at the KUA. I have failed to discover the origin of this concept. Literally, the first word, *ta'kīd*, is associated with the Arabic word *tawkīd*, meaning endorsement or ratification.[39] *Ta'kīd al-nikāḥ* could be interpreted as officiating a marriage (*pengukuhan pernikahan*). It seems that Haji Misbah's idea in coming up with this concept is that an *akad nikah* at the KUA will provide state authentication of a preceding religious marriage. Interestingly, he has also applied this concept in another context, underage marriage. If the bride has not yet reached the legal age of marriage, the couple is first married religiously. Later, when the woman's age qualifies her for legal marriage registration, their marriage is registered at the KUA.

Unsurprisingly, the issue of *akad nikah dua kali* has been raised in a series of meetings between the KUA and *modins*. Pak Yusuf has sternly cautioned the *modins* to discourage this sort of this marriage, saying "Don't ever marry them at home!" Nor do his troubles end there. Besides the thorny issue of competing authorities, another aspect has been causing him and the other *modins* to grow concerned. Note the following statement by Pak Yusuf:

> What they desire is free of charge marriage. Whether they arrive here by motorcycle or by car, I run my eye over them. Sometimes this makes me hesitate to marry them at the office. Just think about it, they have arrived here in a Livina (a minibus). This is nonsensical if they want a *nikah kantor*. I have had to refuse them. Why do you not invite us to come to your home! Have a *nikah bedolan* and, by paying just 600,000, ensure your religious, worldly and Afterlife interests!

In his remark, Pak Yusuf is making a veiled reference to the relationship between *nikah kantor* and the financial capacity of the families concerned. He

---

39 Elsaid M. Badawi and Muhammad Abdel Haleem, "و/ك/د w–k–D," *Arabic-English Dictionary of Qur'anic Usage* (Brill, 2008), 1044.

was questioning why, when people find it hard to find that bit of extra money to hold a *nikah bedolan*, do they not opt to get a marriage certificate which, in his opinion, covers the worldly and religious aspects of marriage for so much less. He said, "*Buku nikah sekali untuk seumur hidup*" (a marriage certificate is for life). Meanwhile, a *penghulu* in the KUA in the town of Jember said to me, "This year (2018), we are targeting 85 percent of *nikah bedolan*." Both statements carry a strong undercurrent that hints that *nikah bedolan* is somehow bound up with economics. There is a logic behind this. However, before I set out my explication, I should say that the existing table of multiple tariffs was the outcome of the absence of any regulation that would cover an incentive for *penghulus* to perform *nikah bedolan*. When it was realised, the central government decided to set tariffs for *nikah bedolan*, legally entitling *penghulus* to supplement their income. This regulation means that, for each *nikah bedolan*, a *penghulu* receives approximately Rp. 100,000 for their transportation and Rp. 150,000, or another amount depending on the KUA category, as an honorarium (*jasa profesi*).[40] Consequently, the fluctuating number of *nikah bedolan* has become a major issue among *penghulus* as they feel it in their pockets.

Pak Syamsu, the head of the KUA in the city of Surabaya, acknowledged that this bureaucratic reform confirms the legal certainty of the rights of *penghulus* in the case of a *nikah bedolan*,[41] but it has not overcome the problem of the organisation of marriage registration in general. He referred to the lack of the KUA in managing its everyday activities as it is forced to fight an uphill battle, frustrated in its efforts by the limited budget allocated by the government. He argued: "The new regulation has undermined our capacity to act. Under the old regulation, we could still donate to social or mosque activities around us. Now, the budget for the KUA is so straightened, we cannot do anything for our non-tenured staff or society in general because we just do not have the money to do this." In the past, the KUA had the autonomy to manage the money it received from people via *modins* and strengthen its institutional power. With Rp. 0 coming in for *nikah kantor* and the incentive for *penghulus* to perform *nikah bedolan* severely curtailed, the head of the KUA is currently besieged by problems arising from the organisation of the office. In their attempts to deal

---

40 Keputusan Direktur Jenderal Bimbingan Masyarakat Islam (the Decree of the Directorate General of Islamic guidance) No. DJ.II/748 Tahun 2014 tentang Petunjuk Teknis Pengelolaan Penerimaan Negara Bukan Pajak atas Biaya Nikah atau Rujuk di luar Kantor Urusan Agama Kecamatan (on the technical procedure of the organisation of non-tax revenue from the fees of marriage or reconciliation outside the sub-district KUA).

41 Interview with him, October 2017.

with this, I witnessed that some KUA offices in other areas have encouraged their *penghulus* not to grab all the incentive, but to distribute some of it in the wider interest of the KUA.

Apart from these financial considerations, based on Migdal's state-in-society, the practice of *akad nikah dua kali* has been a place in which the state has been unable to impose its single-authoritative authority in marriage practice and, consequently, the everyday actor has been able to intervene in the making of the state practice. The practice now provides what Peletz has called "the co-imbrication of law, politics, and religion."[42] *Akad nikah dua kali* encompasses a multiplicity of issues, ranging from state authority, religious authority, the local sense of religious validity and the *penghulus*' economic interests. However, this has been offset by a local development in which people strategise the multiple tariffs for marriage by concluding *akad nikah dua kali*. This tactic allows them to maintain the ideals of the marriage ceremony, which incorporates the religious and social activities so important to them. This is their response to their perception of the lack of religious competency displayed by *penghulus*. The intervention of traditional authority is embedded in this realm. In its turn, this 'deviation' has become a critical stepping-stone for *penghulus* to implement state laws on marriage on a grassroots level. Subtly, the tactics adopted by *penghulus* never mount a direct challenge to the traditional authority. Instead, they tend to present themselves as state agents, exercising their authority by the threat that state recognition of marriage will never be possible without the possession of a marriage certificate that they have signed.

6 Conclusion

Examining the developments in a KUA office in Pasuruan, it seems obvious that the day-to-day running of this state body is not a compartmentalised, isolated aspect of society. In this chapter, Migdal's state-in-society approach has helped reveal the complexities faced by *penghulus* and the KUA in the implementation of legal rules on marriage registration, as they struggle in a web of pressures exerted by societal agencies.

I found that the internal synergy between the KUA officials has been the key to securing the KUA's legitimacy. My principal reasons for this assertion are threefold. Firstly, if they are to fulfil their tasks satisfactorily, the head of the

---

42 Michael G. Peletz, "A Tale of Two Courts: Judicial Transformation and the Rise of a Corporate Islamic Governmentality in Malaysia," *American Ethnologist* 42, no. 1 (2015): 144–160.

KUA and *penghulu*s have to understand the local social life. They then need to transfer this knowledge into the grounds for making balanced decisions. Secondly, it should not be overlooked that the non-tenured local officials at the KUA also play a considerable role in communicating the state's ideas on marriage to social agencies, including *modin*s. Thirdly, the KUA civil servants tend to implement the state rules strictly. Other factors also play a role. In Pasuruan villages, local people regard marriage registration as a transactional relationship between state-citizen. *Modin*s are the key agents in this brokerage. This KUA-*modin*-society relationship has produced the remarkable development of registered marriages and remarriages. In a nutshell, this triangular relationship demonstrates the effective functioning of the state.

In spite of these changes, the Indonesian central government has not given up its own ideas about how to manage marriage registration. Consequently, the central government has drafted a regulation that draws a stricter boundary between *nikah kantor* and *nikah bedolan, expecting* that this would be effective in eradicating the custom of earning gratification among *penghulu*s. This has not been plain sailing. This regulation has intensified the tension between religious authority and the state agency and led to *akad nikah dua kali*. It seems fair to argue that *akad nikah dua kali* is an outgrowth of the multiple tariff system for marriage ceremonies. Be that as it may, it also has to do with the local conceptualisation of the function of marriage. In everyday Muslim life, a marriage ceremony entails not only religious but importantly also social activities, both of which require the intervention of religious leaders. At the same time, we have also been witnessing situations in which *penghulu*s are challenged by accusations of their lack of competency in Islam. *Penghulu*s need to redefine their position if they were to be accepted as legitimate agents competent to deal with Muslim marriages. Heeding the warning, *penghulu*s have transformed their authority to provide state recognition of marriage into their source of power.

To conclude, in Pasuruan, *penghulu*s tend not to identify themselves as 'ulama', even though their identity as a religious authority remains important. This differs from Nurlaelawati's finding in West Java. *Penghulu*s in East Java identify themselves as state agents, wielding their authority to provide state recognition of a marriage as a resource to reinforce their influence. This suggests two interrelated aspects: Firstly, they invariably speak on behalf of the state. Secondly, a marriage certificate has become an important instrument in bolstering their authority. Finally, *modin*s are apparently playing a greater role in bridging the relationship between the state and society. *Modin*s are finding themselves the subject of a compromise between competing legal orders, a situation which has given rise to the production of new legal norms, such as *ta'kīd al-nikāḥ*, to make their intermediary role possible. However, turning to the nub of the problem, the fact that *penghulu*s have not been successful in persuading society to marry according to the State law suggests that, in the first place, they do not enjoy a solidly entrenched position in society. This is in contrast to the *modin*s who, with the rise of interest in *ta'kīd al-nikāḥ*, have created a semi-autonomous social field, which sustains customs and rules symbols internally but is nevertheless vulnerable to rules and decisions from outside the field.[43] In other words, the idea of *ta'kīd al-nikāḥ* has been effective in touching the meaning of marriage as the local people perceive it on the one hand and in ensuring the implementation of the state legal norms on marriage on the other hand.

The following chapter will problematise social and legal meaning of marriage legalisation for villagers who have made unregistered marriages. It seeks to understand people's motives and the ways people try to have state recognition of unregistered marriages.

43 Sally Falk Moore, "Law and Social Change: The Semi-Autonomous Social Field as an Appropriate Subject of Study," *Law and Society Review* 7, no. 4 (1973): 720.

CHAPTER 7

Legalising Unregistered Marriage: Reasons and Strategies

1 Introduction

Abdullah (44 years) is the husband of Jamilah (40 years). They have been married for twenty-one years in a traditional way. Their marriage was not registered at the KUA.[1] Consequently, they do not have a marriage certificate. Nevertheless, Abdullah has somehow been registered as the *kepala keluarga* (head of household) and Jamilah as the *istri* (wife) on their Kartu Keluarga (KK, family card). Normally, this would not have been possible because they are not legally a couple. When I asked him how this could happen, Abdullah replied, "I just received it from the village official (*pamong*). He organised everything."[2] In possession of this KK, they are accordingly recognised as a legal couple in the civil administration.[3] Similarly, on their Kartu Tanda Penduduk (KTP, identity card), their marital status is listed as *kawin* (married).

Although their status is recognised as *kawin*, Abdullah and Jamilah encountered a problem when they went on the *ḥajj* (pilgrimage). The KK or the KTP, which confirmed their status as *kawin*, did not suffice as a required document for the *ḥajj* visa application. Under state law, they had to submit a marriage certificate to prove that they were in a lawful marital relationship. Their predicament was that they were not qualified to apply for it. The 1991 Kompilasi, which acts as the reference for Islamic judges, stipulates that Muslims can legalise their unregistered marriages through a judicial procedure called retrospective marriage legalisation (*isbat nikah*). Although this legal norm was formulated to accommodate marriages concluded before 1974 when the legal obligation of marriage registration came into force, judicial practice in the Islamic courts nowadays will legalise unregistered marriage whenever it has been concluded in accordance with Islamic precepts.[4]

1 A marriage without registration is locally referred to as *nikah sirri*.

2 Interview with Abdullah, November 2017.

3 It is worth noting that, in the old KK version, the date of marriage was not mentioned.

4 Nurlaelawati, *Modernization, Tradition and Identity: The Kompilasi Hukum Islam and Legal Practice in the Indonesian Religious Courts*, 202–203.

 | DOI:10.1163/9789004516113_008

Given this choice, instead of proposing an *isbat nikah*, Abdullah opted to apply for marriage registration at the KUA. This meant that he would have a newly registered marriage date, erasing any prior marital relationship between him and his wife. Abdullah had no concerns or the least objection to the new date of marriage, although it would give consequences, particularly on the legal position of their children. The children cannot state the names of both parents on their birth certificates because, as far as the bureaucracy is concerned, they were born before the registration of their parent's marriage. Welchman remarks that one distinct manifestation of the bureaucratisation and the centralisation of the state authority against what the Sharīʿa postulates in marriage is the validity or otherwise of acts performed in accordance with traditional law but in violation of state law. Registration serves several objectives, principally extending state control over the private affairs of citizens.[5]

Abdullah's experience illuminates the array of problems plaguing the state-citizen relationship in contemporary Indonesia. Their possession of a KK allows Abdullah's family to enjoy certain benefits from the state. However, the legal status as husband and wife on the KK was not sufficient to meet the requirements for *ḥajj* documentation. Harbitz and Boekle-Giuffrida remark that "every day in any given country around the world, individuals are denied access to fundamental services and rights because they cannot present positive proof of identity."[6]

In short, Abdullah needed a marriage certificate from the KUA to obtain a *ḥajj* visa. It was actually not Abdullah who was in need of a marriage certificate because he could have applied for a *ḥajj* visa on his own. However, since he wanted to go together with his wife, it was actually his wife who needed a legal marriage certificate. According to Saudi Arabian regulations, any woman under the age of 45 who wants to apply for a *ḥajj* visa needs to indicate by whom she will be accompanied (*yurāfiquhā*) as her male guardian (*maḥram*).[7] In this case, this role was obviously to be assumed by Abdullah, but since he was not officially registered as her husband, this was impossible.

One interesting point emerging from this story is that Abdullah used the KK—showing his status as married—to apply for marriage registration. The responsible authority at the KUA was aware of this anomalous situation, yet

---

5 See Welchman, *Women and Muslim Family Laws in Arab States: A Comparative Overview of Textual Development and Advocacy*, 53.

6 Mia Harbitz and Bettina Boekle-Giuffrida, *Democratic Governance, Citizenship, and Legal Identity* (New York, 2009), 5.

7 Saudia.com, *Hajj Visa*, https://www.saudia.com/before-flying/travel-information/hajj-and-umrah/hajj-visa?sv_lang=en&sv_cn=ID

proceeded with the registration. I shared this case with a close friend of mine who is a *penghulu* in another town and he responded spontaneously "*KUAnya harus ditegur itu*" (the KUA should be rebuked). He argued that the KUA was obliged to reject Abdullah's application and should have encouraged him to go to the Islamic court to request an *isbat nikah*.[8] I also tried to obtain clarification on this decision with a person from the KUA, who said: "We just wanted to help him. It was a pity that he should have to go to court because this takes money and time. Abdullah only needed an official marriage certificate."[9] For Abdullah, the expedient of registering his marriage at the KUA meant having to spend less money and being assisted more efficiently than if he had gone to the Islamic court.

2 Why Legalising an Unregistered Marriage?

There has been a widespread public assumption that assuring the legal status of marriage is important to the protection of rights to state services for family members and, more widely, to ensuring public order. Marriage registration means that women and their children are entitled to state services and protected by law against the disadvantageous consequences of a divorce or a husband's death, such as being unable to claim alimony and maintenance. However, it appears that Abdullah was not interested in the legal validity of a marriage. All he wanted was state recognition of his marriage, in the form of a marriage certificate, purely and simply to be able to go to Mecca.

In his case, marriage registration sounds as if it is a purely administrative affair. Nonetheless, it has a wider dimension. A marriage certificate is part of a person's legal identity. In Abdullah's case, possession of a marriage certificate was the solution he needed so that he and his wife could go on the *ḥajj*. However, from the state perspective, when he registered his marriage Abdullah clearly (re)negotiated his sense of self as a citizen.[10] In day-to-day reality, the absence of proof of legal identity can disqualify a citizen from access to rights or state protection. Legal identity is as much about being a citizen as about one's sense of belonging and ability to exercise his or her rights and obligations.[11]

---

8 Interview with Pak Multazam, a *penghulu* in Jember.

9 Interview with Pak Zaki, a KUA official in Sumbersari.

10 Deepta Chopra, Philippa Williams, and Bhaskar Vira, "Politics of Citizenship: Experiencing State-Society Relations from the Margins," *Contemporary South Asia* 19, no. 3 (2011): 243.

11 Harbitz and Boekle-Giuffrida, *Democratic Governance, Citizenship, and Legal Identity*, 5.

Consequently, legal identity influences citizenship. Following Van Klinken, I wish to emphasise that citizenship develops in relation to the specific way the state and local societies reshape each other.[12]

For Abdullah, and many other Indonesians, religious legitimacy which constitutes the social acceptance of a marriage is more important than state recognition.[13] Sonneveld has remarked that, from a legal point of view, it is not difficult to differentiate between formal marriages and informal marriages.[14] However, from a social perspective, the difference is hardly visible. Platt confirms this statement when she argues that, where the reach of the state is limited, marriage remains largely a community-based affair.[15] Bedner and Huis also claim that, in West Java, state recognition of a marriage is considered unimportant from a social perspective.[16]

On the law-making level, debates about family law in Muslim majority countries have paid great attention to the matter of how the state should deal with religious norms. By contrast, when it comes to marriage registration, my observation on the grassroots level in Pasuruan villages shows that these issues revolve around the significance of the state recognition of marriages which have been accorded social recognition based on community-based legal norms, which in turn are grounded in religion. This begs the question of in what ways is the legal validity of marriage relevant? This is the core of this chapter. I argue that state recognition of a marriage cannot entirely substitute community-based legal norms. The state's ideas of recognition and protection might diverge quite sharply from what people imagine. For Abdullah, registration served as legitimate proof that he could use it to claim certain rights. This reflects an emic point of view in which the local people of Sumbersari, Pasuruan, refer to the notions of *keperluan* (necessity) or *sedang butuh* (in need).

Nowadays Indonesia offers an array of mechanisms to which people can resort to be able to adjust their situation so that it dovetails with the state framework. When it issues legal documents, the state is aiming to protect cer-

12 Gerry van Klinken, "Citizenship and Local Practices of Rule in Indonesia," *Citizenship Studies* 22, no. 2 (2018): 114.

13 In Java, and in Indonesia in general, marriage is performed according to the social norm which in practice involves informal religious leaders. Living together outside wedlock is a taboo. The local belief is that the extent to which a marriage is valid merely depends on whether it has been concluded in conformity with Islamic law.

14 Sonneveld, "Rethinking the Difference Between Formal and Informal Marriages in Egypt."

15 Platt, *Marriage, Gender and Islam in Indonesia: Women Negotiating Informal Marriage, Divorce and Desire*, 5.

16 Bedner and van Huis, "Plurality of Marriage Law and Marriage Registration for Muslims in Indonesia: A Plea for Pragmatism," 187.

tain rights, in particular those of women. However, providing certain people with a legal document is only possible if state marriage functionaries are sympathetic to and flexible in implementing the regulation.[17] To a certain degree, they have to come up with discretionary policies and are prepared to commit legal transgressions. When they do this, these functionaries feel privileged to be able to help people obtain their due right to state services. This explains why Abdullah's submission for marriage registration was accepted. This situation necessarily relates to the 1980 work by Michael Lipsky. His book *Street-level bureaucracy: Dilemmas of the individual in public services* is meaningful as it examines the behaviour of frontline workers in policy delivery agencies. He refers to these frontline workers as 'street-level bureaucrats.' They are public employees whose job is to cope directly with citizens and they are permitted considerable discretion in the implementation of their work.[18] Certainly their job is to implement public policies but, at the same time, they have to respond to citizens' requirements on the basis of a limited amount of information or time in which to make a decision.[19]

The attitudes adopted by state agencies are necessarily based on the local situation. In an interview, Haji Hamim, a village religious official, said, "*di sini belum tertib, masih kocar-kacir*" (documentation here is not yet well organised, it is still a mess).[20] While the head of the KUA said, "*di sini sulit, karena* (*mohon maaf*) SDM [sumber daya manusia] *masyarakat sini kurang*" (It is not easy here because (I do apologise) local human resources are not yet up to scratch). The variety of problems that arise from legal documents has to have been subject to discretion and negotiation. This negotiation has also turned out to be a means by which informal marriage functionaries can maintain their vital position. In these sorts of situations, citizens' rights are somehow constituted by the intervention of these informal leaders. In their work, Berenschot and Van Klinken have underlined the importance of informal connections in the shaping of state-citizen interactions.[21] Bedner and Van Huis have dealt with this issue too.[22] They have emphasised the pragmatism which inevitably underlies a situation in which state officials prioritise the interests of the weaker party.

17 Lipsky, *Street-Level Bureaucracy: Dilemmas of the Individual in Public Services*, 105.

18 Ibid., 3.

19 Lars Tummers and Victor Bekkers, "Policy Implementation, Street-Level Bureaucracy, and the Importance of Discretion," *Public Management Review* 16, no. 4 (2014): 527–547.

20 Interview with Haji Hamim, a *modin* in Sumbersari, February 2017.

21 Ward Berenschot and Gerry van Klinken, "Informality and Citizenship: The Everyday State in Indonesia," *Citizenship Studies* 22, no. 2 (2018): 95–111.

22 Bedner and van Huis, "Plurality of Marriage Law and Marriage Registration for Muslims in Indonesia: A Plea for Pragmatism."

This chapter demonstrates how state recognition of marriage works. It will address the different ways people strategize to obtain state recognition of their marriage and examine the ways the state accords the recognition they crave. Through extensive observation at the KUA and a close reading of marriage registration documents, I have managed to identify the kind of administrative transgressions to which a marriage registrar resorts. In addition to my investigations at the KUA, I also analysed conversations in Islamic courtrooms and the legal reasoning used by Islamic judges in cases of marriage legalisation and the legitimation of children.

The following section deals with the theoretical framework of this chapter. Section 3 on legal identity and citizens' rights is especially relevant in approaching the issues arising from marriage registration. Section 4 is concerned with administrative transgressions in marriage registration in the KUA. Section 5 examines the ways Islamic court handles cases of marriage legalisation. Section 6 elucidates the roles of Islamic courts in the case of the legitimation of children. Section 7 concludes.

3 Legal Identity and Citizens' Rights

Legal identity has become an important issue in Indonesia over the last few years. According to the Institute on Statelessness and Inclusion, legal identity is defined as: "a set of elements and characteristics, the combination of which is unique to every person, which defines each person and governs their relationship, obligations and rights under both private and public law."[23] In simple terms, it refers to the recognition of an individual as a person before the law. Recognition of legal identity often depends on individual possession of valid legal identity documentation or other forms of proof of legal identity. The United Nations has incorporated legal identity into the Sustainable Development Goal (SDG). Goal 16 emphasises the promotion of peaceful and inclusive societies, which will encourage sustainable development and the protection of access to justice for all.

Because legal identity is an important starting point in realising personal rights, human rights activists pay great attention to the term of legal identity. In Indonesia, a number of human rights and international donor organisations have launched a campaign to bring home the importance of legal

23 The Insitute on Statelessness and Inclusion, *Sustainable Development Goal 16.9: "Legal Identity", Nationality & Statelessness* (London: Institute on Statelessness and Inclusion, 2018), 7.

identity. One is the Australia Indonesia Partnership for Justice (AIPJ). For a couple of years now, the AIPJ has been focusing on the problem of the absence of legal identity documents, which can limit access to civil rights and services. Some of their contributions were incorporated into the law of Population Administration 23/2006. Hence for the last fourteen years, the state has had a national reference for population administration and civil registration.

Studies about legal identity are closely connected to the problem of statelessness. This is a problem worldwide. Millions of people are stateless and an estimated 1.1 billion lack legal identity documentation. Having to live undocumented lives or without effective citizenship prevents them from reaching their full human potential as they are cut off from access to healthcare, education and other services. Making sure that every individual is recognised as belonging and capable of accessing the documents to prove their legal status is important. Documents like birth certificates serve as foundational proof of citizenship. Marriage certificates are another inseparable proof of legal identity.

Although marriage registration and citizenship are two distinct concerns and represent different fields of enquiry, they are fundamentally related to one another. Both are about the recognition of a particular status of its subject by the state. Citizenship concerns the relationship between the state and its citizens. It is of utmost importance because it provides citizens with a sense of identity which enables them to exercise a wide range of basic social, economic and political rights. Without a doubt, people's participation in acquiring legal identity has been important in enhancing the quality of citizenship in post-*reformasi* Indonesia.

An abundance of scholarly works has underlined the rise in citizens' rights in the wake of the collapse of the Soeharto regime in 1998. Its fall paved the way for democratisation and a series of decentralisation reforms, which extended greater autonomy to local governments and introduced bureaucratic reform. This change seemed to offer great opportunities to transform public administration and public service. The issuance of a series of laws such as the Presidential Regulation 81/2010 on bureaucratic reform and Law 25/2009 on public service has marked this transformation. However, we know that citizenship in Indonesia was, and is, being challenged by the rise of a wave of religious, ethnic and regional identity politics.[24] *Reformasi* in 1998 has allegedly intensified these fragmented identities.

---

24 Henk Schulte Nordholt, "Identity Politics, Citizenship and the Soft State in Indonesia: An Essay," *Journal of Indonesian Social Sciences and Humanities* 1 (2008): 1–21.

I should argue that the desire of the state to protect its citizens' rights has made marriage registration increasingly effective. The insistence by the state that possession of proof of legal identity defines certain rights gives people with limited choices a chance. People can argue that the state validity of a marriage does not necessarily improve the validity and social acceptability of a religious marriage. However, the current problem does not lie in whether the marriage is valid, but in the extent to which a citizen can claim rights from a marriage. The absence of legal identity could disqualify a citizen from access to rights. Here, linking in with my argument in Chapter 1, a rights-to-obtain-the-state-services approach has been effective in changing people's ideas about accepting the state's orientation. Importantly, this approach circumvents the necessity for the state to speak out on religious issues concerning marriage, in which it might have to challenge religious authorities.

4 Administrative Transgressions in Marriage Registration

Besides demonstrating the insoluble relationship between legal identity and citizenship, Abdullah's case also reflects the degree of pragmatism practised in the field. My close reading of marriage registration documents has uncovered what can be called a kind of administrative transgression resorted to by *penghulus*. The importance of administrative transgression was apparent in the everyday functioning of the marriage bureaucracy at the KUA.

To understand how administrative transgression works at the KUA, it is helpful to have a picture of the marriage registration procedure. In 1990, the Minister issued a regulation setting out the obligations of the marriage registrar.[25] This regulation maintained the requirement that an oral application for a marriage is made. More than a decade later, the Decree of the Minister of Religion 298/2003 signified major changes as it re-standardised the documents for marriage registration previously required. This Decree can be considered the first regulation to use the term *pencatatan nikah* (marriage registration), although it was amended a year later by the Decree of the Minister of Religion 477/2004.[26] Currently, marriage registration is undertaken on the basis of the Regulation of the Minister of Religion 11/2007 on marriage registration. The regulations of 2004 and 2007 stipulated that a marriage application must be submitted in written form. It set out the requisite documents as follows:

---

25 PMA No. 2/1990 tentang Kewajiban Pegawai Pencatat Nikah (the obligations of marriage registrar).

26 KMA No. 477/2004 tentang Pencatatan Nikah (marriage registration).

- Letters from the village administration which give the personal details of the bride (*keterangan untuk nikah* or Model N1), the bride's and the groom's origin (*keterangan asal usul* or Model N2) and the details of the parents (*keterangan orang tua* or Model N4).
- Application for marriage submitted in a letter (Model N7)
- Letters confirming the spouses' consent (*persetujuan mempelai* or model N3).
- A letter of permission from the parents if the ages of the bride and groom are under 21 (Model N5).
- If the bride is a widow (or the groom is a widower), she (or he) has to submit a death certificate (Model N6).

In Sumbersari society, as I mentioned in the previous chapter, the administrative side of marriage registration is handled by a *modin*. He takes all the documents to the KUA; rarely do the ordinary people come to the KUA themselves. They attend only if the KUA invites them. This invitation is extended after the KUA official has verified their documents. Sometimes, a complication arising from the verification process means that the couples have to personally attend the KUA office. According to the Regulation of the Minister of Religion 11/2007, marriage registration generally requires five steps: submission of a proposal for marriage registration, document assessment, an announcement of the marriage ceremony, marriage ceremony (*akad nikah*) and the signing of the marriage certificate (*penandatanganan akta nikah*). The second step, the process known locally as *rafak* (*pemeriksanaan*, observation) is crucial. The *rafak* is conducted to examine the conformity of the data written on the forms with the documents enclosed. This term is understood and used differently in other areas in Java. In Central Java, *rafak* means a divorce initiated by the wife.[27]

To support the validity of all the forms, the bride has to enclose certain documents, namely an identity card and a birth certificate or a diploma. In Sumbersari, not all brides have a birth certificate, among other reasons, because of the legal status of their parents' marriage. In this case, a birth certificate can be replaced by a diploma. So, a diploma can substitute for other missing documents.

At this point, it is worth mentioning that the number of marriage registrations in Sumbersari has escalated dramatically since 2010. It is safe to assume that, before that year, numerous marriages went unregistered. The limited number of documents available for examination made it hard to determine

27 Hisako Nakamura, *Perceraian Orang Jawa: Studi Tentang Pemutusan Perkawinan Di Kalangan Orang Islam Jawa* (Yogyakarta: Gadjah Mada University Press, 1990), 66.

who was qualified to act as the *wali* (marriage guardian). In interviews, the head of KUA Sumbersari complained about the validity of the *wali* as written on the form. He pointed out that in some cases the *modin* had been slapdash about this. He was worried about how it was possible to know if someone was a proper *wali* according to Islamic law, saying:

> If someone else were to take over my position, he might not be acquainted with the area. Imagine you are the head of the KUA and you do not know that a particular person is the proper *wali* of the bride? A birth certificate is no guarantee. The only document you can refer to is a copy of the parents' marriage certificate. This cannot lie. The parents are noted on the N2 form and the N4 form. But, how can this be proved? In Surabaya, the marriage certificate of the parents must be handed in.

The problem of the *wali* is one that often arises. Let me explain the first case to unravel the problem. Aisya is a daughter of Muhdor and Maimunah, born in a marriage that was not registered. The marriage, which took place in early 2000, was not her first marriage for Maimunah because she was a widow. Aisya attached her family's KK and a diploma in her application for marriage registration. The KK had been issued years ago. In the KK, Muhdor was listed as the head of the household and Maimunah as his wife. Since the government has changed its policy, nowadays, this confusion is unlikely to happen: if a family cannot present a marriage certificate at the civil registration office, the legal status of the parents must be registered as *belum kawin* (unmarried). The mother appears as the head of the household and the husband appears in the bottom row as *lainnya* (the other). Therefore, the status of Muhdor as the head of household does not automatically guarantee his position as Aisya's biological father in the KK because of the absence of the marriage certificate. According to the KK, Aisya is fatherless. Her diploma also mentions only the name of her mother.[28]

In the marriage application forms submitted to the KUA, she was required to mention her father, who would also serve as her *wali*. On account of the ambiguous position of her father, Aisya was invited to come to the KUA to have *rafak* (pemeriksaan). As Aisya did not have a marriage certificate for her parents, the *modin* provided Aisya with two letters from the village administration. The first was a letter declaring the marital relationship between her father and

28 It is interesting to note that the newest version of the KK now includes the date of the marriage ceremony. It would be impossible for couples in an unregistered marriage to manipulate the data in the KK as happened in the solution to Muhdor's problem.

her mother was valid according to Islamic law. The second was a letter that declared that Muhdor was her biological father who had the right to marry her off. These letters did the trick. At this point, we see how an administrative transgression proved an important element in coping with cases that fell outside the box. As a street-level bureaucrat, the *penghulu*'s position is critical, as he plays a crucial role in settling problems arising from these citizen entitlements. He either directly provides public benefits through the services he offers or mediates between citizens.[29] The immediacy of a change in policy in his interaction with citizens and its impact on people's lives is of vital importance.[30] The head of the KUA went ahead with the marriage registration on the basis of letters that should not have existed according to the standard procedure. Bedner and Van Huis have remarked that the bureaucrats on the lowest levels of state administration play crucial roles in providing documentation for those who do not qualify.[31]

Administrative transgression also came into play in Abdullah's case. As I claimed earlier, according to Indonesian law, the KUA has no authority to legalise a marriage which had been concluded earlier but had not been registered. This authority is the prerogative of the Islamic court. Although he must have been aware of this, the head of the KUA chose to exercise his discretion and agreed to register the marriage. At the time, because the KK had their status as *kawin* (married), the KUA asked Abdullah to declare on paper that he had never registered his marriage before. Abdullah asked the village administration to issue the required letter. The letter declared that Abdullah had never registered his marriage at any KUA office and, therefore, under the provisions of the marriage law, his legal status was *perjaka* (unmarried). Of course, this letter contradicts the legal status written in the KK.

Yet another transgression was committed in the case of Syamsul. Syamsul's problem arose from his divergent birthdates. The *penghulu*s ensured a synchronisation of dates. Interestingly, these dates were not necessarily based on the real situation. When there is a conflict of data, the validity of the data is usually based on other data obtained from a diploma. The argument was that it is uncommon to change the data on a diploma, but it is not that difficult to change the data in the civil registration documents as long as another legal proof can be produced. Since the government implemented the NIK (Nomor Induk Kepen-

29 Lipsky, *Street-Level Bureaucracy: Dilemmas of the Individual in Public Services*, 6.

30 Ibid., 8.

31 Bedner and van Huis, "Plurality of Marriage Law and Marriage Registration for Muslims in Indonesia: A Plea for Pragmatism," 187.

SURAT PERNYATAAN BELUM PERNAH MENCATATKAN PERNIKAHAN

Yang bertanda tangan di bawah ini saya :

1. Nama lengkap dan alias :
2. Bin :
3. Tempat dan tanggal lahir : Pasuruan, 15 April 1974
4. Nomor Induk Kependudukan :
5. Warga Negara : Indonesia
6. Agama : Islam
7. Pekerjaan : Wiraswasta
8. Tempat tinggal :

Bersama ini menyatakan dengan sebenarnya bahwa saya sampai saat ini benar benar belum pernah mencatatkan pernikahan saya di kantor urusan agama manapun, dan menurut undang undang perkawinan saya masih berstatus : *Jejaka*

Apabila di kemudian hari ada pihak lain maupun keluarga yang mempermasalahkan pencatatan pernikahan saya, maka saya akan mempertanggung jawabkannya sendiri serta akan menanggung segala akibatnya dan tidak akan melibatkan pihak lain maupun pejabat terkait/instansi manapun.

Demikian Surat pernyataan ini saya buat dengan sebenarnya dan tanpa ada paksaan dari pihak manapun, dan apabila dikemudian hari ternyata tidak benar maka saya bersedia di tuntut sesuai Hukum yang berlaku

Pasuruan, 13 April 2017

Mengetahui
Kepala Desa

Yang Menyatakan

FIGURE 14 A letter from the village administration declaring that a person is not legally married.

dudukan, single identity number) policy, the validity of the data has become a crucial issue. To give an example, now a parent cannot easily change the birthdate of their son or daughter to obfuscate child marriage to ensure qualification for marriage registration, because the KUA official will check his/her birthdate in the civil administration office database. So, if he wants to pursue his nefarious purpose, he has to make the change at the civil administration office by presenting reasonable arguments and adequate evidence to convince the officials there to do so. For this reason, since 2015, the NIK of a couple and the *wali* is written on the marriage certificate and the KK also mentions the marriage date. Below is empirical evidence of this practice.

Syamsul was born in 1993. However, the KK and his diploma gave different versions of his birthdate. I clarified this with the *modin* and he said that neither version was legally valid. The birthdate on the diploma had been noted by the teacher at primary school because Syamsul's parents had not submitted a birth certificate when he was first registered; the birthdate in the KK had been entered by the parents. When he wanted to marry, Syamsul referred to the birthdate written on his diploma. This case suggests that a citizen can use marriage registration as an opportunity to synchronise all his or her personal details. This attitude is quite common among villagers. They usually come to the civil administration office to affirm their marital status as 'married,' and take the opportunity to adjust the names and birthdates according to the marriage certificate.

This section has shown the importance of a marriage certificate as a means of proving legal identity. However, because of the complexity of the documents required to obtain a marriage certificate, from time to time, *penghulu*s have to commit an administrative transgression and turn a judicious blind eye. This transgression is an impromptu solution to a particular situation that has escaped the regulations. *Penghulu*s execute a degree of autonomy and transform it into policy. In the following section, we turn to the way in which marriage registration is dealt with in Islamic courts. Does transgression take place there too?

5 *Isbat Nikah* by Islamic Courts

In the previous section, I paid attention to the roles played by *penghulu*s and the KUA in marriage registration. We have seen how transgression is important in dealing with anomalies in the documentation required for marriage registration. Without this transgression, marriage registration would not be possible. Regardless of this solution, as I mentioned earlier, people in marriages that have not been sanctioned by state legality can request retrospective legitimisation by applying for *isbat nikah* from the Islamic court. This section will elucidate how *isbat nikah* works. In the Bangil Islamic court, *isbat nikah* appears to be a very workable solution for people who need to declare the legal status of their children, but it is not the only solution. In the case of Abdullah above, he did manage to register his unregistered marriage at the KUA. If he had just wanted to have state recognition for his children, he could have opted for the judicial instrument known as the legalisation of children's status (*asal usul anak*). An explanation of this child's legitimation follows.

There are varied reasons people might have not registered for their marriage. Any correlations with economic or other factors, such as access to the office, are not very convincing. No one would that dispute that marriage registration is not affordable. In Sumbersari, the KUA is located at the heart of the sub-district and it is not that difficult to access the office. As far as I could see, almost all first marriages are registered because they are handled by *modins*. Most of the time, non-registration arises in cases of remarriage. If we look at the data in Sumbersari in 2015, 78 percent of all marriages were first marriages, while 22 percent were remarriages for either one or both spouses. In 2016, the data indicates pretty much the same number. First marriages made up 77 percent of all marriages, while 23 percent were remarriages. My materials indicate that 67 percent in 2016 and 77 percent in 2017 of all remarriages were between people who had been divorced. In 2017 33 percent in 2016 and 23 percent in 2017 were of people whose previous spouse was deceased.[32]

The Marriage Law stipulates that women cannot register a remarriage as long as their divorce from their first husband has not been processed by the court. Although people now often register their first marriage, they fail to go through the relatively complicated process of judicial divorce when they break up. Consequently, under state law, they are still married to the spouse from whom they have divorced in a socially accepted manner. On this basis, we can conclude that unregistered marriage is influenced by two factors. Firstly, if one of the spouses has a legal reason not to register, this will almost certainly be the absence of a divorce decree. Secondly, local norms pertaining to the legality of marriage derive predominantly from religious doctrine, and this contributes to the reason certain marriages are not registered. It seems that there is no urgency to register a remarriage as long as it has conformed to Islamic principles and, hence, is socially acceptable.

The Kompilasi regards marriage registration merely as an administrative obligation but does emphasise the solid legal status of marriage when it is registered. The legal draftsmen have included an article on *isbat nikah*. This article was included to help those who had not yet registered their marriage as required by the marriage law when it came into force.[33] In practice, however, because the formulation of the provision in the Kompilasi is ambiguous, judges

32 This data is collected from SIMKAH KUA Sumbersari.

33 Bedner and van Huis, "Plurality of Marriage Law and Marriage Registration for Muslims in Indonesia: A Plea for Pragmatism," 187.

also apply this legal norm to legalise marriages that occurred after 1974 retrospectively. Article 7 (2) of the Kompilasi states "In the context of marriages that do not have a marriage certificate, one can ask for an *isbat nikah*." The Kompilasi then explains the types of marriages eligible for *isbat nikah*. These conditions are: a) a marriage in which the spouses are seeking a divorce; b) the loss of a marriage certificate; c) doubts about whether or not a marriage is valid; d) a marriage concluded prior to the 1974 Marriage Law; and e) a marriage concluded by those who have no legal impediment according to the Marriage Law. Nurlaelawati has noted that these provisions are phrased ambiguously and are indecisive about who is qualified for registration by the Islamic court. She argues that the loose implementation of the marriage registration provisions contradicts the stated goal of marriage registration itself because non-registration can easily be registered retroactively.[34]

5.1 *Polygynous Marriage*

In the Bangil Islamic court, there is an irrefutable correlation between *isbat nikah* and legal identity. *Isbat nikah* appears to present a workable solution for those wishing to claim a legal identity for their children. Almost all *isbat nikah* cases are driven by the need to obtain children's birth certificates. This is what happened to Pak Salim. He works as an official in the village administration. Pak Salim was married to Samsia in June 1990 but the marriage was not performed before a marriage registrar. It was actually not the first marriage for Pak Salim. In short, this was unregistered polygyny. Pak Salim, who has a son with Samsia, wanted to claim legal status for his child as he thought that his son had the potential to make a good career. In fact, he was planning to apply for the military and needed a birth certificate mentioning the names of both his parents (*asal usul*). In the absence of the marriage certificate of his parents, the son could actually apply for a birth certificate, but it would only mention the name of his mother. This is definitely not enough for the requirements demanded when applying for a position as a civil servant or joining the military.

In his hour of need, Pak Salim turned to a *modin* to help him. The *modin* suggested he request an *isbat nikah* from the Islamic court. Of course, this contravened the conditions enshrined in the Kompilasi. The purpose of *isbat nikah* is not to legalise a polygynous marriage. Nevertheless, the *modin* went ahead with all the necessary arrangements to make this mission possible. A letter of application (*surat permohonan*) was drawn up to expedite this purpose. In the

34 Nurlaelawati, *Modernization, Tradition and Identity: The Kompilasi Hukum Islam and Legal Practice in the Indonesian Religious Courts*, 202–203.

letter, the status of both Salim and Samsia is declared to be unmarried (*perjaka* or *perawan*). The letter clearly states that the applicants need a marriage certificate to have the legal certainty (*kepastian hukum*) that they could use it to apply for the birth certificate of their son. Pak Salim also included a letter from the village head declaring that their marriage had never been registered before.

I asked the *modin* who assisted Pak Salim why he had acted as he did as the matter involved a polygynous marriage. The *modin* argued that proposing to obtain an *isbat nikah* of the marriage would serve the bigger *maṣlaḥa*. He backed up his statement by associating *isbat nikah* with an Islamic legal maxim: If many *maṣlaḥa* contradict one another, the one offering the greatest benefits should be prioritised. If many wrongs contradict each other, the lesser of these evils should be given priority.[35] The legal status of polygyny should be accorded less significance because legalising the marriage would bring a bigger benefit. He was well aware that Pak Salim's son required his parents' marriage certificate so that he could have a birth certificate mentioning the names of both his parents.

Most court hearings are usually quite short, around 15–20 minutes, and the judgement is read out directly at the end of the hearing. However, perhaps because I was attending the hearing, the judges tended to stick to the procedure more strictly. The hearing was then adjourned for a week before being reconvened to hear the result of the *musyawarah majlis* (judge deliberation). This hearing was presided over by three judges, one of whom was female. In the court hearing, the judges asked Pak Salim about how the marriage had been concluded. He explained that it had been conducted by Ustad Syafi'i in the presence of Samsia's father, the *wali* and two witnesses. The judges also asked about Pak Salim's relationship with Samsia, specifically if they had a degree of consanguinity that made it unlawful for them to have sexual intercourse. In Islamic law, this relationship is known as *maḥram*, a person that is not permitted to marry due to a close blood relationship. It delineates the prohibited degrees of consanguinity within which marriage or sexual intercourse would be considered illegal. Pak Salim replied that they did not. The judges also asked them if the marriage would have no social consequences and that no one would have any objection if their marriage were legalised. Again, Pak Salim answered that the marriage was fine as far as the local people were concerned.

Pak Salim presented two witnesses to support his claim. The night before, the *modin* had coached them on potential questions and the answers they needed to give. The judges invited them to enter the courtroom one by one. After they

---

35 Interview with Haji Misbah, January 2019.

had taken the oath, the judges asked about their identity and their relationship with the applicants. After this, the judges asked if they had known about and attended the marriage at the time it was concluded. They answered in the affirmative. The judges moved on to the next stage, which was asking them if they thought the marriage would cause any social problems. They also verified if there was no close kinship relationship between the applicants. This was followed by questions about the religious status of the applicants; whether or not they were converts to Islam. Although the legal status of the applicants had been registered as unmarried, the judges still questioned them about their marital status. The witnesses said that both Pak Salim and Samsia were unmarried. This prevarication meant that the witnesses were hiding the fact that it was a second marriage for Pak Salim. Eventually, both witnesses convinced the judges that the right decision was to legalise Pak Salim's marriage because he needed the marriage certificate to acquire the birth certificate of his son.

This application was finally accepted.[36] A week later, the judges declared that there was no conflict between all the information given by the applicants and the witnesses. The decision asserted that the marriage had been conducted according to both Islamic law and national law, had no relationship with other marriages and had not been concluded within the period of *ʿidda* (waiting period). It then affirmed that the family had led a harmonious existence and that a son had been born. As its legal basis, the decision mentions Article 2 of the Marriage Law which states marriage is valid when it has been concluded according to the religious requirements of the parties involved. The decision also referred to Article 14 of the Kompilasi on the conditions of marriage to declare that the marriage had met all the requisite conditions. To strengthen its legitimacy, the decision also referred to the Shāfiʿī classical treatise on *fiqh*.[37]

An important point is the judges pragmatically used article 7 (3) point e of the Kompilasi to approve the claim. In most *isbat nikah* verdicts, point e acts as legal consideration for judges. As long as the marriage is proved to have been concluded between people who have no legal impediment to their matrimony, the judges must accept it. Indonesian legal scholars have problematised this

36 Verdict no. 0091/Pdt.P/2018/PA.Bgl.

37 This fact confirms Nurlaelawati's finding that, in the judicial practice of Islamic courts, a *fiqh* book is important in the decision making. She claims that some judges argue that, because the Kompilasi has not been accorded statutory status, its legal position is the same as that of the *fiqh* books. In this reference to the *fiqh* books, the judges seem to have elevated the Kompilasi to the status of an unwritten source, like that of the *fiqh* books, and they feel that the *fiqh* books embrace a more certain legal position. Nurlaelawati, *Modernization, Tradition and Identity: The Kompilasi Hukum Islam and Legal Practice in the Indonesian Religious Courts*, 163.

point because they see it as conflicting.[38] Point d clearly sets the limits for *isbat nikah* at marriages concluded prior to the legal obligation of marriage registration coming into force. The Law of Islamic court also limits *isbat nikah* to marriages before 1974. However, in this case, the verdict ignored this limitation and sought confirmation by citing article 7 (3) point e of the Kompilasi. Point e opens the door for all marriages, without any restrictions, to request an *isbat nikah*. The judges used this 'ambiguous' point to legitimate their decision.

The verdict also argues that unregistered marriages cause severe problems in society. Interestingly, the decision also relates the claim to the problems of citizenship and child protection. In this particular instance, the judges also used Law 23/2002 on Child Protection to legitimate their decision. The elucidation of this Law states that parents, family and society are responsible for protecting children and providing facilities for them. It was drawn up with the idea of ensuring the best life for children so as to make them potentially, capable citizens whose nationalism is based on good behaviour. The judges concurred with the reason submitted by the applicant that the *isbat nikah* was required to seek a birth certificate, presented as a guarantee of the protection of a child. Quite clearly, the judges incorporated citizens' rights into their judicial practice.

The accommodation of citizens' rights in the judicial decision has been a matter of heated debate among scholars. Judicial practice in Islamic courts in Indonesia has undergone significant changes. Although Van Huis looks at the decline of the *fiqh* tradition, that is *khulʿ* (the wife pays compensation to the husband for a divorce) in the legal practice of divorce in Islamic courts,[39] he does not overlook the fact that *fiqh*-based divorce mechanisms can still play a significant role. This finding is quite similar to Nurlaelawati's study in which she found the judges are committed to *fiqh* as the right and proper means to secure a religious identity. Nevertheless, Van Huis suggests that most of the elements in current wife-petitioned judicial divorces have their roots in the *syiqaq* divorce mechanism, not in *khulʿ* as practised in the past. Both the Supreme Court and the Law on Islamic courts interpret the meaning of the phrase 'continuous and irreconcilable marital discord' in a manner close to that of *syiqaq*.

In the Bangil Islamic court, *isbat nikah* cases are few and far between. There were six cases in 2016, none in 2017 and seven in 2018. In interviews, the head

---

38 Euis Nurlaelawati, "Pernikahan Tanpa Pencatatan: Isbat Nikah Sebuah Solusi?," *Musâwa* 12, no. 2 (2013): 261–277.

39 Stijn Cornelis van Huis, "Khulʿ over the Longue Durée: The Decline of Traditional Fiqh-Based Divorce Mechanisms in Indonesian Legal Practice," *Journal of Islamic Law* 25, no. 2 (2018): 1–25.

of Bangil Islamic court said: "*Kebutuhan masyarakat dilayani saja*" (we are just there to serve the people's needs).[40] He qualifies *isbat nikah* as one of these. He expounded on his view by saying that in principle the court cannot reject applications submitted by members of the society. This attitude raises the problem of whether or not the application is based on sound legal proof and this is if it can be proved that marriage had met the conditions of marriage stipulated by Islamic law. This solution conforms to Rosen's concept which argues that the concept of law is a manifestation of a larger socio-cultural reality, simply referred to as law as a culture.[41] Studying the local Sharīʿa court records (*sijill*) in the city of Sefrou, Morocco, he found that neither the oaths sworn nor the use of professional witnesses was not truly objective, but the outcome of the *qadi*'s construction and the result of a process of negotiation which allows him to make convenient decisions.[42] His finding, therefore, situated the *qadi* in a wider cultural dimension in the city. In Bangil, the judges were perfectly well aware that unregistered marriages are a common practice. The state has no choice but to accord them legal recognition when it is requested. Any application of a strict interpretation of the conditions of *isbat nikah* does not address problems in society. The judges pragmatically implemented article 7 (3) point e of the Kompilasi to accommodate the applicant's wishes.

5.2 *Underage Marriage*

Isbat nikah appears to be a legitimate solution to the legalisation of unregistered marriages. The above case demonstrates how *isbat nikah* was used to legitimise a polygynous marriage. In the following case, we see *isbat nikah* was also an effective instrument in legalising a marriage that contravened the law because the groom was underage. This was a marriage between Hasan (17 years) and Jamilatul (17 years) which took place in January 2013. Although the groom was not yet nineteen which is underage according to state law, his parents did not request a marriage dispensation. Their reason was that the bride was three months pregnant. This pregnancy does not make any sense as a reason, but it is in fact mentioned in the decision. The child was born in June 2013. The couple applied for an *isbat nikah* in early 2014 because they needed to raise the legal status of their daughter. The judges eventually granted legalisation of their marriage. They seemed to ignore the fact that, at the time, Hasan was still underage and not legally eligible to enter into a marriage.

40 Interview with Pak Purnomo, the head of Bangil religious court, January 2019.

41 Lawrence Rosen, *Law as Culture: An Invitation* (Princeton: Princeton University Press, 2006).

42 Rosen, *The Anthropology of Justice: Law as Culture in Islamic Society*.

Article 7 of the Marriage Law provides leeway for those who performed underage marriages to request marriage dispensation. However, there is a tendency in Islamic courts not to make this dispensation too easy to acquire. In my interview with Wahyu Widiana, the former Director-General of Religious Courts under the Supreme Court, he expressly stated that he suggested judges should be stricter in their acceptance of petitions for marriage dispensation. His argument for taking this stance was that, in a normal situation, such a marriage was undesirable. However, as he saw it, besides dispensing justice, Islamic courts should also educate people in legal matters. If for some reason a delay of the marriage is unavoidable, they still have the option to ask for an *isbat nikah*.[43] This view was confirmed by Pak Purnomo, the head of Bangil Islamic court. He argues that Islamic courts are put on the horns of a dilemma when a petition for marriage dispensation is submitted. Nevertheless, the judges are still inundated by complaints from women activists who say that they are far too ready to grant the dispensation. In his view, marriage dispensation should only be granted if the bride has been proven to be pregnant on the basis of a letter from a doctor.[44]

The verdict in this case also problematises whether or not the marriage deserved an *isbat nikah* (retrospective legalisation) because it was concluded in 2013. The verdict begins by emphasising that only marriages conducted before the issuance of the 1974 Marriage Law are eligible for retrospective legalisation, but then proceeds to clarify that article 7 (3) point e in the Kompilasi does open the possibility of legalising all marriages submitted for their consideration. In a nutshell, the verdict declares that such a marriage is eligible for state legal protection. Furthermore, it also confirms that the Law of the Age of Marriage is intended to protect the rights of children as stated in article 3 of Law 3/2002 on Child Protection. The judges were perfectly well aware that legalising a marriage in which the bride is underage violates the law. However, they thought that prioritising the rights of the son was even more important.

Even more interestingly, the judges argued that the absence of an affirmation of the legal age for marriage in classical Islamic law is not an omission. They consider marriage a biological need of humanity, concluded not only on the basis of maturity and logic but to constrain the biological urges of the individual which can be observed from the biological signs of physical maturity. Nevertheless, the fulfilment of the sacred and noble objectives of marriage is a necessity. In this argument, the judges seem to have a tendency towards ambi-

43 Interview with Wahyu Widiana, November 2018.

44 Interview with Pak Purnomo, January 2019.

valence. On the one hand, they are definitely adhering to the state law but, on the other, they are ignoring the marriageable age enshrined in the Marriage Law by proposing arguments from viewpoint of Islamic law. In the end, the judges did accept the application and granted the legalisation of the marriage.

Legal anthropologists emphasise the multiplicity of legal bases and institutions which co-determine the structure, norms and interpretations of the law.[45] *Isbat nikah* provides a space in which judges can exploit the plurality of legal orders.[46] The judges examined 'the dialectic, mutually constitutive relation between state law and other normative orders.'[47] Legal pluralism is justified on pragmatic grounds as a technique of governance.[48] From the decision handed down, we see that the law offers a legitimate frame of reference in which political, economic and legal interests can be defended.[49] The judges also found it important to be able to consult a different legal norm, that is, traditional *fiqh* or theological doctrines. However, this is not to say that the judges were ultra-conservative as they interpreted these sources liberally to support their judgement.

6 Child Legitimation

Is it possible for Abdullah's children who were born before their father's registered marriage to acquire a legal status as a legitimate child? The answer is definitely yes. As I have mentioned earlier, spouses in a marriage which has lately been registered at the KUA can still make an application to have the status of the children legalised. This is pursued through a legal procedure called legitimation of children (*asal usul anak*). I have observed that this tendency has become an alternative solution for those who do not petition for an *isbat nikah* or do so only to have it rejected. The Indonesian judicial system grants the Islamic court the judicial authority to examine and declare the legitimacy of children.[50] In most cases, these children are born in an unregistered marriage.

45 Fernanda Pirie, *The Anthropology of Law* (Oxford: Oxford University Press, 2013).

46 Arskal Salim, "Dynamic Legal Pluralism in Indonesia: Contested Legal Orders in Contemporary Aceh," *Journal of Legal Pluralism and Unofficial Law* 42, no. 61 (2010): 1–29.

47 Sally Merry, "Legal Pluralism," *Law and Society Review* 22 (1988): 869–896.

48 John Griffiths, "What Is Legal Pluralism?," *The Journal of Legal Pluralism and Unofficial Law* 24 (1986): 5.

49 Keebet Von Benda-Beckmann, "Transnational Dimensions of Legal Pluralism," in *Begegnung Und Konflikt—Eine Kulturanthropologische Bestandsaufnahme*, ed. Wolfgang Fikentscher (Munich: C.H. Beck, 2001), 44.

50 See the Elucidation of Law No. 3/2006 on Religious Courts Number 37 point (a).

In the Bangil Islamic court, the number of cases of *asal usul anak* does not differ much from that of *isbat nikah* cases. There were six cases in 2016, eight in 2017, and six in 2018.

In this section, I would like to analyse the legal reasoning applied by judges of Islamic courts in granting a decision in an *asal usul anak* case. In this analysis, I turn to Verdict 230/Pdt.P/2016/Pa.Bgl. The application was submitted by Nizar and Jubaidah.[51] They were married religiously on 30 April 2003 and later had two children. The first child was born in 2005, while the second was born in 2007. On 9 December 2016, they applied for a registered marriage at their local KUA. Bringing with them their children's birth certificates (*surat keterangan kelahiran*) issued by the village administration, they submitted a request for the children to be legitimated by the Bangil Islamic court.

At the time he married Jubaidah, Nizar was informally divorced. Because it was an informal divorce, his marriage to his first wife was still legal according to state law. His first wife petitioned the Islamic court for divorce some months after his remarriage. Some months later, Nizar submitted a request for *isbat nikah* to validate his remarriage to the Bangil Islamic court. The court rejected his request because he could not be recognised as legally divorced. The judges considered his marriage to Jubaidah not a remarriage, but a polygynous marriage. They took only written legal proof into consideration. Their decision meant that Nizar could be married to Jubaidah only if he had permission to enter into a polygynous marriage from the Islamic court. The absence of this permission invalidated his marriage according to statutory law.

It is worth noting that, before the 1974 Marriage Law was implemented, polygynous marriages did not require the permission of an Islamic court. Marriages and polygynous marriages had to be registered, but this registration was just considered an administrative obligation, not a requirement for a valid marriage. In my interviews, one of the judges argued that he and his colleagues often rejected a request for *isbat nikah*. After all, the marriage had been concluded prior to the issuance of a divorce certificate terminating the previous marriage.[52] He acknowledged that this was a tricky situation, especially when it happens to the woman because a wife cannot have two husbands at the same time.

Although *nikah sirri* is not legally recognised in the Indonesian legal system, the judges still thought it important to examine the religious validity of this marriage, to discover whether or not it has been in accordance with Islamic

51 Verdict No. 230/Pdt.P/2016/Pa.Bgl.

52 Interview with Pak Rasid, a judge of Bangil Religious Court, January 2018.

law. The judges asked the parents, Nizar and Jubaidah, about who had acted as the marriage guardian, the witnesses and who had attended the marriage ceremony. The trouble they took shows that an unregistered marriage is considered valid by Islamic courts.[53] This examination was undertaken because, despite this case being *voluntair* (petition, *gugatan permohonan*), which did not demand other parties rebut it, the judges were still required to examine whether or not the parties had an adequate reason to petition. Therefore, the judges examined the unregistered marriage and, on the basis of their conclusions, validated it. They did not assess the (second) registered marriage. Van Huis has found that marriage legalisation can be rejected by a Islamic court if the said marriage fails to meet the religious requirements.[54]

The judges also asked them the reason they wanted this legitimation of their children. Their verdict states they wanted to acquire the birth certificates of their children. This reason was more than enough for the judges to go ahead with the hearing. The judges referred to article 49 in Law 3/2006 on Islamic courts and its elucidation which states that an Islamic court is authorised to adjudicate this case. The parties presented proof which included letters from the village head declaring the birth of their children. As part of legal reasoning, the judges referred to a Prophetic tradition that asserts "children born are to a man who has a wife (*al-waladu li al-firāsh*) and death by stoning is for indulging in extramarital relations (*wa al-ḥajaru li al-ʿāhir*)." The judges also considered the common good (*maṣlaḥa*) as well as the harm (*ḍarar*) which might ensue in the future if they did not accept this petition.

The judges confirmed the legal status of the children with a reference to article 99 in the Kompilasi which stipulates "a legal child is who is born within or as a consequence of a valid marriage." In another case, the judges also referred to article 103 of the Kompilasi. This article is specifically about *asal usul anak* (the legal origin of the child). It says that *asal usul anak* is proved by a birth certificate. However, in the absence of a birth certificate, the Islamic court might be able to issue a declaration confirming the legal status of a child after examining relevant proof. On the basis of the declaration of the Islamic court, the civil administration can issue a birth certificate.

In this section, I have argued that the legitimation of children is the last resort for a family. The decision made by Islamic courts is essential as it serves

---

53 van Huis and Wirastri, "Muslim Marriage Registration in Indonesia: Revised Marriage Registration Laws Cannot Overcome Compliance Flaws"; van Huis, "Islamic Courts and Women's Divorce Rights in Indonesia: The Cases of Cianjur and Bulukumba," 97.

54 van Huis, "Islamic Courts and Women's Divorce Rights in Indonesia: The Cases of Cianjur and Bulukumba," 228.

as a legitimate basis for the issuance of a birth certificate. No necessary judicial discretion is exercised by the judges during the hearing. They just accept both the letter of birth issued by the village administration and the marriage certificate issued by the KUA as the legal evidence on which to base their decision. In addition, these suggestions put us on safe ground to suggest that the Islamic court has interpreted the 1974 Marriage Law and the 1991 Kompilasi in a relatively liberal way. This progressive stance is believed to have considerable influence on their legal reasoning. It is relevant to relate this situation to Bowen's remarks that gender equality, fairness and consensus-seeking are an integral part of legal reasoning in Indonesia.[55]

7 Conclusion

In this chapter, I have shown some of the different paths villagers can take to legalise their unregistered marriages and their children. It seems that they are not concerned about whether or not their marriages are legally valid according to national laws. As long as the marriage is socially accepted, they feel content. Scholars have emphasised how much more heavily the significance of social acceptance weighs than considerations of state legality.[56] However, they are brought back down to earth about the need for the legalisation of marriage when their children require a birth certificate which cannot be issued without the marriage certificate of their parents. Several paths are open to them.

The first is to have a 'new' marriage ceremony at the KUA in the presence of a *penghulu*. This marriage is usually undertaken solely for the sake of obtaining the marriage certificate and is, of course, meaningless as far as the legal status of the children is concerned. A number of issues pertaining to transgressions are inevitably part and parcel of this process. As street-level bureaucrats, *penghulus* need to exercise their autonomy in drawing up policy in each individual case to enable a particular marriage to be legally recognised. The second path is to seek legalisation by submitting a petition for an *isbat nikah* to the Islamic court. *Isbat nikah* is an important construct to legalise a marriage, a process which would be otherwise impossible according to the standard procedure set out in state law. This category includes polygynous and underage marriages. Of course, such matters require the utmost discretion of the judges, who tend to

55 Bowen, *Islam, Law, and Equality in Indonesia: An Anthropology of Public Reasoning*, 257.

56 Sonneveld, "Rethinking the Difference Between Formal and Informal Marriages in Egypt"; Bedner and van Huis, "Plurality of Marriage Law and Marriage Registration for Muslims in Indonesia: A Plea for Pragmatism."

work pretty much in line with procedural law. However, the decision to approve legalisation is principally based upon whether or not a marriage has been concluded in line with Sharīʿa law coupled with considerations about the extent to which the marriage impinges on social relationships. This still leaves the problem of the legal status of the children. Parents who opt for the first choice and safely navigated it will then be in the position to take yet another step to legalise their children. With their new marriage certificate as proof, they can submit a request to the Islamic court asking that their children be legally recognised.

The registration is the responsibility of the KUA while the legalisation procedure can be carried out by the Islamic court. This shows that it is often the lowest level of the state administration which is crucial to providing a legal identity to those who would otherwise not qualify.[57] Moreover, these observations show that the way *isbat nikah* works is closely interwoven with Nurlaelawati's findings. She remarks that in many cases judges find it hard to apply the rules by which they should formally abide. Because these judges do not have the power to force society to adhere to the state law, they show the tendency to go along with the temporal interests of those seeking justice in the courts, although they do so in contravention of the rules as interpreted by the state.[58] In this instance, the judges prioritise the public good rather than applying the letter of the law.

These different paths should be understood as the district-level bureaucracy's strategy to regulate marriage and family. Those administering government on a lower level are aware that the strict imposition of a legal norm on the legal obligation to register a marriage has been far from successful. Nevertheless, it is impossible to leave unregistered marriage as it is. Therefore, to protect citizens' rights, these different solutions have been made available. Furthermore, checking on marriage by the state is a tricky task in a country like Indonesia in which there is a wealth of perceptions of both the national law and Islamic law in Muslim society. In response, the Indonesian legal system provides a wide playing field of ample legal and judicial opportunities to solve the problems which arise as long as these support its effort to control. When it is set in motion, these opportunities lead not only to administrative transgressions and the exercise of judicial discretion but also to overlapping authorities. Both the judges of Islamic courts and the *penghulus* of the KUA are street-level bureaucrats who, according to Lipsky, are "the focus of citizen reac-

57 Bedner and van Huis, "Plurality of Marriage Law and Marriage Registration for Muslims in Indonesia: A Plea for Pragmatism," 187.

58 Nurlaelawati, *Modernization, Tradition and Identity: The Kompilasi Hukum Islam and Legal Practice in the Indonesian Religious Courts*, 224.

tions because their discretion opens up the possibility that they will respond favourably on behalf of people."[59] The discretion is not only the outcome of the absence and the vagueness of the legal norms, it is also a deliberate interpretation made by public officials and judges.

59 Lipsky, *Street-Level Bureaucracy: Dilemmas of the Individual in Public Services*, 9.

CHAPTER 8

Conclusion

This book has approached Muslim marriage from an array of different perspectives. It has examined how the Indonesian state has endeavoured to regulate Muslim marriage and how a local society in East Java has gone about dealing with the regulation to have their marriages recognised by the state. I have looked not only at the law as interpreted by the central state, but also at the law as perceived and implemented by different actors in the lower strata of society, namely ordinary people, judges, marriage registrars and religious leaders. Following Sally Moore, I have simultaneously looked at the rules, the occasions on which they are communicated and invoked, what actual behaviour they have had to address, the contexts in which this takes place and the ideas and assumptions which have accompanied their introduction.[1] This has yielded a number of insights that I have discussed in the chapters of this book and which I shall now re-address in this conclusion. However, I would like to begin by setting out the key findings of my study.

Instead of reforming the substance of the marriage law at the law-making level, which would only stir up controversy and debates, the Indonesian government has used a citizens' rights approach to control marriage practice. This citizens' rights approach helps guide people towards compliance with the state legal framework. Recent legal reforms reveal that the judiciary and the civil bureaucracy have been crucial to secure legal reform. The legal reform on Muslim marriage no longer hinges on the religious and legal validity of marriage but is about the consequences of marriage registration for citizens' rights.

Furthermore, the bureaucratic reform of the administration of Muslim marriage has still left some leeway in which informality can function. Berenschot and Van Klinken have remarked that, in post-colonial states like Indonesia, the experience of state-citizen interaction depends not just on the content of the law but also on the strength of personal connections.[2] This informality has certainly shaped the practice of marriage registration, which initially presented a major problem as it has inexorably led to the bureaucratisation of Muslim marriage.[3] The idea of marriage registration as an element of social reform militates

1 Sally Falk Moore, *Law as Process: An Anthropological Approach* (London: Routledge & Kegan Paul, 1983), 3.

2 Berenschot and van Klinken, "Informality and Citizenship: The Everyday State in Indonesia."

3 Nisa, "The Bureaucratization of Muslim Marriage in Indonesia," 309.

 | DOI:10.1163/9789004516113_009

against the convictions of conservative Muslims who believe that Muslim marriage should be regulated by 'ulama' only, not by the state. In this study, I have discovered that this informality has produced a mediating sphere that contains the potential to align state law and religious law, allowing people to adjust their religiously oriented attitudes to the state law. Informal religious leaders, represented by *modin*s are the main actors in this sphere. Their role is key to helping citizens negotiate their interest in obtaining state recognition and to facilitate their ability to realise their rights. On the central government level, this informality is mistakenly viewed as corruption and therefore rejected. It provided an excuse for the government to remove the *modin*s from the governmental apparatus. However, the local levels of government (district and sub-district), as in East Java, prefer to keep these informal actors in place as it is realised that they assist in aligning people's behaviour with the state legal framework.

The central government assumes that the lower levels of government are capable of building a direct relationship with ordinary people without necessarily involving intermediaries. However, in practice, it does not work that way. Effective marriage registration needs these intermediaries, particularly in communities in which religious leaders command great respect. Moreover, the Marriage Law still defines marriage as a religious ceremony. In these communities, marriage registration includes two inseparable dimensions. Firstly, it is just an administrative matter. The second dimension has to do with aspects related to the religious validity of a marriage and the proper conclusion of a marriage ceremony. Some state *penghulu*s are considered to lack religious legitimacy to perform the second dimension. Traditionally *modin*s do have such legitimacy. This is why informality survives.

While these findings might seem to indicate competition between state and local religious leaders, I want to underline that the relationship between the state and religion in Muslim marriage, at least in the cases I examined, is actually a matter of mutual adjustment. Religious authorities do indeed accept the state's intervention in marriage law if this is limited to marriage registration. Simultaneously, local people are increasingly eager to register marriages as this makes them eligible to have access to state services. Of course, there is a small segment of religious leaders who oppose the state law, especially those who do not accept the democratic foundation of the nation state and propagate the idea of a so-called Islamic state. However, the large majority can accept some level of intervention of the nation state in Muslim marriage if two conditions are met. Firstly, the state law cannot challenge the fundamental principles of Sharīʿa law or introduce something impermissible according to the classical understanding of Sharīʿa law, such as allowing same-sex marriage or totally prohibiting polygyny. However, this is hardly ever the case in Indonesia as to a large extent the legal reforms have taken into account what is permissible and impermissible according to the common understanding of Sharīʿa law. Secondly, when the state law is too rigid to deal with some particular practices which are socially and religiously acceptable when religious law is applied. To local people, religious law is a more responsive instrument for handling problems of sexual morality such as *zinā* and teenage pregnancy. They prioritise the religious validity of marriage rather than its legal validity.

In response to the continuing informality and the relationship between the state law and religious law, the state officials in charge of marriage registration on the frontier levels, namely the sub-district office of Muslim marriage registration and the Islamic courts, are amenable to adopting a lenient approach towards regulations on marriage.[4] They do not interpret and implement the rules strictly. This attitude is of great assistance to those people who want to seek state recognition of their marriages so that they can have access to their citizens' rights. The lenient approach applies in particular in two conditions. Firstly, as street-level bureaucrats of marriage registration, *penghulu*s at the KUA are willing to register an unregistered marriage. Their acquiescence means that people do not have to file a formal request for the legalisation of their unregistered marriage with Islamic courts as decreed by the law. Here, *penghulu*s transgress the rules on marriage registration in the name of humanity. Secondly, judicial practice also shows that judges resort to judicial discretion in the case of *isbat nikah* (retrospective marriage legalisation) to prioritise the interest of the weaker party.[5] These differences in interpretation between the central government and the lower levels of government lead to legal plurality within the state. However, the existence of these legal mechanisms is the key to securing the functioning of state law. In practice, if lower levels of government and judges of Islamic courts did not do this, people would turn away from the state.

The willingness of the state officials to give a less than strict interpretation of legal rules on personal status has become a major trend in other Muslim countries as well. In the case of Tunisia, Voorhoeve remarks that, despite the 'progressive' direction of the reform of its family law, the state-promoted family law is relative because there is much diversity in its application. Judicial discre-

4 van Huis, "Islamic Courts and Women's Divorce Rights in Indonesia: The Cases of Cianjur and Bulukumba," 263.

5 It is worth noting that the procedure for *isbat nikah* as set out in the Kompilasi was initially meant to be a transitional article for those who had not yet registered their marriage prior to the ratification of the Marriage Law. Bedner and van Huis, "Plurality of Marriage Law and Marriage Registration for Muslims in Indonesia: A Plea for Pragmatism," 187.

tion exists on different levels.[6] Vincent-Grosso has also indicated the same. In the Tunisian divorce court, because of the complexity of documents brought to the court, the judges find it difficult to make a decision within the law. Consequently, the judges use the personal narratives of the litigants in making their judgement.[7] In addition, in the Egyptian context, Lindbekk suggests that the judicial practice has developed its order of discourse. She argues that the judicial practice in divorce shows a move towards increased standardisation in the implementation of family law. This standardisation has come about through a closer union between law and religious morality.[8]

The abovementioned findings are the most fundamental issues of the four points which constitute my study. They are the legal reform of marriage rules, the reform of the bureaucracy of marriage registration, changing social practices in marriage, the position of *penghulus* and the legalisation of unregistered marriage. What follows are more detailed conclusions of each of them.

1 Regulating Muslim Marriage and a Shifting Approach

The first point involves the political, religious, and legal debates about how Muslim marriage in Indonesia should be regulated. The reform of the marriage law has become an arena of contesting ideas between Muslim groups.[9] Within the framework of a nation state, legal reforms of marriage in post-independence Indonesia concentrate on the debate about how the religious norms governing marriage can be transformed into state law (*hukum negara*), or what positive law should look like. The debate has revolved around what constitutes a valid (*sah*) marriage. It centres on the demand common among Muslims in Indonesia that the codification of Islamic marriage law by the state should not reduce the religious character of marriage.

Historically speaking, family law reform in Indonesia has addressed sensitive issues such as polygyny, the minimum age of marriage and the legal obligation of marriage registration. Under the terms of the 1974 Marriage Law, the Indonesian state embraces the principle of monogamy but still provides room

6 Voorhoeve, "Judicial Discretion in Tunisian Personal Status Law."

7 Sarah Vincent-Grosso, "Maktub: An Ethnography of Evidence in a Tunisian Divorce Court," in *Family Law in Islam: Divorce, Marriage and Women in the Muslim World*, ed. Maaike Voorhoeve (London: I.B. Tauris, 2012), 171–198.

8 Monika Lindbekk, "Inscribing Islamic Shariʿa in Egyptian Divorce," *Oslo Law Review* 3, no. 2 (2016): 103–135.

9 Bowen, *Islam, Law, and Equality in Indonesia: An Anthropology of Public Reasoning*, 10.

for those who wish to have more than one wife. Regarding minimum age, the Law has introduced the prescription that the bride must not be younger than sixteen years and the groom must be at least nineteen (now both changed to nineteen years). Before this law came into force, these two issues blew up into a heated debate between female activists and religious leaders in the early years of the twentieth century.[10] Up to now, the norms concerning polygyny and minimum age remain a subject of deliberation and negotiation involving state officials, religious leaders, feminist activists and other interested parties. Turning to the question of registration, the Marriage Law stipulates that marriage must first be solemnised in accordance with the religious teachings of the parties, after which the legal obligation of registration can be taken care of.

After the 1998 *reformasi*, the marriage law has increasingly been an arena of contestation between different groups in Islam.[11] On the sub-national level, we come across the politicisation of Islamic issues. Several Islam-based regional regulations covering ruling on public morality have been enacted and these have complicated the procedure of Muslim marriage as stipulated by the national law. For instance, a local regulation obliges both the bride and the groom to be able to read the Quran. On the national level, the legal reform of Muslim marriage has been continued through the drafting of the bill on the substantive law of Islamic courts. The purpose of this legal reform is to introduce legal sanctions on those who do not register their marriage. This reform led to a public debate and certain Islamic groups urged people to resist it. The reform ended in a deadlock.

Earlier, the Law on Civil Administration has introduced legal sanctions in the form of fines for those who fail to register their marriage, but these scarcely raised an eyebrow. Moreover, as Van Huis and Wirastri have argued, legal sanctions are never a sufficient deterrent to stop people from opting for unregistered marriages.[12] Ironically, at the same time, the Ministry of Home Affairs drafted a regulation that assists people in unregistered marriages to obtain birth certificates for their children mentioning the names of both parents. Once again, this shows the ambiguity of the state when it comes to dealing with informality.

10 Susan Blackburn, *Women and the State in Modern Indonesia* (Cambridge: Cambridge University Press, 2004); Susan Blackburn and Sharon Bessell, "Marriageable Age: Political Debates on Early Marriage in Twentieth-Century Indonesia," *Indonesia* 63 (1997): 107–141.

11 See Fauzi, "Islamic Law in Indonesia: Recent Debates on Islamic Family Law in the Reformasi Era (1998–2007)."

12 van Huis and Wirastri, "Muslim Marriage Registration in Indonesia: Revised Marriage Registration Laws Cannot Overcome Compliance Flaws," 14.

The debate on legal reform also involved 'ulama'. They use their organisations and *fatwās* to claim and reinforce their religious authority. Their *fatwās* demonstrate how the concept of *maṣlaḥa* (public good) in Islamic law has become increasingly important in supporting the state to establish its control of marital relations. Despite its success, this *maṣlaḥa* orientation has been challenged by those Islamic groups which take a literal approach to classical Islamic texts. In the case of the registration of polygyny, such texts suggest that neither judges nor the state should exert exaggerated (*ishrāf*) control over personal relations.

In spite of these religious debates, the state is still determined to extend its power to control Muslim marriage to protect the rights of women and children. Therefore, legal reform is still a work in progress. The judiciary and the civil bureaucracy have been important to achieve the goal. I classify this new direction as a citizens' rights approach. In this approach, both members of the judiciary and the civil service are key actors. One important feature has concerned the judiciary's examination of the legal status under the Constitution of children born out of legal wedlock. Court decisions grant children born out of wedlock paternal recognition as long as there is sufficient proof that they have a blood relationship with the father, a decision that directly contravenes classical Islamic law. The civil bureaucracy has also been seriously addressing the consequences of unregistered marriage for the registration of the birth of a child. Its efforts have led to the mapping out of a new policy, namely letters of absolute responsibility (*Surat Pernyataan Tanggungjawab Mutlak*) which declare the religious validity of the marital relationship of the parents and hence the legitimacy of the child. Armed with these letters, the parents are able to claim the birth certificate of a child born out of legal wedlock. The letters can be used as a substitute for a marriage certificate, but they do not legalise the marital relationship of the parents. This policy would seem to have reduced the significance of marriage registration. In other words, this policy explicitly challenges the reason for the regulation of marriage registration. Nevertheless, by implementing this policy, the state is able to control marriage practice in society and bestow individual rights and obligations concomitant with national identity. Such a process is categorised by Peletz as an inseparable part of state formation.[13]

To sum up, a new trend in family law reform is currently underway in Indonesia. Instead of reforming the content of the Marriage Law, which inevitably ignites heated debates, the government has adopted a citizens' rights approach to deal with the problems arising from unregistered marriage. Far-reaching

13 Peletz, *Islamic Modern: Religious Courts and Cultural Politics in Malaysia.*

reforms of the rules on marriage have been achieved without secularising the main elements of Muslim family law. These reforms indirectly improve the position of women in the matrimonial sphere and protecting the rights of children. However, the issue of parents whose marriage is not legal under state law still face limitations in claiming certain citizens' rights is still the elephant in the room. The legal status of a marriage can only be proven by producing a marriage certificate. However, new obstacles have arisen as the citizen's approach, as I explained earlier, is undermining the importance of the marriage certificate. Nevertheless, despite this new development, the recompenses accruing from the possession of a marriage certificate still pressures people to comply with the state's regulation of marriage. On these grounds, it is safe to suggest that the legal debate about Muslim marriage in Indonesia has shifted from the issue of the validity of Muslim marriage to the problems for citizens' rights caused by the consequences of marriage registration. Since its implementation of the citizens' rights approach, the government has become much more effective in managing marriage and controlling people's marital practices.

2 Corruption, Informality, and the Reformed Fees

The second important set of findings of this study is related to the bureaucratisation of marriage in the wake of the government's insistence on marriage registration and the subsequent issuing of a marriage certificate, considered to be the instrument that determines the legal validity of a marriage. Failure to register a marriage makes a union legally invalid in the eyes of the state. The KUA, which is headed by a PPN (*Petugas Pencatat Nikah*, marriage registrar), is in charge of the registration of Muslim marriage. In the past, no special qualifications were needed to be appointed as a PPN. Now, only a *penghulu* can act as a PPN, a move which is part of the state's strategy to boost the legitimacy of the KUA.

Over the past few years, in efforts to improve its performance, the government has attempted to introduce bureaucratic reform in the KUA. This bureaucratic reform has been devised for the simultaneous attainment of two objectives: the government wants all its citizens to register their marriages and that this registration should not be dependent on religious actors operating outside the state framework. This reform was introduced after an incident in East Java in which *penghulu* Romli was sued for corruption just because he recorded the customary extra-legal payment he collected for conducting a marriage ceremony outside the office. Determined to eradicate this extra-legal payment, the government (the Ministry of Religious Affairs) issued a new regulation in

2014 that clearly differentiates between *nikah kantor* (marriage in the office) and *nikah bedolan* (marriage out of the office). *Nikah kantor* is free of charge because a marriage certificate is treated in the same way as other civil documents. For *nikah bedolan*, people have to pay Rp. 600,000-, replacing the contested informal payment, to cover the *penghulus*' expenses.

However, the matter of extra-legal payment has not yet been properly solved. It is particularly complicated because it is also linked to the position of the *modins* who, in the past, acted as the PPPN (*Pembantu Petugas Pencatat Nikah*, the marriage registrar's assistant). *Modins* are usually persons with a high reputation for religious scholarship.[14] The Ministry of Religious Affairs decided to eliminate the institution of the marriage registrar's assistant in 2010. As a consequence, the marriage registrar's assistant was no longer an official marriage registration functionary. The dismissal of the marriage registrar's assistant caused no problems in an urban community like in Yogyakarta in which dependence on *modins* was not particularly strong. However, it was less effective in rural contexts. Sumbersari in East Java provides a good example. Although the institution of the marriage registrar's assistant has officially disappeared, *modins* still survive. By involving *modins* in the process of marriage, people manage to combine the religious aspect of the marriage ceremony and the administrative aspect of the marriage registration. This kind of situation arises in most areas in East Java. Grijns and Horii have demonstrated that *amil* play a similar role in West Java.[15]

A similar reform has been the integration of marriage registration into the civil administration. The thinking behind this reform was to prevent any modification of the ages of couples, usually of the brides, to make these comply with the Marriage Law. This reform has caused new problems. Although a bride might be legally underage, she, or her family, still seek state recognition of her marriage. Currently, the government officials are unlikely to be prepared to negotiate in this situation because the system uses the data filed under a single identification number (NIK, *Nomor Induk Kependudukan*) to calculate her age. If her age does not comply with the legal requirement, the system will automatically reject the registration. Once again, *modins* can alleviate this situation by performing a religious marriage with a delayed registration, meaning that the marriage will be registered as soon as the spouses have reached the required minimum age.

14 To become PPPN, *modins* were appointed by the village head and then confirmed by the head of the KUA to assist the PPN in his work.

15 Grijns and Horii, "Child Marriage in a Village in West Java (Indonesia): Compromises between Legal Obligations and Religious Concerns."

This series of reforms leads us to the conclusion that the central government is heavily influenced by the idea of rationalisation as defined by Weber.[16] In the eyes of the government, modern bureaucratic reform simply means eliminating values embedded in a religious/ethical context. Efficiency and effectiveness have been the keywords from the government's point of view. However, as I explained in Chapter 5, Muslim marriage can never be completely rational in Max Weber's sense, since it must invariably be based on core Islamic norms and values if it is to retain its Islamic character. The success of the reform is indeed dependent on the situation prevailing in each society. For Pasuruan people in general, the involvement of a *modin* is fundamental because people consider the religious elements of marriage more important than any requirements which might be imposed by the state administration. Unlike the *modin*, the state does not have the leeway to make suitable adjustments.

3 Present-Day Islam and Cultural Life in Pasuruan

The centrality of *modin*s and religious leaders, in general, is reasonable if we look at how Islam extends its influence in the Pasuruan social life. Pasuruan is a regency in the province of East Java which is inhabited by a majority of Muslim communities which generally show a tendency towards practising the traditional Islam encouraged by the NU. This religious orientation draws strength from the fact that many Pasuruan residents have historical roots in the island of Madura. The migrants have acculturated with the Javanese, a mingling which led to a distinct sub-culture called *pedalungan* or *pendhalungan*. This community has been established on the basis of patron-client relationships in which *kyai*s or the leaders of *pesantren* act as the patron. The commitment to practising Islamic traditions and the strongly inculcated obedience to religious leaders (*kyai*s) have led to a complicated relationship between religion and the state. This social configuration appears to have infiltrated and influenced political life too.

Furthermore, Sumbersari, the area in Pasuruan in which I have been conducting my fieldwork, as is common in Maduro-Javanese areas, has to contend with an array of social problems, chief among them poverty and a tendency

16 Tony Waters and Dagmar Waters, "Max Weber's Sociology in the Twenty-First Century," in *Weber's Rationalism and Modern Society New Translations on Politics, Bureaucracy, and Social Stratification*, ed. Tony Waters and Dagmar Waters (New York: Palgrave Macmillan, 2015), 4; Max Weber, *Economy and Society: An Outline of Interpretive Sociology*, ed. Guenther Roth and Claus Wittich (Berkeley: University of California Press, 1978), 889.

not to participate in formal education. This avoidance of the established formal educational system has made *pesantren* a central institution. *Pesantren* serves as an alternative educational institution that is perceived to be adequate to fulfil their needs as it inculcates in students not only the knowledge they require to function in society but also instils religion and character-building in them. However, the winds of change have been coming for the last decade. *Pesantren* has been expanding curricula to respond to a new aspiration, i.e., providing general knowledge and practical skills. This is coincident with the development on the national level which has shown a growing tendency for Islamic schools to be more open to change.

4 Everyday Practice of Marriage and the Functioning of the Bureaucracy of Marriage

The fourth set of findings in this study is centred on two issues: the everyday practice of marriage in rural society and the functioning of the marriage registration bureaucracy—which is not the same as its bureaucratisation, which I discussed in the previous section. I have put these aspects into the same category because both relate to how marriage is practised by local people. It encompasses how people perceive marriage and determine whom and when to marry as well as how they perceive marriage registration.

In the eyes of the people of Sumbersari, and many others in Indonesia, marriage is a purely religious affair. People set tremendous store by the involvement of religious authorities in the sacred ceremony, far more than they are bothered about state involvement. Nevertheless, despite the homogenous tradition of Islam in the area, I encountered internal heterogeneity in the relationship between the agency of the actors involved, cultural norms and the social structure in the selection of whom to marry. It is important to note that, in all social classes, the ideas about an ideal spouse have been shaped by the discourses circulating within traditional Islam. These ideas include preserving chastity (*kesucian*) and playing according to the rules (*apik*). *Pesantren* plays an important role in maintaining this *fiqh*-based understanding of marriage. Being a *santri* means a guarantee of the purity and good morals of a girl.

Marriage practice in Sumbersari shows that the negotiations in which these ideas are dominant are dependent on the role of the *pengarep* (traditional marriage broker). Entrusted with the principal role of mediating the communication of the two families concerned, the work of *pengarep* is mainly important to those families whose daughters have been educated in *pesantren*. In these families, girls have limited agency and restricted room when it comes to finding a suitable future husband. It is the parents, not always the father, who determine to whom and when they will be married to. Arranged marriage is quite common. In this situation, marriage has become a marketplace in which a *pengarep* is essential to achieving the expectations of the parents.

Another key actor in marriage is the *kyai*. Marriage practice in Sumbersari shows the on-going centrality of the role of *kyai*s in the production of an Islam-based legal norm to safeguard sexual morality. This is a tricky point as a decision based on these norms sometimes conflicts with the state legal norms. "Preventing harm (extramarital sex and unwanted pregnancy) should be the priority" is always the overriding argument presented. Differences of opinions between traditional *fiqh* doctrines are essential to the construction of the *kyai*s' legal reasoning, which should comply with the interests of the people concerned. From a social perspective, religious marriage has been an effective way to tackle the problems caused by religious morality and female sexuality when the state law is difficult to comply with.

In Sumbersari, modernity manifests itself in the form of increasing participation in formal education and the rise in female mobility. As the younger generations acquire more room to exercise agency in the selection of a possible spouse, the role of the *pengarep* will decrease. Nevertheless, even if girls do have the agency to find a suitable partner this does not mean that they can also determine the timing of the marriage. In certain cases, the decision about the timing of a marriage is subject to the parents' authority. This is grounded on the idea of preserving the social honour of a family. Indeed, even if women are able to articulate consent to a marriage, they will still need to resort to religion-inspired reasons to justify their choices.

In Sumbersari a woman who has divorced informally (out of court) and wants to remarry will have no problem in finding an Islamic leader willing to marry her traditionally. This is in line with Van Huis's finding in Cianjur, West Java.[17] Furthermore, the centrality of religion and cultural norms corroborates earlier research findings. These issues are becoming more prominent as Sumbersari is being confronted with 'modern' development. As argued by Nancy Smith-Hefner, modernity has become a space of moral and political contestation when the ideals of a family come up for discussion.[18] Reassured by the presence of *kyai*s and *pengarep*, to solve their problems, villagers almost always resort to the community-based legal system, eschewing any involvement of the

17 van Huis, "Islamic Courts and Women's Divorce Rights in Indonesia: The Cases of Cianjur and Bulukumba," 271.

18 Smith-Hefner, "The New Muslim Romance: Changing Patterns of Courtship and Marriage Among Educated Javanese Youth," 458.

state apparatus. In West Java, Grijns and Hori suggest the same development.[19] Platt has also underlined that the dominant influence of community-based law undermines the efficacy of the Marriage Law.[20]

Examining the history of the KUA in Sumbersari, I found evidence of the continuing intervention of religious leaders in the (re)making of the KUA. Their undiminished authority means that the KUA cannot ignore them but has to reach a compromise with these leaders. *Penghulu*s discover the importance of maintaining a good relationship with religious leaders and local elites if they want to maintain their power. In addition, non-tenured workers at the KUA, who are local villagers, play a significant role in bridging the distance between *penghulu*s and the local population.

In Sumbersari, marriage registration is regarded by the common people as a commercial relationship between the state and society. Their argument is simple: the state provides recognition by means of a marriage certificate and people have to spend a sum of money to acquire this document. Given this perception, *penghulu*s consistently find that they run into complications when they try to implement the central government regulation which differentiates between *nikah kantor* and *nikah bedolan*. Before this policy came into force, nearly all marriage ceremonies were concluded at home (*nikah bedolan*). By making *nikah bedolan* much more expensive, the state pressures its citizens to have their marriage ceremony performed in the office. The thinking behind the state's insistence was to make people fully dependent on its services. However, people challenge this policy and negotiate it to fit their interests.

In most cases, people differentiate between a marriage ceremony as a religious and social process in which a *kyai* or a *modin* is involved and a marriage ceremony as an administrative process in which *penghulu*s play a role. People do not want to spend much money on conducting a *nikah bedolan*, which is why there has been a tendency to arrange *akad nikah dua kali* (twofold marriage ceremonies). The first marriage ceremony, held at home, is the one in which they can satisfy their religious obligations, while the second is carried out at the KUA solely for the sake of registration. Of course, as the mediator between the state and society, *modin*s play an important role in this and they have constructed a religious argumentation to justify these people's choices. Their solution is the idea of a *ta'kīd al-nikāḥ* (authenticating a marriage, *pengukuhan pernikahan*) to refer to the second marriage ceremony in the KUA. They have needed

19 Grijns and Horii, "Child Marriage in a Village in West Java (Indonesia): Compromises between Legal Obligations and Religious Concerns," 12.

20 Maria Platt, *Marriage, gender and Islam in Indonesia: women negotiating informal marriage, divorce and desire* (Oxon. and New York: Routledge, 2017), p. 149.

to invent such a new legal norm to sustain their intermediating role. The idea of *ta'kīd al-nikāḥ* is an undisputed outcome of the negotiations between religious law and state law. It has been effectively used to achieve the religious significance of marriage as the local people perceive it and to ensure the implementation of the state legal norms on marriage.

As street-level bureaucrats,[21] *penghulu*s have to struggle to expand their influence and naturally they are opposed to the idea of *ta'kīd al-nikāḥ*. Nevertheless, they are also aware that *ta'kīd al-nikāḥ* has been the only way to make people conform to the legal obligation of marriage registration. Therefore, *ta'kīd al-nikāḥ* can be identified as a product of a semi-autonomous social field, in which the customs and symbols based on religious law are maintained on the one hand but which also harbours the potential to bring them into line with rules and decisions from outside the field, the state law.[22]

Furthermore, this research has discovered that *penghulu*s do not work the same way as 'ulama'. This differs from Nurlaelawati's study which suggests that *penghulu*s pretend to act as religious authorities.[23] In my study, by contrast, *penghulu*s are identifying themselves as a representative of the state. My study corroborates Van Huis's finding about the competing authorities in West Java. Religious leaders there perceived the state as a threat to their authority which led to a situation in which religious leaders in West Java denied the authority of the state in Islamic matters.[24] This outcome suggests two interrelated aspects: firstly, *penghulu*s always speak on behalf of the state and treat the state law as the source of their authority; secondly, they use a marriage certificate as an important instrument to support their authority. In other words, to maintain their legitimacy, *penghulus* consistently advocate state recognition of a marriage, arguing that it contributes to the protection of citizens' rights. The fact that *penghulu*s are not always successful in persuading society to marry according to the state law in the first place suggests that they do not yet enjoy a solid position in society. When it is all said and done, the legitimacy of *penghulu*s' authority to control people's behaviour is dependent upon the extent to which *modin*s play their roles. *Modin*s are the key to bridging the relationship between the state and society, thereby securing the *penghulus*' position.

---

21 Lipsky, *Street-Level Bureaucracy: Dilemmas of the Individual in Public Services*.

22 Moore, "Law and Social Change: The Semi-Autonomous Social Field as an Appropriate Subject of Study," 720.

23 Nurlaelawati, *Modernization, Tradition and Identity: The Kompilasi Hukum Islam and Legal Practice in the Indonesian Religious Courts*, 189.

24 van Huis, "Islamic Courts and Women's Divorce Rights in Indonesia: The Cases of Cianjur and Bulukumba," 139–140.

5 Unregistered Marriages and Seeking State Recognition

The last set of findings in this study relates to the process of legalising unregistered marriage. It probes into the problem of how people deal with unregistered marriage, that is, a marriage that has been concluded in accordance with the religious requirements but has not been registered at the KUA. The reason they want to legalise an unregistered marriage usually revolves around an emic account of the necessity (*kebutuhan*) of obtaining requisite legal documents, such as marriage or birth certificates mentioning the names of both the parents. The Kompilasi decrees that unregistered marriage can be legalised retrospectively by following the process of *isbat nikah* in Islamic courts. Consequently, *isbat nikah* is the only judicial procedure available to people to legalise unregistered marriages retrospectively and is the only possible legal way to cope with unregistered marriages.

However, in practice, people have yet another way to have their unregistered marriages legalised. Instead of going to the Islamic court, they approach *penghulu*s to register it at the KUA office. In other words, the choice between *isbat nikah* in Islamic courts or registering unregistered marriage in the KUA is dependent on the needs of particular people. *Isbat nikah* is meaningful only to people who seek the legalisation of unregistered marriages to obtain a birth certificate for children born out of legal wedlock. If their concern is obtaining a marriage certificate only, they do not go to Islamic courts but solicit the help of *penghulus*. *Penghulu*s at the KUA acquiesce in the legalisation although they know it is a violation of the law. Their justification is that they are simply helping the people to procure a required document. *Penghulu*s usually demand that the couples present a letter from the village administration declaring that their marriage has never been registered. Of course, this marriage registration will not change the legal status of children born before the marriage was registered.

Another relevant finding is that, in practice, the judicial procedure of *isbat nikah* can be used to legalise marriages that are not actually permissible under the terms of the Marriage Law, that is, illegal polygyny and underage marriage. In cases of polygyny, judges do not put much effort into uncovering how the marriage ceremony concerned was performed. They just consider that legalisation is more important for the sake of children's legal status. In other words, *isbat nikah* is accepted on humane grounds. The judges make use of article 7 (3) point e "marriage which is concluded between those who do not have any impediment according to the Marriage Law," but they interpret it more widely. In addition to these two mechanisms, Indonesian law now provides another legal opportunity for people, who do not request *isbat nikah* from Islamic courts or register unregistered marriage in the KUA, to validate the legal status of children. This is done by submitting a proposal for the children's legalisation (*asal usul anak*) to an Islamic court.

This sort of *isbat nikah* supports Nurlaelawati's finding that, in many cases, judges find it hard to apply the rules which they are formally expected to observe. Because the judges cannot force society to adhere to the state law, they have the tendency to go along with the temporal interests of those seeking justice in the courts, although what they do is contradictory to the rules expounded by the state.[25] Here we see that the judges prioritise *maṣlaḥa* of the people rather than enforcing the letter of the law as intended by the legislator.

The frontier agencies of marriage, the judges of the Islamic courts and *penghulu*s at the KUA, seem aware that the judicial norm requiring the legal obligation of marriage registration has not been entirely successful. Many Indonesians still prioritise religious validity and are not particularly bothered about the legal validity of marriage. They are willing to comply with the state law only when they are in need of state services. The state has devised the *isbat nikah* procedure to cope with this situation. Judges of the Islamic courts have to exercise their judicial discretion and *penghulu*s at the KUA deliberately transgress the law to help citizens comply with the requirements of the state legal framework. The implementation of these procedures is important to leverage in edging people towards the state.

To sum up, with regard to my findings, taken as a whole what we have witnessed is a continuing process of the penetration of state law into Indonesian society. Instead of reforming the substance of the marriage law, which would only stir up controversy and debates, the government has used a citizens' rights approach to control marriage practice. This citizens' rights approach is helpful in guiding people towards compliance with the state legal framework. People have no option but to legalise their marriages. However, as long as the dualism of religious validity and legal validity remains an issue, many marriages will remain unregistered. Furthermore, the central state is also endeavouring to remove all forms of informality from the procedures involved. Nevertheless, although the central government has officially removed the informal authority to act from marriage functionaries, in practice it seems it is an uphill battle to reduce the latter's intervention.

Moreover, in terms of the legalisation of unregistered marriages, we have also witnessed the decision by judges of Islamic courts and *penghulu*s at the KUA to adopt a lenient approach toward the rules governing marriage. In cer-

---

25 Nurlaelawati, *Modernization, Tradition and Identity: The Kompilasi Hukum Islam and Legal Practice in the Indonesian Religious Courts*, 224.

tain cases, *penghulus* turn a blind eye to the rules, while the judges are ready to exercise judicial discretion to enable them to grant state recognition to a marriage. This situation has led to continuing legal plurality within the state. The willingness of the state officials to give a less than strict interpretation of legal rules is key to guaranteeing the functioning of the state law and will be good for the legal development of Indonesia in the future.

Glossary

abangan a group of Muslims who practise a syncretic form of Islam
adat local customary practises and traditions
ajuddhuagi married-off by parents
akad nikah a marriage ceremony
apik good manner
aurat shame
akta kelahiran birth certificate
akta nikah marriage certificates
aḥwāl shakhṣiyya Islamic personal status
Bahtsul Masail producing *fatwā*s within NU
bikr a single/virgin woman
bebet, bobot, bibit descent, wealth, and moral character
Bupati Government official in charge of a district (*kabupaten*)
cerai gugat state legal term for Muslim divorce initiated by the wife, stipulated by the Law 7/1989 on Religious courts in 1989 as an umbrella term to encompass *khulʿ* and *faskh*
cerai hidup dissolution of marriage while both spouses are alive
cerai mati dissolution of marriage due to death of one of the spouses
cerai talak Indonesian legal term for Muslim divorce initiated by the husband
dhanyang a sacred place
dhikr remembrance of Allah
elek ugly
fatwā nonbinding legal opinions on a point of Sharīʿa
fiqh Islamic jurisprudence
cerai guga a divorce petition claimed by the wife
guru bantu a teacher assistant
ḥadīth the traditions of the Prophet Muhammad, based on his sayings and actions
iʿlān publicity
ibadah an act of worship
iftāʾ *fatwā* giving
ijtihād process of legal reasoning deriving law on the basis of the Quran and the Sunna
ījāb qabūl offer and acceptance
ijbār compelling power
isbat nikah retrospective legalisation of a marriage concluded by Islamic courts
janda mati widow
janda cerai divorcee

juddhu divine destiny
kartu keluarga family card
kejawen Javanism
kesucian purity, chastity
khulʿ a divorce in which the wife offers compensation to the husband in return for his pronunciation of divorce
Kompilasi Kompilasi Hukum Islam, the Compilation of Islamic law that serves as a reference for judges in Islamic courts
kitab kuning (lit. means 'yellow books') Islamic literature, mainly in Arabic and other local languages, like Javanese and Malays, refers to the traditional set of Islamic texts used by the educational curriculum of *pesantren* in Indonesia
kyai traditional religious leaders
kufu' a man of her social status
kumpul kebo sex out of wedlock
lamaran proposing a marriage (a betrothal)
langgar a small mosque
la padeh senneng mutual love
madhhab school in Islamic legal jurisprudence
madrasah diniyah an out-of-school institution teaching subjects related to Islam
mahr dower
maḥram a person that is not permitted to marry due to a close blood relationship
Majelis Tarjih a *fatwā* body of Muhammadiyah
manut following the parents' decision
mapolong tolang collecting the scattered bones
maqāṣid higher aims-based approach to Sharīʿa
maṣlaḥa common good
modin a village religious official; in marriage, it refers to a person whose authority was given by the state as PPPN (Pembantu Petugas Pencatat Nikah, the marriage registrar's assistant); currently, they are not officially recognised
mompong good fortune
Muhammadiyah a reformist organisation and the second biggest Indonesian Muslim organisation founded by Ahmad Dahlan (d. 1923) in 1912
mukena the costume worn by women during Islamic prayers
munakkiḥ one who solemnises a marriage contract
nafkah the financial support of a husband for a wife
namu visiting a girl's house
neket to engage a girl
ngredit paying off a lease
ngen-angen sending a marriage proposal by a marriage broker
nikah sirri religious marriages that are not registered
nikah di bawah tangan unofficial marriage

nontoni viewing
oreng bhagus a good man
oreng lowar outsiders
pacaran courtship
pamong village officials
pejabat official
pendhalungan a mixed community, acculturation between Javanese and Madurese cultures
pengajian religious gatherings
pengarep a voluntarily traditional marriage broker
Pengadilan Agama district-level Islamic court.
penghulu a religious scholar and a leader of community; in current practice, it refers to a person whose authority is given by the state as officials of the state religious affairs offices (Kantor Urusan Agama/KUA) in charge of Muslim marriage
pesantren traditional Islamic boarding school
praban maiden
qiyās analogy, the deduction of legal prescriptions from the Quran or Sunnah by analogic reasoning
rafak the verification of documents
reformasi Indonesian political period that results from the reign of Soeharto administration in 1998
rujuk reconciliation
rushd legal capacity or financial competency
sadd al-dharīʾa blocking the means to unexpected evil
santri students of Islamic boarding schools (*pesantren*); It also refers to an orthodox form of Islam in contrast to the syncretic *abangan*
sarong a length of fabric wrapped and tied around the body at the waist
sedah betel
sijill court records
siyāsa sharʾiyya Muslim law as expressed in regulatory decisions or policy of government.
sangkal karma that a proposed daughter will become a spinster
Sharīʿa God's law for the way of living as a Muslim
solawatan reciting prayers for the Prophet
shuhadāʾ witnesses
siyasa sharʿiyya legal-cum-political right of the ruler
sumpah jabatan an oath of the office
suróh betel
tahlil taken from the Arabic sentence *lā ilāha illā Allāh*, no god but Allah. It is a set of litanies recited in a communal gathering (*tahlilan*)

talak a divorce pronounced by a husband

taklik talak conditional divorce

tarjīḥ an examination of various Muslim jurists' opinions to determine which is most truthful to the original Sharī'a source

tegal dry cultivation

'ulama' religious leaders

walī a marriage guardian

walīma marriage feast

warung a small restaurant

zinā adultery or premarital sex

Bibliography

Books, Journal Articles, and Newspapers

Abaza, Mona. "Perceptions of 'Urfi Marriage in the Egyptian Press." *ISIM Newsletter* 7 (2001): 20–21.

Abdurrahman. *Kompilasi Hukum Islam Di Indonesia*. Jakarta: Akademika Pressindo, 1992.

Alami, Dawoud Sudqi el-. *The Marriage Contract in Islamic Law in the Sharīʿah and Personal Status Laws of Egypt and Morocco*. London: Graham & Trotman, 1992.

Ali, Kecia. "Marriage in Classical Islamic Jurisprudence: A Survey of Doctrines." In *Islamic Marriage Contract: Case Studies in Islamic Family Law*, edited by Asifa Quraishi and Frank E. Vogel, 11–45. Cambridge, MA: Harvard Law School, Islamic Legal Studies Program, 2008.

Alimi, Moh Yasir. "Rethinking Anthropology of Shariʿa: Contestation over the Meanings and Uses of Shariʿa in South Sulawesi, Indonesia." *Contemporary Islam*, no. 2 (2018): 123–151.

Anwar, Syamsul. "Fatwā, Purification and Dynamization: A Study of Tarjīh in Muhammadiyah." *Islamic Law and Society* 12, no. 1 (2005): 27–44.

Arabi, Oussama. *Studies in Modern Islamic Law and Jurisprudence*. The Hague: Kluwer Law International, 2001.

Arifianto, Alexander R. *Islam Nusantara & Its Critics: The Rise of NU's Young Clerics*. RSIS Comentary. Singapore, 2017.

Arifin, Achmad Zainal. "Defending Traditions, Countering Intolerant Ideologies: Re-Energizing the Role of Modin in Modern Java." *Al-Jamiʿah: Journal of Islamic Studies* 55, no. 2 (2017): 265–292.

Arifin, Muhajir. "Gara-Gara Postingan Di Medsos, Ansor Dan FPI Pasuruan Bersitegang." *Detik.Com*. Accessed October 14, 2018. https://news.detik.com/berita-jawa-timur/d-3495695/gara-gara-postingan-di-medsos-ansor-dan-fpi-pasuruan-bersitegang.

Aripin, Jaenal. *Jejak Langkah Peradilan Agama Di Indonesia*. Jakarta: Kharisma Putra Utama, 2013.

Az-Zuḥailī, Wahbah. *Al-Fiqh Al-Islāmī Wa Adillatuh*. Vol. 7. Beirut: Dār al-fikr, 1985.

Azra, Azyumardi. "The Indonesian Marriage Law of 1974: An Institutionalization of the Shariʿa for Social Changes." In *Shariʿa and Politics in Modern Indonesia*, edited by Arskal Salim and Azyumardi Azra, 76–95. Singapore: Institute for Southeast Asian Studies, 2003.

Azra, Azyumardi, Dina Afrianty, and Robert W. Hefner. "Pesantren and Madrasa: Muslim Schools and National Ideals in Indonesia." In *Schooling Islam: The Culture and Politics of Modern Muslim Education*, edited by Robert W. Hefner and Muhammad Qasim Zaman, 172–198. Princeton: Princeton University Press, 2010.

Badareen, Nayel. "Identity and Authority: Changes in the Process of Debates over the Islamic Marriage Contract among Contemporary Muslim-Arab Intellectuals." PhD Dissertation. The University of Arizona, 2014.

Badawi, Elsaid M., and Muhammad Abdel Haleem. "و/ك/د w–k–D." *Arabic-English Dictionary of Qur'anic Usage*. Brill, 2008.

Barlas, Asma. *"Believing Women" in Islam: Unreading Patriarchal Interpretations of the Qur'an*. Austin, TX: University of Texas Press, 2002.

Bass, Jerome R. "The PKI and the Attempted Coup." *Journal of Southeast Asian Studies* 1, no. 1 (1970): 96–105.

Beatty, Andrew. "Feeling Your Way in Java: An Essay on Society and Emotion." *Ethnos: Journal of Anthropology* 70, no. 1 (2005): 53–78.

Beatty, Andrew. *Varieties of Javanese Religion: An Anthropological Account*. Cambridge: Cambridge University Press, 1999.

Bedner, Adriaan W., and Stijn Cornelis van Huis. "Plurality of Marriage Law and Marriage Registration for Muslims in Indonesia: A Plea for Pragmatism." *Utrecht Law Review* 6, no. 2 (2010): 175–191.

Von Benda-Beckmann, Franz. *Property in Social Continuity: Continuity and Change in the Maintenance of Property Relationships through Time in Minangkabau, West Sumatra*. The Hague: Martinus Nijhoff, 1979.

Von Benda-Beckmann, Franz, and Keebet Von Benda-Beckmann. "Islamic Law in a Plural Context: The Struggle over Inheritance Law in Colonial West Sumatra." *Journal of the Economic and Social History of the Orient* 55, no. 4/5 (2012): 771–793.

Von Benda-Beckmann, Keebet. "Transnational Dimensions of Legal Pluralism." In *Begegnung Und Konflikt—Eine Kulturanthropologische Bestandsaufnahme*, edited by Wolfgang Fikentscher, 33–48. Munich: C.H. Beck, 2001.

Benda, Harry J. *The Crescent and the Rising Sun: Indonesian Islam under the Japanese Occupation, 1942–1945*. Dordrecht: Foris Publications, 1983.

Benda, Harry J. "The Pattern of Administrative Reforms in the Closing Years of Dutch Rule in Indonesia." *The Journal of Asian Studies* 25, no. 4 (1966): 589–605.

Benda, Harry J. "The Structure of Southeast Asian History: Some Preliminary Observations." *Journal of Southeast Asian History* 3, no. 1 (1962): 106–138.

Bennett, Linda Rae. *Women, Islam and Modernity: Single Women, Sexuality and Reproductive Health in Contemporary Indonesia*. London and New York: RoutledgeCurzon, 2005.

Berenschot, Ward, and Gerry van Klinken. "Informality and Citizenship: The Everyday State in Indonesia." *Citizenship Studies* 22, no. 2 (2018): 95–111.

Berger, Peter L. "The Desecularization of the World: A Global Overview." In *The Desecularization of the World: Resurgent Religion and World Politics*, edited by Peter L. Berger, 1–18. Washington: Ethics and Public Policy Center, 1999.

Bijsterveld, Melissa Christina van. "Continuation and Change on Dutch Plantations in Indonesia." Leiden University, 2018.

Bisri, Cik Hasan, ed. *Kompilasi Hukum Islam Dan Peradilan Agama Dalam Sistem Hukum Nasional*. Jakarta: Logos, 1999.

Black, Ann, Hossein Esmaeili, and Nadirsyah Hosen. *Modern Perspectives on Islamic Law*. Cheltenham: Edward Elgar Publishing, 2013.

Blackburn, Susan. *Women and the State in Modern Indonesia*. Cambridge: Cambridge University Press, 2004.

Blackburn, Susan, and Sharon Bessell. "Marriageable Age: Political Debates on Early Marriage in Twentieth-Century Indonesia." *Indonesia* 63 (1997): 107–141.

Bosma, Ulbe. "The Cultivation System (1830–1870) and Its Private Entrepreneurs on Colonial Java." *Journal of Southeast Asian Studies* 38, no. 2 (2007): 275–291.

Bowen, John R. "Fairness and Law in an Indonesian Court." In *Islamic Law in Contemporary Indonesia: Ideas and Institutions*, edited by R. Michael Feener and Mark E. Cammack, 170–192. Cambridge, MA: Harvard University Press, 2007.

Bowen, John R. *Islam, Law, and Equality in Indonesia: An Anthropology of Public Reasoning*. Cambridge: Cambridge University Press, 2003.

Bowen, John R. *Shariʿa, State, and Social Norms in France and Indonesia*. ISIM Paper No. 3. Leiden: Institute for the Study of Islam in the Modern World, 2001.

BPS Kab. Pasuruan. *Kabupaten Pasuruan Dalam Angka 2016*. Pasuruan: BPS Kab. Pasuruan, 2017.

BPS Kab. Pasuruan. *Kecamatan Rembang Dalam Angka 2015*. Pasuruan: BPS Kab. Pasuruan, 2015.

Bruinessen, Martin van. "Islamic State or State Islam? Fifty Years of State-Islam Relations in Indonesia Hamburg: Abera-Verlag." In *Indonesien Am Ende Des 20. Jahrhunderts*, edited by Ingrid Wessel, 19–34. Hamburg: Abera-Verlag, 1996.

Bruinessen, Martin van. "Kitab Kuning: Books in Arabic Script Used in the Pesantren Milieu, Comments on a New Collection in the KITLV Library." *Bijdragen Tot de Taal-, Land- en Volkenkunde* 146, no. 2 (1990): 226–269.

Bruinessen, Martin van. *Tarekat Naqsyabandiyah Di Indonesia*. Bandung: Mizan, 1992.

Buehler, Michael. "Elite Competition and Changing State–Society Relations: Shariʿa Policymaking in Indonesia." In *Beyond Oligarchy: Wealth, Power, and Contemporary Indonesian Politics*, edited by Michele Ford and Thomas B. Pepinsky, 157–175. Ithaca, New York: Cornell Southeast Asia Program Publications, 2014.

Buehler, Michael. "The Rise of Shariʿa by-Laws in Indonesian Districts: An Indication for Changing Patterns of Power Accumulation and Political Corruption." *South East Asia Research* 16, no. 2 (2008): 255–285.

Bush, Robin. *Nahdlatul Ulama and the Struggle for Power within Islam and Politics in Indonesia*. Singapore: Institute of Southeast Asian Studies, 2009.

Buskens, Léon. "A Medieval Islamic Law? Some Thoughts on the Periodezation of the History of Islamic Law." In *O Ye Gentlemen: Arabic Studies on Science and Literary Culture. In Honour of Remke Kruk*, edited by A. Vrolik and J.P. Hogendijk, 469–484. Leiden: Brill, 2007.

Buskens, Léon. "An Islamic Triangle: Changing Relationships between Sharia, State Law, and Local Customs." In *ISIM Newsletter*, 5:8. Leiden: Institute for the Study of Islam in the Modern World, 2000.

Buskens, Léon. "Recent Debates on Family Law Reform in Morocco: Islamic Law as Politics in an Emerging Public Sphere." *Islamic Law and Society* 10, no. 1 (2003): 70–131.

Buskens, Léon. "Sharia and the Colonial State." In *The Ashgate Research Companion to Islamic Law*, edited by Rudolph Peters and Peri Bearman, 209–221. Surrey, England: Ashgate, 2014.

Buskens, Léon, and Baudouin Dupret. "The Invention of Islamic Law: A History of Western Studies of Islamic Normativity and Their Spread in the Orient." In *After Orientalism: Critical Perspectives on Western Agency and Eastern Re-Appropriations*, edited by Jean-Claude Vatin and François Pouillion, 31–47. Leiden: Brill, 2014.

Butt, Simon. "Islam, the State and the Constitutional Court in Indonesia." *Pacific Rim Law & Policy Journal* 19, no. 2 (2010): 279–301.

Butt, Simon. *The Constitutional Court and Democracy in Indonesia*. Leiden/Boston: Brill Nijhoff, 2015.

Cammack, Mark. "Indonesia's 1989 Religious Judicature Act: Islamization of Indonesia or Indonesianization of Islam?" *Indonesia* 63, no. April (1997): 143–168.

Cammack, Mark. "Islam, Nationalism and the State in Suharto's Indonesia." *Wisconsin International Law Journal* 17 (1999): 27–63.

Cammack, Mark. "Islamic Law in Indonesia's New Order." *International and Comparative Law Quarterly* 38, no. 1 (1989): 53–73.

Cammack, Mark. "The Indonesian Islamic Judiciary." In *Islamic Law in Contemporary Indonesia: Ideas and Institutions*, edited by R. Michael Feener and Mark Cammack, 146–169. Cambridge (Mass): Harvard University Press, 2007.

Cammack, Mark, Adriaan W. Bedner, and Stijn Cornelis van Huis. "Democracy, Human Rights, and Islamic Family Law in Post-Soeharto Indonesia." *New Middle Eastern Studies* 5 (2015): 1–32.

Cammack, Mark, Helen Donovan, and Tim B. Heaton. "Islamic Divorce Law and Practice in Indonesia." In *Islamic Law in Contemporary Indonesia: Ideas and Institutions*, edited by R. Michael Feener and Mark Cammack, 99–127. Cambridge, MA: Harvard University Press, 2007.

Cammack, Mark, and R. Michael Feener. "The Islamic Legal System in Indonesia." *Pacific Rim Law & Policy Journal* 21, no. 1 (2012): 13–42.

Cammack, Mark, Lawrence A. Young, and Tim B. Heaton. "Legislating Social Change in an Islamic Society: Indonesia's Marriage Law." *The American Journal of Comparative Law* 44, no. 1 (1996): 45–74.

Ch, Mufidah. "Complexities in Dealing With Gender Inequality: Muslim Women and Mosque-Based Social Services in East Java Indonesia." *Journal of Indonesian Islam* 11, no. 2 (2017): 459–488.

Chopra, Deepta, Philippa Williams, and Bhaskar Vira. "Politics of Citizenship: Experiencing State-Society Relations from the Margins." *Contemporary South Asia* 19, no. 3 (2011): 243–247.

Clarke, Morgan. *Islam and Law in Lebanon: Sharia within and without the State*. Cambridge: Cambridge University Press, 2018.

Cornelis, Fasseur. "The Cultivation System and Its Impact on the Dutch Colonial Economy and the Indigenous Society in Nineteenth-Century Java." In *Two Colonial Empires. Comparative Studies in Overseas History*, edited by Bayly C.A. and Kolff D.H.A., 137–154. Dordrecht: Springer, 1986.

Cott, Nancy F. *Public Vows: A History of Marriage and the Nation*. Cambridge, MA: Harvard University Press, 2002.

Curnow, Jayne. "Legal Support Structures and the Realisation of Muslim Women's Rights in Indonesia." *Asian Studies Review* 39, no. 2 (2015): 213–228.

Daniels, Timothy P. "Introduction: Sharia Dynamics and the Anthropology of Islam." In *Sharia Dynamics: Islamic Law and Sociopolitical Processes*, edited by Timothy P. Daniels, 1–27. Cham: Springer International Publishing, 2017.

Davis, D.E. "Informality and State Theory: Some Concluding Remarks." *Current Sociology* 65, no. 2 (2017): 315–324.

Departemen Agama RI. *Bimas Islam Dalam Angka 2007*. Jakarta: Direktorat Jenderal Bimbingan Masyarakat Islam, 2007.

Dhofier, Zamakhsyari. "Kinship and Marriage among the Javanese Kyai." *Indonesia* 29 (1980): 47–58.

Dhofier, Zamakhsyari. *The Pesantren Tradition: The Role of the Kyai in the Maintenance of Traditional Islam in Java*. Tempe: Arizona State University, 1999.

Dirdjosanjoto, Pradjarta. *Memelihara Umat: Kiai Pesantren-Kiai Langgar Di Jawa*. Yogyakarta: LKiS, 1999.

Drake, Phillip. *Indonesia and the Politics of Disaster: Power and Representation in Indonesia's Mud Volcano*. New York: Routledge, 2016.

Dupret, Baudouin. "Legal Pluralism, Plurality of Laws, and Legal Practices: Theories, Critiques, and Praxiological Re-Specification." *European Journal of Legal Studies* 1, no. 1 (2007): 1–26.

Dupret, Baudouin. "What Is Islamic Law? A Praxiological Answer and an Egyptian Case Study." *Theory, Culture & Society* 24, no. 2 (2007): 79–100.

Elsam. *Monitoring Perda Syariat Islam Di Bulukumba: Perda Nomor 06 Tahun 2003 Tentang Pandai Baca Tulis Al-Qur'an Bagi Siswa Dan Calon Pengantin*. Jakarta, 2008.

Elson, R.E. "Sugar and Peasants: The Social Impact of the Western Sugar Industry on the Peasantry of the Pasuruan Area, East Java, from the Cultivation System to the Great Depression." Monash University, 1979.

Fadel, Mohammad. "State and Sharia." In *The Ashgate Research Companion to Islamic Law*, edited by Rudolph Peters and Peri Bearman, 93–107. Surrey, England: Ashgate, 2014.

Fauzi, Muhammad Latif. "Islamic Law in Indonesia: Recent Debates on Islamic Family Law in the Reformasi Era (1998–2007)." Leiden University, 2008.

Fauzi, Muhammad Latif. "Traditional Islam in Javanese Society: The Roles of Kyai and Pesantren in Preserving Islamic Tradition and Negotiating Modernity." *Journal of Indonesian Islam* 6, no. 1 (2012): 125–144.

Fealy, Greg, and Robin Bush. "The Political Decline of Traditional Ulama in Indonesia." *Asian Journal of Social Science* 42, no. 5 (2014): 536–560.

Feener, R. Michael. *Muslim Legal Thought in Modern Indonesia*. Cambridge: Cambridge University Press, 2007.

Fogg, Kevin W. "Islam in Indonesia's Foreign Policy, 1945–1949." *Al-Jamiʿah* 53, no. 2 (2015): 303–335.

Gaus, Nurdiana, Sultan Sultan, and Muhammad Basri. "State Bureaucracy in Indonesia and Its Reforms: An Overview." *International Journal of Public Administration* 40, no. 8 (2017): 658–669.

Geertz, Clifford. "Local Knowledge: Fact and Law in Comparative Perspective." In *Local Knowledge: Further Essays in Interpretive Anthropology*, 167–234. New York: Basic Books, 1983.

Geertz, Clifford. "The Javanese Kijaji: The Changing Role of a Cultural Broker." *Comparative Studies in Society and History* 2, no. 2 (1960): 228–249.

Geertz, Clifford. *The Religion of Java*. Illinois: The Free Press, 1960.

Geertz, Hildred. *The Javanese Family: A Study of Kinship and Socialization*. New York: The Free Press of Glencoe, 1961.

Gennep, Arnold van. *The Rites of Passage*. London: Routledge & Kegan Paul, 1960.

Giddens, Anthony. *The Consequences of Modernity*. Chicester: Polity Press, 1991.

Gilsenan, Michael. *Recognizing Islam: Religion and Society in the Modern Middle East*. London: I.B. Tauris, 1982.

Griffiths, John. "What Is Legal Pluralism?" *The Journal of Legal Pluralism and Unofficial Law* 24 (1986): 1–56.

Grijns, Mies, and Hoko Horii. "Child Marriage in a Village in West Java (Indonesia): Compromises between Legal Obligations and Religious Concerns." *Asian Journal of Law and Society* 5, no. 2 (2018): 1–14.

Hadiz, Vedi R. "A New Islamic Populism and the Contradictions of Development." *Journal of Contemporary Asia* 44, no. 1 (2013): 125–143.

Haeri, Shahla. *Law of Desire: Temporary Marriage in Shiʿi Iran*. Syracuse, N.Y.: Syracuse University Press, 2014.

Hallaq, Wael B. "Can the Shariʿa Be Restored?" In *Islamic Law and the Challenges of Modernity*, edited by Yvonne Y. Haddad and Barbara F. Stowasser, 21–53. Walnut Creek: Altamira Press, 2004.

Hallaq, Wael B. *Sharīʿa: Theory, Practice, Transformations*. Cambridge: Cambridge University Press, 2009.

Hallaq, Wael B. *The Origins and Evolution of Islamic Law*. Cambridge: Cambridge University Press, 2005.

Hamidah, Tutik. "The Rights of Children Born out of Wedlock: Views of Muslim Women's Organizations on Constitutional Court Judgement 46/2010." In *Women and Property Rights in Indonesian Islamic Legal Contexts*, edited by John Bowen and Arskal Salim, 47–68. Leiden: Brill, 2018.

Harbitz, Mia, and Bettina Boekle-Giuffrida. *Democratic Governance, Citizenship, and Legal Identity*. New York, 2009.

Hasan, Noorhaidi. "The Making of Public Islam: Piety, Agency, and Commodification on the Landscape of the Indonesian Public Sphere." *Contemporary Islam* 3, no. 3 (2009): 229–250.

Hasyim, Syafiq. "Majelis Ulama Indonesia and Pluralism in Indonesia." *Philosophy & Social Criticism* 41, no. 4–5 (2015): 487–495.

Hefner, Robert W. "Islam, State, and Civil Society: ICMI and the Struggle for the Indonesian Middle Class." *Indonesia* 56, no. October (1993): 1–35.

Hefner, Robert W. "Islamizing Java? Religion and Politics in Rural East Java." *The Journal of Asian Studies* 46, no. 3 (1987): 533–554.

Hefner, Robert W. "Reimagined Community: A Social History of Muslim Education in Pasuruan, East Java." In *Asian Visions of Authority: Religion and the Modern States of East and Southeast Asi*, edited by Charles F. Keyes, Laurel Kendall, and Helen Hardacre, 75–95. Honolulu: University of Hawaii Press, 1994.

Hefner, Robert W. "Sharia Law and Muslim Ethical Imaginaries in Modern Indonesia." In *Sharia Dynamics: Islamic Law and Sociopolitical Processes*, edited by Timothy P. Daniels, 91–115. Cham: Springer International Publishing, 2017.

Hefner, Robert W. *The Political Economy of Mountain Java: An Interpretive History*. Berkeley: University of California Press, 1990.

Herawati, Etty. *Kain Dan Pakaian Tradisional Madura*. Jakarta: Dinas Museum dan Sejarah, Pemerintah DKI Jakarta, 1979.

Hisyam, Muhamad. *Caught between Three Fires: The Javanese Pangulu under the Dutch Colonial Administration, 1882–1942*. Jakarta: INIS, 2001.

Hoel, N. "Engaging Islamic Sexual Ethics: Intimacy, Pleasure and Sacrality." *Sexualities* 18, no. 1–2 (2015): 80–99.

Hoel, Nina, and Sa'diyya Shaikh. "Sex as Ibadah: Religion, Gender, and Subjectivity among South African Muslim Women." *Journal of Feminist Studies in Religion* 29, no. 1 (2013): 69–91.

Hooker, M.B. *Islamic Law in Southeast Asia*. Singapore: Oxford University Press, 1984.

Hooker, M.B. "State and Syarîah in Indonesia, 1945–1995." In *Indonesia: Law and Society*, edited by Timothy Lindsey. Sydney: Federation Press, 1999.

Horikoshi, Hiroko. *Kiai Dan Perubahan Sosial*. Jakarta: P3M, 1987.

Huis, Stijn Cornelis van. "Islamic Courts and Women's Divorce Rights in Indonesia: The Cases of Cianjur and Bulukumba." PhD Dissertation. Leiden University, 2015.

Huis, Stijn Cornelis van. "Khulʿ over the Longue Durée: The Decline of Traditional Fiqh-Based Divorce Mechanisms in Indonesian Legal Practice." *Journal of Islamic Law* 25, no. 2 (2018): 1–25.

Huis, Stijn Cornelis van, and Theresia Dyah Wirastri. "Muslim Marriage Registration in Indonesia: Revised Marriage Registration Laws Cannot Overcome Compliance Flaws." *Australian Journal of Asian Law* 13, no. 1 (2012): 1–17.

Hussin, Iza R. *The Politics of Islamic Law: Local Elites, Colonial Authority, and the Making of the Muslim State*. Chicago and London: The University of Chicago Press, 2016.

Husson, Laurence. "Eight Centuries of Madurese Migration to East Java." *Asia and Pacific Migration Journal* 6, no. 1 (1997): 77–102.

Ibn Ḥajar al-ʿAsqalānī, Aḥmad ibnʿAlī. *Bulūgh Al-Marām Min Adillat Al-Aḥkām*. Riyadh: Maktaba al-Rushd, 2005.

Ibn Mājah, Muḥammad ibn Yazīd. *English Translation of Sunan Ibn Majah with Commentary*. Vol. 3. Riyadh: Darussalam, 2007.

Ichwan, Moch Nur. "Official Reform of Islam: State Islam and the Ministry of Religious Affairs in Contemporary Indonesia, 1966–2004." Tilburg University, 2006.

Idrus, Nurul Ilmi. *Gender Relations in an Indonesian Society: Bugis Practices of Sexuality and Marriage*. Leiden: Brill, 2016.

Ismail, Faisal. "The Nahdlatul Ulama: Its Early History and Contribution to the Establishment of Indonesian State." *Journal of Indonesian Islam* 5, no. 2 (2011): 247–282.

Jones, Gavin. "Which Indonesian Women Marry Youngest, and Why?" *Journal of Southeast Asian Studies* 32, no. 1 (2001): 67–78.

Kalanges, Kristine. *Religious Liberty in Western and Islamic Law: Toward a World Legal Tradition*. Oxford: Oxford University Press, 2012.

Katz, June S., and Ronald S. Katz. "Legislating Social Change in a Developing Country: The New Indonesian Marriage Law Revisited." *American Journal of Comparative Law* 26, no. 2 (1978): 309–320.

Katz, June S. "The New Indonesian Marriage Law: A Mirror of Indonesia's Political, Cultural, and Legal Systems." *American Journal of Comparative Law* 23, no. 4 (1975): 653–681.

Kemenag. "Tiga Tahun Jokowi-JK: Kemenag Pemrakarsa Dan Investor Terbesar SBSN." Last modified 2017. Accessed May 7, 2018. https://kemenag.go.id/berita/read/505984/tiga-tahun-jokowi-jk--kemenag-pemrakarsa-dan-investor-terbesar-sbsn.

Kementerian Agama. *Profil Direktorat Urusan Agama Islam Dan Pembinaan Syariah*. Jakarta: Kementerian Agama RI, 2013.

van Klinken, Gerry. "Citizenship and Local Practices of Rule in Indonesia." *Citizenship Studies* 22, no. 2 (2018): 112–128.

van Klinken, Gerry, and Joshua Barker. "Introduction: State in Society in Indonesia." In *State of Authority: The State in Society in Indonesia*, edited by Gerry van Klinken and Joshua Barker, 1–16. Ithaca, NY: Cornell University, 2009.

Koentjaraningrat. "Family and Religion in Indonesia." *East Asian Cultural Studies* 13, no. 1/4 (1974): 59–68.

Koentjaraningrat. *Javanese Culture*. Singapore: Oxford University Press, 1985.

KPAI. "Akta Kelahiran Adalah Hak Setiap Anak Indonesia, Batalkan UU Yang Persulit Pembuatan Akta Kelahiran!" Accessed March 4, 2019. http://www.kpai.go.id/tinjauan/akta-kelahiran-adalah-hak-setiap-anak-indonesia-batalkan-uu-yang-persulit-pembuatan-akta-kelahiran.

Kroef, Justus M. van der. "Indonesia's First National Election: A Sociological Analysis." *The American Journal of Economics and Sociology* 16, no. 3 (1957): 237–249.

Künkler, Mirjam. "The Bureaucratization of Religion in Southeast Asia: Expanding or Restricting Religious Freedom?" *Journal of Law and Religion* 33, no. 2 (2018): 192–196.

Kurasawa, Aiko. "Mobilization and Control: A Study of Social Change in Rural Java, 1942–1945." Cornell University, 1988.

Layish, Aharon. "The Transformation of the Sharīʿa from Jurists' Law to Statutory Law in the Contemporary Muslim World." *Die Welt des Islams* 44, no. 1 (2004): 85–113.

Lev, Daniel S. "Colonial Law and the Genesis of the Indonesian State." *Indonesia* 40, no. 2 (1985): 57–74.

Lev, Daniel S. *Islamic Courts in Indonesia: A Study in the Political Bases of Legal Institutions*. Berkeley: University of California Press, 1972.

Lev, Daniel S. "Judicial Authority and the Struggle for an Indonesian Rechtsstaat." *Law & Society Review* 13, no. 1 (1978): 37–71.

Liddle, R. William. "The Islamic Turn in Indonesia: A Political Explanation." *Journal of Asian Studies* 55, no. 3 (1996): 613–634.

Lindbekk, Monika. "Inscribing Islamic Shariʿa in Egyptian Divorce." *Oslo Law Review* 3, no. 2 (2016): 103–135.

Lindsey, Tim. *Islam, Law and the State in Southeast Asia*. Vol. 1: In. London: Tauris, 2012.

Lipsky, Michael. *Street-Level Bureaucracy: Dilemmas of the Individual in Public Services*. New York: Russell Sage Foundation, 2010.

Lith, P.A. van der, and Joh. F. Snelleman. *Encyclopaedie van Nederlandsch-Indië*. Vol. 3. Amsterdam: KIT Royal Tropical Institute, 2010.

Lombardi, Clark B. *State Law as Islamic Law in Modern Egypt: The Incorporation of the Sharīʿa into Egyptian Constitutional Law*. Leiden: Brill, 2006.

Lubis, Nur Ahmad Fadhil. *Islamic Justice in Transition: A Socio-Legal Study of the Agama Court Judges in Indonesia*. Los Angeles: University of California, 1994.

Lucas, Scott C. "Justifying Gender Inequality in the Shāfiʿī Law School: Two Case Studies of Muslim Legal Reasoning." *Journal of the American Oriental Society* 129, no. 2 (2009): 237–258.

Lukens-Bull, Ronald Alan. "A Peaceful Jihad: Javanese Islamic Education and Religious Identity Construction." Arizona State University, 1997.

Lukito, Ratno. "Sacred and Secular Laws: A Study of Conflict and Resolution in Indonesia." PhD Dissertation. McGill University, 2006.

Lund, Christian. "Rule and Rupture: State Formation through the Production of Property and Citizenship." *Development and Change* 47, no. 6 (2016): 1199–1228.

Maarif, Ahmad Syafii. *Islam Dan Politik: Teori Belah Bambu, Masa Demokrasi Terpimpin, 1959–1965*. Jakarta: Gema Insani Press, 1996.

Manan, Abdul. *Pembaruan Hukum Islam Di Indonesia*. Depok: Kencana, 2017.

Mansurnoor, Iik Arifin. *Islam in an Indonesian World: Ulama of Madura*. Yogyakarta: Gadjah Mada University Press, 1990.

Masud, Muhammad Khalid. "Gender Equality and the Doctrine of Wilāya." In *Gender and Equality in Muslim Family Law: Justice and Ethics in the Islamic Legal Tradition*, edited by Ziba Mir-Hosseini, Kari Vogt, Lena Larsen, and Christian Moe, 127–152. London: I.B. Tauris, 2013.

Menchik, Jeremy. *Islam and Democracy in Indonesia: Tolerance without Liberalism*. New York: Cambridge University Press, 2016.

Merry, Sally. "Legal Pluralism." *Law and Society Review* 22 (1988): 869–896.

Merry, Sally Engle. "Law, Culture, and Cultural Appropriation." *Yale Journal of Law & the Humanities* 10, no. 2 (1998): 575–603.

Migdal, Joel S. *State in Society: Studying How States and Societies Transform and Constitute One Another*. Cambridge: Cambridge University Press, 2001.

Mir-Hosseini, Ziba. "Marriage." *Encyclopedia of Islam and the Muslim World*. New York: Macmillan, 2004.

Mir-Hosseini, Ziba. *Marriage on Trial: Islamic Family Law in Iran and Morocco*. London and New York: I.B. Tauris, 2000.

Mir-Hosseini, Ziba. "Nikah." *Encyclopedia of Islam and the Muslim World*. New York: Macmillan, 2004.

Mohamad, Maznah. "Malaysian Sharia Reforms in Dlux: The Changeable National Character of Islamic Marriage." *International Journal of Law, Policy and the Family* 25, no. 1 (2011): 46–70.

Moore, Sally Falk. "Law and Social Change: The Semi-Autonomous Social Field as an Appropriate Subject of Study." *Law and Society Review* 7, no. 4 (1973): 719–746.

Moore, Sally Falk. *Law as Process: An Anthropological Approach*. London: Routledge & Kegan Paul, 1983.

Muhammad, Husein. *Fiqh Perempuan: Refleksi Kiai Atas Wacana Agama Dan Gender*. Yogyakarta: LKiS, 2001.

Mujiburrahman. *Feeling Threatened: Muslim-Christian Relations in Indonesia's New Order*. Amsterdam: Amsterdam University Press, 2006.

Mulia, Siti Musdah, and Mark Cammack. "Toward a Just Marriage Law: Empowering Indonesian Women through a Counter Legal Draft to the Indonesian Compilation of Islamic Law." In *Islamic Law in Contemporary Indonesia: Ideas and Institutions*, 129–145. Cambridge, MA: Harvard University Press, 2007.

Müller, Dominik M. *The Bureaucratization of Islam and Its Socio-Legal Dimensions in Southeast Asia: Conceptual Contours of a Research Project*. Halle, 2017.

Nakamura, Hisako. *Conditional Divorce in Java*. Harvard: Islamic Legal Studies Program Harvard Law School, 2006.

Nakamura, Hisako. *Divorce in Java: A Study of the Dissolution of Marriage among Javanese Muslims*. Yogyakarta: Gadjah Mada University Press, 1983.

Nakamura, Hisako. *Perceraian Orang Jawa: Studi Tentang Pemutusan Perkawinan Di Kalangan Orang Islam Jawa*. Yogyakarta: Gadjah Mada University Press, 1990.

Nasir, Mohamad Abdun. "Islamic Law and Paradox of Domination and Resistance." *Asian Journal of Social Science* 44, no. 1–2 (2016): 78–103.

Nasution, Khoiruddin. *Status Wanita Di Asia Tenggara: Studi Terhadap Perundang-Undangan Perkawinan Muslim Kontemporer Di Indonesia Dan Malaysia*. Leiden: Indonesian-Netherlands Cooperation in Islamic Studies (INIS), 2002.

Nawāwī, Muḥammad ibnʿUmar al-. *ʿUqūd Al-Lujayn Fī Bayān Ḥuqūq Al-Zawjayn*. al-Qāhira, 1919.

Nichols, Joel A. "Religion, Family Law, and Competing Norms." In *Negotiating State and Non-State Law: The Challenge of Global and Local Legal Pluralism*, edited by Michael A. Helfand, 197–214. Cambridge: Cambridge University Press, 2015.

Niehof, Anke. *Women and Fertility in Madura (Indonesia)*. Leiden: Instituut voor Culturele Antropologie en Sociologie der Niet-Westerse Volken, 1985.

Niehof, Anke. *Women and Fertility in Madura (Indonesia)*. Leiden: Instituut voor Culturele Antropologie en Sociologie der Niet-Westerse Volken, 1985.

Nieuwenhuijze, C.A.O. van. "The Legacy of Islam in Indonesia." *The Muslim World* 59, no. 3–4 (1969): 210–219.

Nilan, Pam. "Youth Transitions to Urban, Middle-Class Marriage in Indonesia: Faith, Family and Finances." *Journal of Youth Studies* 11, no. 1 (2008): 65–82.

Nisa, Eva F. "Marriage and Divorce for the Sake of Religion: The Marital Life of Cadari in Indonesia." *Asian Journal of Social Science* 39, no. 6 (2011): 797–820.

Nisa, Eva F. "The Bureaucratization of Muslim Marriage in Indonesia." *Journal of Law and Religion* 33, no. 2 (2018): 291–309.

Noer, Deliar. *Administrasi Islam Di Indonesia*. Jakarta: Rajawali, 1983.

Noer, Deliar. *The Administration of Islam in Indonesia*. Ithaca, NY: Cornell Modern Indonesia Project, 1978.

Nooteboom, Gerben. *Forgotten People: Poverty, Risk and Social Security in Indonesia, the Case of the Madurese*. Leiden/Boston: Brill, 2015.

Nordholt, Henk Schulte. "Identity Politics, Citizenship and the Soft State in Indonesia: An Essay." *Journal of Indonesian Social Sciences and Humanities* 1 (2008): 1–21.

Nurlaelawati, Euis. *Modernization, Tradition and Identity: The Kompilasi Hukum Islam and Legal Practice in the Indonesian Religious Courts*. Amsterdam: Amsterdam University Press, 2010.

Nurlaelawati, Euis. "Muslim Women in Indonesian Religious Courts: Reform, Strategies, and Pronouncement of Divorce." *Islamic Law & Society. 2013* 20, no. 3 (2013): 242–271.

Nurlaelawati, Euis. “Pernikahan Tanpa Pencatatan: Isbat Nikah Sebuah Solusi?” *Musâwa* 12, no. 2 (2013): 261–277.

O'Shaughnessy, Kate. *Gender, State and Social Power in Contemporary Indonesia: Divorce and Marriage Law*. London and New York: Routledge, 2009.

Oetomo, Dédé. “The Chinese of Pasuruan: Their Language and Identity.” Australian National University, 1987.

Ophuijsen, A.H. van. *De Huwelijksordonnantie En Hare Uitvoering*. Leiden: Firma P.W.M. Trap, 1907.

Opwis, Felicitas. “Maṣlaḥa in Contemporary Islamic Legal Theory.” *Islamic Law and Society* 12, no. 2 (2005): 182–223.

Otto, Jan Michiel. “Introduction: Investigating the Role of Sharia in National Law,” in *Sharia Incorporated: A Comparative Overview of the Legal Systems of Twelve Muslim Countries in Past and Present*, ed. Jan Michiel Otto (Leiden: Leiden University Press, 2010), 17–49.

Otto, Jan Michiel. “Sharia and National Law in Indonesia.” In *Sharia Incorporated: A Comparative Overview of the Legal Systems of Twelve Muslim Countries in Past and Present*, edited by Jan Michiel Otto, 433–490. Leiden: Leiden University Press, 2010.

Otto, Jan Michiel. ed. *Sharia Incorporated: A Comparative Overview of the Legal Systems of Twelve Muslim Countries in Past and Present*. Leiden: Leiden University Press, 2010.

Panggabean, Samsu Rizal. “Policing Sectarian Conflict in Indonesia: The Case of Shi'ism.” In *Religion, Law and Intolerance in Indonesia*, edited by Tim Lindsey and Helen Pausacker, 271–288. London: Routledge, 2016.

Parker, Lyn, Irma Riyani, and Brooke Nolan. “The Stigmatisation of Widows and Divorcees (Janda) in Indonesia, and the Possibilities for Agency.” *Indonesia and the Malay World* 44, no. 128 (2016): 27–46.

Pausacker, Helen. “Pink or Blue Swing? Art, Pornography, Islamist and the Law in Reformasi Indonesia.” In *Religion, Law and Intolerance in Indonesia*, edited by Tim Lindsey and Helen Pausacker, 289–316. London: Routledge, 2016.

Peacock, James Lowe. *Purifying the Faith: The Muhammadijah Movement in Indonesian Islam*. Chapel Hill: University of North Carolina Press, 1978.

Peletz, Michael G. “A Tale of Two Courts: Judicial Transformation and the Rise of a Corporate Islamic Governmentality in Malaysia.” *American Ethnologist* 42, no. 1 (2015): 144–160.

Peletz, Michael G. *Islamic Modern: Religious Courts and Cultural Politics in Malaysia*. Princeton: Princeton University Press, 2002.

Pemda Kab Pasuruan. *The Present Day of Kab Pasuruan*. Pasaruan: Pemda Kab Pasuruan, 1974.

Peters, Rudolph. “From Jurists' Law to Statute Law or What Happens When the Shari'a Is Codified.” *Mediterranean Politics* 7, no. 3 (2002): 82–95.

Pirie, Fernanda. *The Anthropology of Law*. Oxford: Oxford University Press, 2013.

Platt, Maria. *Marriage, Gender and Islam in Indonesia: Women Negotiating Informal Marriage, Divorce and Desire*. Oxon and New York: Routledge, 2017.

Pranowo, M. Bambang. "Pesantren, Traditional Islam in Contemporary Rural Java: The Case of the Tegal Rejo Pesantren." In *Islam in the Indonesian Social Context*, edited by M.C. Ricklefs, 39–56. Clayton: Monash University Centre of Southeast Asian Studies, 1991.

Prettitore, Paul Scott. "Family Law Reform, Gender Equality, and Underage Marriage: A View from Morocco and Jordan." *Review of Faith and International Affairs* 13, no. 3 (2015): 32–40.

Pribadi, Yanwar. *Islam, State and Society in Indonesia: Local Politics in Madura*. London and New York: Routledge, 2018.

Pribadi, Yanwar. "Religious Networks in Madura: Pesantren, Nahdlatul Ulama, and Kiai as the Core of Santri Culture." *Al-Jami'ah: Journal of Islamic Studies* 51, no. 1 (2013): 1–32.

Raharjo, Christanto P. *Pendhalungan: Sebuah 'Periuk Besar' Masyarakat Multikultural*. presented in Jelajah Budaya 13 August, 2006.

Retsikas, Konstantinos. *Becoming—An Anthropological Approach to Understandings of the Person in Java*. London: Anthem Press, 2012.

Retsikas, Konstantinos. "The Power Of The Senses: Ethnicity, History and Embodiment in East Java, Indonesia." *Indonesia and the Malay World* 35, no. 102 (2007): 183–210.

Ricklefs, M.C. *A History of Modern Indonesia*. Bloomington: Indiana University Press, 1981.

Ricklefs, M.C. *Polarising Javanese Society: Islamic and Other Visions, c. 1830–1930*. Leiden: KITLV Press, 2007.

Rinaldo, Rachel. *Mobilizing Piety: Islam and Feminism in Indonesia*. New York: Oxford University Press, 2013.

Rosen, Lawrence. *Law as Culture: An Invitation*. Princeton: Princeton University Press, 2006.

Rosen, Lawrence. *The Anthropology of Justice: Law as Culture in Islamic Society*. Cambridge: Cambridge University Press, 1989.

Rozario, Santi. "Islamic Marriage: A Haven in an Uncertain World." *Culture and Religion* 13, no. March 2015 (2012): 159–175.

Rozario, Santi. "Islamic Piety against the Family: From 'Traditional' to 'Pure' Islam." *Contemporary Islam* 5, no. 3 (2011): 285–308.

Rubaidi. "East Java: New Clientalism and the Fading of Aliran Politics." In *Electoral Dynamics in Indonesia: Money Politics, Patronage and Clientelism at the Grassroots*, edited by Edward Aspinall and Mada Sukmajati, 264–278. Singapore: NUS Press, 2016.

Rumadi. *Islamic Post-Traditionalism in Indonesia*. Singapore: ISEAS-Yusof Ishak Institute, 2015.

Rusyeni, Rini. "Fragmented Voices: The Personal Archives of the Advisors of Inlandsche Zaken, 1899–194." Leiden University, 2017.

Salim, Arskal. *Challenging the Secular State: The Islamization of Law in Modern Indonesia*. Honolulu: University of Hawai'i Press, 2008.

Salim, Arskal. *Contemporary Islamic Law in Indonesia: Shariʿah and Legal Pluralism*. Edinburgh: Edinburgh University Press, 2015.

Salim, Arskal. "Dynamic Legal Pluralism in Indonesia: Contested Legal Orders in Contemporary Aceh." *Journal of Legal Pluralism and Unofficial Law* 42, no. 61 (2010): 1–29.

Salim, Delmus Puneri. *The Transnational and the Local in the Politics of Islam: The Case of West Sumatra, Indonesia*. Cham: Springer International Publishing, 2015.

Salvatore, Armando, and Dale F. Eickelman. "Muslim Publics." In *Public Islam and the Common Good*, edited by Armando Salvatore and Dale F. Eickelman, 3–27. Leiden: Brill, 2004.

Sartori, Paolo, and Ido Shahar. "Legal Pluralism in Muslim-Majority Colonies: Mapping the Terrain." *Journal of the Economic and Social History of the Orient* 55, no. 4/5 (2012): 637–663.

Schacht, Joseph. "Shariʿa." In *First Encyclopedia of Islam*, edited by M.Th. Houstma, Wensinck A.J., T.W. Arnold, W. Heffening, and E. Lévi-Provençal, 320–324. Leiden: Brill, 1987.

Schielke, Samuli. "Second Thoughts about the Anthropology of Islam, or How to Make Sense of Grand Schemes in Everyday Life." *ZMO Working Papers*, no. 2 (2010): 1–16.

Schielke, Samuli, and Liza Debevec. "Introduction." In *Ordinary Lives and Grand Schemes: An Anthropology of Everyday Religion*, edited by Samuli Schielke and Liza Debevec, 1–16. New York and Oxford: Berghahn Books, 2012.

Schielke, Samuli, and Liza Debevec. eds. *Ordinary Lives and Grand Schemes: An Anthropology of Everyday Religion*. New York and Oxford: Berghahn Books, 2012.

Scott, Elizabeth S. "Social Norms and the Legal Regulation of Marriage." *Virginia Law Review* 86, no. 8 (2000): 1901–1970.

Scott, James C. "Patron-Clients Politics and Political Change in Southeast Asia." *The American Political Science Review* 66, no. 1 (1972): 91–113.

Seo, Myengkyo. "Falling in Love and Changing Gods: Inter-Religious Marriage and Religious Conversion in Java, Indonesia." *Indonesia and the Malay World* 41, no. 119 (2013): 76–96.

Sezgin, Yüksel, and Mirjam Künkler. "Regulation of Religion and the Religious: The Politics of Judicialization and Bureaucratization in India and Indonesia." *Comparative Studies in Society and History* 56, no. 2 (2014): 448–478.

Sirry, Mun'im. "The Public Expression of Traditional Islam: The Pesantren and Civil Society in Post-Suharto Indonesia." *The Muslim World* 100, no. 1 (2010): 60–77.

Smith-Hefner, Nancy J. "The New Muslim Romance: Changing Patterns of Courtship and Marriage Among Educated Javanese Youth." *Journal of Southeast Asian Studies* 36, no. 3 (2005): 441–459.

Smith, Bianca J. "Sexual Desire, Piety, and Law in a Javanese Pesantren: Interpreting Varieties of Secret Divorce and Polygamy." *Anthropological Forum* 24, no. 3 (2014): 37–41.

Smith, Bianca J., and Mark Woodward. "Introduction, Decolonizing Islam and Muslim Feminism." In *Gender and Power in Indonesian Islam: Leaders, Feminists, Sufis and Pesantren Selves*, edited by Bianca J. Smith and Mark Woodward, 1–21. London and New York: Routledge, 2014.

Soares, Benjamin F. "Notes on the Anthropological Study of Islam and Muslim Societies in Africa." *Culture and Religion* 1, no. 2 (2000): 277–285.

Soares, Benjamin, and Filippo Osella. "Islam, Politics, Anthropology." In *Islam, Politics, Anthropology*, edited by Benjamin Soares and Filippo Osella, 1–22. London: Royal Anthropological Institute, 2010.

Soewondo, Nani. "The Indonesian Marriage Law and Its Implementing Regulation." *Archipel* 13 (1977): 283–294.

Sonneveld, Nadia. "Rethinking the Difference Between Formal and Informal Marriages in Egypt." In *Family Law in Islam: Divorce, Marriage and Women in the Muslim World*, edited by Maaike Voorhoeve, 77–107. London: I.B. Tauris, 2012.

Spectorsky, Susan A. *Women in Classical Islamic Law: A Survey of the Sources*. Leiden/Boston: Brill, 2010.

Srimulyani, Eka. *Women from Traditional Islamic Educational Institutions in Indonesia: Negotiating Public Spaces*. Amsterdam: Amsterdam University Press, 2012.

Starrett, Gregory. *Putting Islam to Work: Education, Politics, and Religious Transformation in Egypt*. Berkeley: University of California Press, 1998.

Steenbrink, Karel A. *Beberapa Aspek Tentang Islam Di Indonesia Abad Ke-19*. Jakarta: Bulan Bintang, 1984.

Stryber, R. "Legitimacy." *International Encyclopedia of the Social & Behavioral Sciences* (2001): 8700–8704.

Stumpo, Pamela J. "Challenging the Practice of the State, but Beholden to Its Image: Women's Activists, Academics, and the Public Take on Egypt's Citizenship Laws." In *The Everyday Life of the State: A State-in-Society Approach*, edited by Adam White, 189–204. Seattle: University of Washington Press, 2013.

Suminto, Husnul Aqib. *Politik Islam Pemerintah Hindia Belanda: Het Kantoor Voor Inlandsche Zaken*. Jakarta: LP3ES, 1985.

Sumner, Cate, and Tim Lindsey. *Courting Reform: Indonesia's Islamic Courts and Justice for the Poor*. New South Wales: Lowy Institute for International Policy, 2010.

Sutarto, Ayu. "Becoming a True Javanese: A Javanese View of Attempts at Javanisation." *Indonesia and the Malay World* 34, no. 98 (2006): 39–53.

Tempo.co. "Kasus Fany, Bupati Garut Terancam Kena Sanksi Golkar." *Tempo.Co*. Last modified 2012. Accessed March 15, 2016. https://nasional.tempo.co/read/445735/kasus-fany-bupati-garut-terancam-kena-sanksi-golkar/full&view=ok.

Tempo.co. "Pembagian Zakat Haji Syaikhon Fikri Tidak Haram." *TEMPO Interaktif*. Last modified 2008. Accessed June 15, 2017. https://m.tempo.co/read/news/2008/09/16/058135791/pembagian-zakat-haji-syaikhon-fikri-tidak-haram.

Tempo.co. "Tebar Zakat Ala Haji Syaikhon Tak Sesuai Quran." *TEMPO Interaktif*. Last modified 2008. Accessed June 15, 2017. https://nasional.tempo.co/read/news/2008/09/16/058135727/tebar-zakat-ala-haji-syaikhon-tak-sesuai-quran.

Tempo.co. "Trauma 'Zakat Maut', Haji Syaichon Salurkan Zakat Ke Badan Amil." *TEMPO Interaktif*. Last modified 2009. Accessed June 15, 2017. https://m.tempo.co/read/news/2009/09/07/151196632/trauma-zakat-maut-haji-syaichon-salurkan-zakat-ke-badan-amil.

The Insitute on Statelessness and Inclusion. *Sustainable Development Goal 16.9: "Legal Identity", Nationality & Statelessness*. London: Institute on Statelessness and Inclusion, 2018.

The Jakarta Post. "Paternity Ruling to Apply in Rape Cases," April 7, 2012.

Tirmidhī, Abī 'Īsā al-. *Jāmi' Al-Tirmidhī*. Riyadh: Bayt al-Afkār al-Dawliyya, 1999.

Tummers, Lars, and Victor Bekkers. "Policy Implementation, Street-Level Bureaucracy, and the Importance of Discretion." *Public Management Review* 16, no. 4 (2014): 527–547.

Turmudi, Endang. *Struggling for the Umma: Changing Leadership Roles of Kiai in Jombang, East Java*. Canberra: ANU E Press, 2006.

Ufen, Andreas. "From Aliran to Dealignment: Political Parties in Post-Suharto Indonesia." *South East Asia Research* 16, no. 1 (2008): 5–41.

Vignato, Silvia. "'Men Come In, Men Go Out': Single Muslim Women in Malaysia and Aceh." *Social Identities* 18, no. 2 (2012): 239–257.

Vincent-Grosso, Sarah. "Maktub: An Ethnography of Evidence in a Tunisian Divorce Court." In *Family Law in Islam: Divorce, Marriage and Women in the Muslim World*, edited by Maaike Voorhoeve, 171–198. London: I.B. Tauris, 2012.

Vogel, Frank E. *Islamic Law and Legal System Studies of Saudi Arabia*. Leiden/Boston: Brill, 2000.

Voorhoeve, Maaike. "Judicial Discretion in Tunisian Personal Status Law." In *Family Law in Islam: Divorce, Marriage and Women in the Muslim World*, edited by Maaike Voorhoeve, 199–229. London: I.B. Tauris, 2012.

Wainscott, Ann Marie. *Bureaucratizing Islam: Morocco and the War on Terror*. Cambridge: Cambridge University Press, 2017.

Waters, Tony, and Dagmar Waters. "Max Weber's Sociology in the Twenty-First Century." In *Weber's Rationalism and Modern Society New Translations on Politics, Bureaucracy, and Social Stratification*, edited by Tony Waters and Dagmar Waters, 1–17. New York: Palgrave Macmillan, 2015.

Weber, Max. *Economy and Society: An Outline of Interpretive Sociology*. Edited by Guenther Roth and Claus Wittich. Berkeley: University of California Press, 1978.

Weber, Max. "Politics as a Vocation." In *From Max Weber: Essays in Sociology*, edited by Hans H. Gerth and C. Wright Mills, 77–128. New York: Oxford University Press, 1946.

Weiss, Bernard G. *The Search for God's Law: Islamic Jurisprudence in the Writing of Saif Al-Dīn Al-Āmidī*. Salt Lake and Herndon: University of Utah Press and International Institute of Islamic Thought, 2010.

Welchman, Lynn. *Women and Muslim Family Laws in Arab States: A Comparative Overview of Textual Development and Advocacy*. Amsterdam: Amsterdam University Press, 2007.

Westendorp, Ingrid. "Personal Status Law and Women's Right to Equality in Law and in Practice: The Case of Land Rights of Balinese Hindu Women." *Journal of Human Rights Practice* 7, no. 3 (2015): 430–450.

White, Adam. "Introduction. A State-in-Society Agenda." In *The Everyday Life of the State: A State-In-Society Approach*, edited by Adam White, 1–12. Seattle: University of Washington Press, 2013.

Widjojoatmojo, R. Abdoelkadir. "Islam in the Netherlands East-Indies." *The Far Eastern Quarterly* 2, no. 1 (1942): 48–57.

Wiyata, A. Latief. *Carok: Konflik Kekerasan Dan Harga Diri Orang Madura*. Yogyakarta: LKiS, 2002.

Zahro, Ahmad. *Tradisi Intelektual NU: Lajnah Bahtsul Masa'il, 1926–1999*. Yogyakarta: LKiS, 2004.

"557 Pasangan Sudah Mendaftar Di Acara Nikah Massal Dan Isbat Nikah Di Malam Tahun Baru." *Tribunnews*. Accessed March 4, 2019. http://www.tribunnews.com/metropolitan/2018/12/31/557-pasangan-sudah-mendaftar-di-acara-nikah-massal-dan-isbat-nikah-di-malam-tahun-baru.

"Pencatatan Nikah Hanya Menggunakan KTP Elektronik." Accessed March 15, 2019. https://bimasislam.kemenag.go.id/post/berita/pencatatan-nikah-hanya-menggunakan-ktp-elektronik.

Laws and Regulations

Law 22/1946 on Pencatatan Nikah, Talak, Rujuk (registration of Islamic marriage, divorce, and reconciliation).

Law 19/1948 on the Judicial Power

Law 1/1951 on the Jurisdiction and Procedures of the Civil Courts

Law 1/1974 on *Perkawinan* (marriage)

Law 5/1975 on *Pemerintahan Desa* (village administration)

Law 23/2006 on *Administrasi Kependudukan* (civil administration)

Law 24/2013 on *Perubahan* UU No. 23/2006 (revision of UU No. 23/2006 on civil administration)

Penetapan Pemerintah (the Government Declaration) No. 1/S.D. 1946 on the establishment of the Department of Religion.

Penetapan Pemerintah No. 5/SD 1946 on the transfer of High Islamic Court (Mahkamah Islam Tinggi) from the Department of Justice to the Department of Religion.

Peraturan Pemerintah (Government Regulation) No. 33/1949 tentang Susunan dan Lapang Pekerjaan Kementerian Agama (on the structure and the task of the Ministry of Religious Affairs)

Peraturan Pemerintah No. 51/2000 on Tarif atas Jenis Penerimaan Negara Bukan Pajak yang berlaku pada Departemen Agama (the non-tax revenue of the Ministry of Religious Affairs).

Peraturan Pemerintah No. 48 Tahun 2014 tentang Perubahan atas Peraturan Pemerintah Nomor 47 Tahun 2004 on Tarif atas Jenis Penerimaan Negara Bukan Pajak yang Berlaku pada Departemen Agama (the Revision of the Government Regulation No. 47/2004 on the non-tax revenue of the Department of Religious Affairs).

PMA (Peraturan Menteri Agama, the Regulation of the Minister of Religion) No. 1/1952 on *wali hakim* (magistrate guardian).

PMA 1/1955 on *kewajiban-kewajiban pegawai pencatat nikah* (the obligations of marriage registrars).

PMA 15/1955 on *Contoh-contoh Buku Pendaftaran Nikah, Talak dan Rujuk* (the examples of registration forms of marriage, repudiation and reconciliation of a marriage).

PMA 11/2007 on *pencatatan pernikahan* (marriage registration).

PMA 34/2016 tentang Organisasi dan Tata Kerja Kantor Urusan Agama Kecamatan (on the organisation and the working procedure of the sub-district KUA).

PMA 42/2016 on Organisasi dan Tata Kerja Kementerian Agama (the organization and the operating procedure of the Ministry of Religious Affairs).

PMA 20/2019 on *pencatatan pernikahan* (marriage registration).

PerMenPAN (Peraturan Menteri Pendayagunaan Aparatur Negara, The Decree of the Minister of State Administrative) no. PER/62 /M.PAN/6/2005 on Jabatan Fungsional Penghulu dan Angka Kreditnya (the functional position of *penghulu* and its credit system).

KMA (Keputusan Menteri Agama, the Decree of the Minister of Religion) 6/1947 on 8 December 1947 on the task division of *penghulu kabupaten* and *penghulu hakim*.

KMA 30/1977 on Penegasan Pengakuan Badan Penasihatan Perkawinan, Perselisihan dan Perceraian (the recognition of board of Board of marriage counselling, dispute, and divorce).

KMA 517/2001 on Penataan Organisasi Kantor Urusan Agama Kecamatan (the reorganization of the sub-district KUA)

KMA 114/2009 on Penetapan Pengurus BP4 Pusat (the Officials of the Central BP4).

Instruksi Menteri Agama (Instruction of the Minister of Religious Affairs) 2/2004 on Peningkatan Pelayanan Pernikahan Pada Kantor Urusan Agama Kecamatan (the improvement of the service of the sub-district KUA).

Peraturan Daerah Kabupaten Subang (the local regulation of Subang) 22/2006 on Biaya Pencatatan Nikah Bedolan (the *bedolan* fee).

Keputusan Bupati Sidoarjo (the Regent's decree of Sidoarjo) 29/2003 on Penyesuaian Biaya Nikah Bedolan dan Honorarium Pembantu Pegawai Pencatat Nikah (PPPN) Kabupaten Sidoarjo (the synchronization of the bedolan fee and the honorarium of PPPN in Sidoarjo).

Surat Gubemur Jawa Timur (the Letter of the Governor of East Java) 45113267/02112002 on Permohonan Persetujuan Penyesuaian Besarnya Biaya Nikah Bedolan dan Honorarium Pembantu Pegawai Pencatat Nikah (PPPN) (the request for the adjustment of *bedolan* fee and the honorarium of PPPN).

RUU HMPA, Rancangan Undang-undang Hukum Materiil Pengadilan Agama Bidang Perkawinan (the Bill of Islamic Court's Material Law on Marriage).

Index

www.ingramcontent.com/pod-product-compliance
Lightning Source LLC
Chambersburg PA
CBHW071435230926
51846CB00001B/246